Learning Music Theory with Logic, Max, and Finale

Learning Music Theory with Logic, Max, and Finale is a groundbreaking resource that bridges the gap between music theory teaching and the world of music software programs. Focusing on three key programs—the Digital Audio Workstation (DAW) Logic, the Audio Programming Language (APL) Max, and the music-printing program Finale—this book shows how they can be used together to learn music theory. It provides an introduction to core music theory concepts and shows how to develop programming skills alongside music theory skills.

Software tools form an essential part of the modern musical environment; laptop musicians today can harness incredibly powerful tools to create, record, and manipulate sounds. Yet these programs on their own don't provide musicians with an understanding of music notation and structures, while traditional music theory teaching doesn't fully engage with technological capabilities. With clear and practical applications, this book demonstrates how to use DAWs, APLs, and music-printing programs to create interactive resources for learning the mechanics behind how music works.

Offering an innovative approach to the learning and teaching of music theory in the context of diverse musical genres, this volume provides game-changing ideas for educators, practicing musicians, and students of music.

Geoffrey Kidde is Professor of Music at Manhattanville College.

Learning Music Theory with Logic, Max, and Finale

Geoffrey Kidde

Routledge
Taylor & Francis Group

NEW YORK AND LONDON

First published 2020
by Routledge
52 Vanderbilt Avenue, New York, NY 10017

and by Routledge
2 Park Square, Milton Park, Abingdon, Oxon, OX14 4RN

Routledge is an imprint of the Taylor & Francis Group, an informa business

Library of Congress Cataloging-in-Publication Data
Names: Kidde, Geoffrey, 1963– author.
Title: Learning music theory with Logic, Max, and Finale / Geoffrey Kidde.
Description: New York : Routledge, 2020. | Includes bibliographical references and index.
Identifiers: LCCN 2019039659 (print) | LCCN 2019039660 (ebook) |
  ISBN 9781138544284 (hardback) | ISBN 9781138544291 (paperback) |
  ISBN 9781351004374 (adobe pdf) | ISBN 9781351004350 (mobi) |
  ISBN 9781351004367 (epub) | ISBN 9781351004381 (ebook)
Subjects: LCSH: Music theory. | Computer composition (Music) |
  Max (Computer file : Cycling '74) | Logic (Computer file) | Finale (Computer file)
Classification: LCC MT6.K47 L43 2020 (print) | LCC MT6.K47 (ebook) | DDC 781.20285—dc23
LC record available at https://lccn.loc.gov/2019039659
LC ebook record available at https://lccn.loc.gov/2019039660

ISBN: 978-1-138-54428-4 (hbk)
ISBN: 978-1-138-54429-1 (pbk)
ISBN: 978-1-351-00438-1 (ebk)

Typeset in Times New Roman
by Apex CoVantage, LLC
Printed and bound by CPI Group (UK) Ltd, Croydon CR0 4YY

Visit the eResources: www.geoffreykidde.com/learningmusictheory.html

Dedicated to

Patricia, Ethan, Devin,
and
Cameron

Contents

Acknowledgments .... *xii*

Introduction .... *xiii*

   0.1 An Overview xiii

   0.2 Transmitting MIDI between Programs xv

   0.3 *Max Patcher 0:* Send and Receive xviii

Chapter 1: Rhythm: Tempo, Meter, Durations 1

   1.1 Tempo 1

   1.2 Meter 3

   1.3 Note Values 4

   1.4 Dotted Rhythms and Pickup 6

   1.5 Triplets 7

   1.6 Quantization 7

   1.7 Inputting Rhythm in Logic 9

   1.8 Meter, Time Signatures, and Rhythmic Durations in Finale 10

   1.9 *Max Patcher I:* Drum Pattern 13

  1.10 Exercises 16

      1.10.1 Exercise 1: Rhythmic Values in Measures 16

      1.10.2 Exercise 2: Practice Rhythm with Logic and Finale 16

      1.10.3 Exercise 3: Modifying Drum Pattern 17

      1.10.4 Exercise 4: Add Tempo Changes in Logic or Finale 19

Chapter 2: Rhythm: Loops and Advanced Rhythm 20

   2.1 Loops in Logic 20

   2.2 Drum Loops in Finale 21

   2.3 Tuplets in Logic 22

   2.4 Tuplets in Finale 25

   2.5 Nested Tuplets 26

   2.6 Metric Modulation 26

   2.7 Rhythm Generator 28

   2.8 *Max Patcher 2*: Rhythm Generator 30

   2.9 Mouse Click Melody 34

  2.10 *Max Patcher 3*: Mouse Click Melody 36

  2.11 Exercises 37

      2.11.1 Exercise 1: Rhythm Generator Drum Loops 37

      2.11.2 Exercise 2: Rhythm Generator for Rhythmic Exercises (Performance

            and Dictation) 38

      2.11.3 Exercise 3: Melodies for Mouse Click Melody 38

Chapter 3: Pitch, Intervals, Scales **40**

3.1 Pitch Notation 40

3.2 Pitch Generator 42

3.3 *Max Patcher 4:* Pitch Generator 43

3.4 Intervals 45

3.5 Creating Intervals in Logic and Finale 47

3.6 Inverting Intervals with Finale and Logic 48

3.7 Major Scales and Keys 49

3.8 Minor Scales and Keys 51

3.9 Intervals in Minor Scales 52

3.10 Creating Major and Minor Scales in Finale 54

3.11 Scale Generator 54

3.12 *Max Patcher 5:* Scale Generator 55

3.13 Chromatic Intervals 58

3.14 Interval Identifier 59

3.15 *Max Patcher 6:* Interval Identifier 60

3.16 Modern Modes 61

3.17 Exercises 63

    3.17.1 Exercise 1: Reading Pitches in Logic 63

    3.17.2 Exercise 2: Reading Natural Intervals in Finale 64

    3.17.3 Exercise 3: Scale Practice 65

    3.17.4 Exercise 4: Change Scale Generator into Mode Generator 67

    3.17.5 Exercise 5: Interval Quiz 67

Chapter 4: Triads **70**

4.1 Constructing Triads 70

4.2 Logic's Chord Trigger 71

4.3 Finale's Chord Tool 74

4.4 Inverting Triads in Finale and Logic 77

4.5 Diatonic Collection of Triads 78

4.6 Triads in Major Keys 80

4.7 Triads in Minor Keys 81

4.8 Triad Generator 84

4.9 *Max Patcher 7:* Triad Generator 86

4.10 Chord Identification in Logic 92

4.11 Chord Identification in Finale 94

4.12 Triad Identifier 96

4.13 *Max Patcher 8:* Triad Identifier 96

4.14 Exercises 100

    4.14.1 Exercise 1: Triad Quiz 100

    4.14.2 Exercise 2: Practice Writing Triads with Finale 103

    4.14.4 Exercise 3: Accompany Songs with Chord Trigger 104

Chapter 5: Seventh Chords and Extensions, Chord Patterns **105**

5.1 Constructing Seventh Chords 105

5.2 Chord Trigger's Seventh Chords 105

5.3 Creating Seventh Chords with Finale 107

5.4 Inverting Seventh Chords with Finale and Logic 107

5.5 Seventh Chords from Major Scales 108

5.6 Seventh Chords from Minor Scales...109
5.7 Seventh Chord Generator..111
5.8 *Max Patcher 9*: Seventh Chord Generator...112
5.9 Chord Patterns, Logic's *Arpeggiator*..115
5.10 Chord Patterns in Finale 118
5.11 Extended Chords...119
5.12 Exercises..121
   5.12.1 Exercise 1: Seventh Chord Quiz...121
   5.12.2 Exercise 2: *12-Bar Shuffle Blues* Accompaniment with Logic
      Chord Trigger..123
   5.12.3 Exercise 3: Create a Finale Song Accompaniment.......................................124

Chapter 6: Melody..**127**
6.1 Melody and Motives...127
6.2 Motives and Transposition...129
6.3 Inversion and Retrograde..131
6.4 Rhythmic Augmentation and Diminution...135
6.5 Canonic Utilities in Finale...136
6.6 Finale Motivic Analysis...136
6.7 Diatonic Melody Generator..138
6.8 *Max Patcher 10*: Diatonic Melody Generator 140
6.9 Exercises...144
   6.9.1 Exercise 1: Create a 4-Measure Melody using Finale or Logic......................144
   6.9.2 Exercise 2: Create Melodies with Diatonic Melody Generator.....................145
   6.9.3 Exercise 3: Create Melodies Algorithmically with *Diatonic
      Melody Generator* 146

Chapter 7: Harmonic Progressions...**149**
7.1 *Chord Trigger* and Progressions..149
7.2 Single-Chord Harmony, Non-Chord Tones..149
7.3 Two-Chord Harmonic Progressions, Chord Functions..151
7.4 Cadences...152
7.5 Creating a Three-Part Progression in Finale...154
7.6 Diatonic Progression Generator...156
7.7 Voice Leading 157
7.8 Inverted Chords...160
7.9 Common Tones..160
7.10 Descending-Fifths Progressions 161
7.11 Harmonic Sequences...162
7.12 Patterns 164
7.13 *Max Patcher 11*: Diatonic Progression Generator 164
7.14 Exercises..173
   7.14.1 Exercise 1: Creating Cadence Progressions with Logic Chord Trigger 173
   7.14.2 Exercise 2: Chord Progression with Transposition and Canonic
      Utilities in Finale..174
   7.14.3 Exercise 3: Diatonic Progression Generator and Roman Numeral
      Progressions 175
   7.14.4 Exercise 4: Modify Diatonic Progression Generator for
      Random Generation 175

Chapter 8: Chromatic Harmony **177**

8.1 Diatonic or Chromatic Harmony, Applied Dominant Chords 177
8.2 Constructing Applied Dominants 178
8.3 Chord Trigger Applied Dominants 178
8.4 Chord Tool Applied Dominants..179
8.5 Copy, Paste, and Transpose Applied Dominants 181
8.6 Applied Leading-Tone Chords..182
8.7 Modulation...183
8.8 Chromatic Progression Generator..183
8.9 Pivot Modulation 184
8.10 Step-Up Modulation 185
8.11 Descending-Fifths Progression with Chromatic Alterations.....................186
8.12 Modal Mixture 187
8.13 Phrygian ♭II...188
8.14 V$^{7(♭5)}$, Tritone Substitution, and Augmented Sixth Chords 189
8.15 *Max Patcher 12:* Chromatic Progression Generator 191
8.16 Exercises 194
  8.16.1 Exercise 1: Chromatic Harmony Progression Keyboard Exercises...........194
  8.16.2 Exercise 2: Chromatic Progression Generator Progressions 195
  8.16.3 Exercise 3: Modify Chromatic Progression Generator for Random
          Generation..196

Chapter 9: Chromatic Music **197**

9.1 Atonal Music...197
9.2 Trichords in Logic..198
9.3 Operations on Trichords 199
9.4 Twelve-Tone Music 201
9.5 Creating Twelve-Tone Music with Finale.....................................201
9.6 Twelve-Tone Matrix 204
9.7 Pitch Sets 205
9.8 Manipulating Pitch Sets in Logic and Finale..................................205
9.9 Chromatic Melody Generator...207
9.10 Two-Part Phrase Based on an All-Interval Tetrachord..........................208
9.11 *Max Patcher 13:* Chromatic Melody Generator 210
9.12 Exercises 211
  9.12.1 Exercise 1: Trichord and Tetrachord Music in Logic 211
  9.12.2 Exercise 2: Use Finale to Create a Twelve-Tone Piano Prelude.............211
  9.12.3 Exercise 3: Bartok's String Quartet No. 5, Finale (Introduction)............211
  9.12.4 Exercise 4: Chopin's Etude, Opus 10, No. 2 in A Minor....................211
  9.12.5 Exercise 5: Modify Chromatic Melody Generator 212

Chapter 10: Sound and Music Theory **213**

10.1 Music as Sound..213
10.2 Sound and Frequency 213
10.3 Waveforms..214
10.4 Overtones and Timbre...216
10.5 Musical Intervals and Just Intonation 217
10.6 Ratios and Intervals 219
10.7 Meantone and Equal Temperaments...220

10.8   Logic Temperaments...222

10.9   *Max Patchers 14 – 17* 223

    10.9.1   *Max Patcher 14*: Summing Sines to Make a Sawtooth Wave 224

    10.9.2   *Max Patcher 15*: Just Intonation A Major Scale 225

    10.9.3   *Max Patcher 16:* Pythagorean Comma...226

    10.9.4   *Max Patcher 17*: Triad with Three Temperaments 226

10.10 Exercises...226

    10.10.1   Exercise 1: Diatonic and Chromatic Music Played with Different

           Temperaments 226

    10.10.2   Exercise 2: Create a Chromatic Scale by Ear in Max............................227

Bibliography..**228**

Max Patchers and Objects **230**

Credits **233**

Index..**234**

Acknowledgments

Thank you to Genevieve Aoki of Routledge for her support and guidance throughout the process of creating this book. Thanks as well to Emily Boyd, Shannon Neill, and Abigail Stanley for their help with this project. Thank you to my colleagues at Manhattanville College for their encouragement, conversation, and good will. Thank you to Diane Guernsey for her expert editing and insights. Thank you to Evan London (EML Consulting) for all things computer related. I thank all my students—past, present, and future. So much of what I've learned has come by way of helping students learn about music and music technology. A special thanks goes to Ethan, Devin, and Cameron for their help with coding, design, and for all their encouragements. And, the biggest thanks (and much love) to Patti.

Introduction

0.1 An Overview

From recording audio to computer-generated soundscapes and beyond, the use of technology in music is expanding. Music students and teachers today have vast resources in technology. As these resources grow, so do the questions about how to use them. Music technology pedagogy often focuses on how to create, record, or modify sounds. With a laptop computer running a **Digital Audio Workstation (DAW)**, musicians today have incredibly powerful tools for accomplishing these tasks. But how does the laptop musician, whose primary instrument is the DAW, develop an understanding of music theory that is based on music notation and the music score? How do computer musicians learn the structures of music, such as scales, chords, progressions, rhythms, meters, and form? Or, to ask it differently, how can we learn music theory using new tools such as DAWs and other kinds of music technology?

This book provides an introduction to music theory utilizing three software applications: **Logic Pro X (Logic)**, **Finale**, and **Max/MSP/Jitter (Max)**. While the programs have some things in common, their primary functions and purpose are different: Logic is a DAW, Finale is a **music-printing** program, and Max is an **Audio Programming Language (APL)**. This book's purpose is not to teach these programs comprehensively (books dedicated to these topics are listed in the bibliography) but rather to focus on how to use these popular software programs to learn music theory. I have chosen Logic, Max, and Finale because they are well suited to our purpose. Logic has many well-loved features and also has the **Score Editor** for music notation. Max is a well-supported and accessible APL, and Finale is a widely popular program with many useful tools.

Music technology has burgeoned as an academic discipline, and many undergraduate and graduate programs have been developed over the past several decades. As the tools of music technology have become more powerful, the software has diversified into many areas: recording and audio production, digital sound synthesis, algorithmic music, MIDI sequencing (MIDI is a computer protocol for music), game audio, film audio, and spectral analysis, to name a few.

The primary software program in music technology is the DAW. Many DAWs have expanded their capabilities since their inceptions. With these expansions, DAWs have become more powerful tools not only for creating but also for learning. DAWs are a universal and multipurpose instrument. Their significance today is on par with that of the piano in the nineteenth century, or tape machines and record players in the twentieth century, and their role in music education will certainly continue to expand.

DAWs were originally created for audio recording and production, but there's no limit to how they can be used. We can use them to record rehearsals or practice sessions, work out arrangements and homework assignments, create sound tracks for video, or create content for presentations. And although today's music students may have experience in instrumental or vocal performance, increasingly students' primary means of music-making is a laptop with a DAW. For some music students, encountering a DAW for the first time is an epiphany. As a student at the college where I teach recently said: "When I first opened the program Logic, I knew I could create the music I wanted to create." With DAWs, musicians can create music on a laptop in ways that have been unimaginable before now. DAWs can play any rhythm and any set of notes or chords, on any instrument type or synthesized sound, at any tempo or speed. Given DAWs' vast potential, it's critical that laptop musicians gain an understanding of music theory in order to make the best use of DAWs.

DAWs, APLs, and music-printing programs can provide the tools to explore music theory, but the programs themselves don't provide ready-made lessons. Needless to say, the software user manuals are packed with information about their capabilities, but most don't address music theory directly.

DAWs and music-printing programs can be helpful to explain music theory concepts at many levels because they can put these concepts into sound examples that can be easily modified. With APLs, we can create interactive programs to learn about rhythms, scales, melodies, chords, and progressions, as well as programs to assist in music analysis. Using these interactive devices in conjunction with DAWs makes musical theory practical and accessible. Conversely, understanding music theory substantially enhances any user's experience with DAWs, APLs, or music notation software. A knowledge of music theory makes using some components of DAWs (Logic's **Chord Trigger**, for example) much easier.

The intended audience for this book includes computer musicians, music educators, music technology and software users, and anyone interested in music theory and the connections between technology and education. Theory concepts, music software techniques, and programming are explained without the expectation of prior knowledge.

Music technology sometimes comes to life in experimental form and eventually becomes implemented commercially. One might say that APLs are the experimental labs for developing digital music technology. In the 1950s at Bell Laboratories, Max Mathews developed the ability to generate synthetic sounds from a digital computer with the computer music language, **Music I**, one of the first APLs. These groundbreaking efforts started the age of digital sound and paved the way for the modern DAWs' main capabilities: digital sound production and recording. Mathews presciently wrote in his 1963 article "The Digital Computer as a Musical Instrument," that the computer was of:

> considerable value in the world of music . . . [because] [t]here are no theoretical limitations to the performance of the computer as a source of musical sounds . . . the computer can also function as a machine for composing music.
>
> (Mathews, 1963, p. 533)

From the early days of digital music, music technology researchers (or experimenters) have used APLs to create devices, some of which have become components of commercial DAWs.

Examples of how researchers use APLs to create capabilities that have subsequently become part of DAWs are found in Todd Winkler's *Composing Interactive Music: Techniques and Ideas Using Max* (2001). For instance, Winkler describes how to create a device that "maps every note input to a predetermined scale, available in a menu" (p. 199). In other words, Winkler demonstrates how to program the computer to constrain any MIDI input (such as notes played on an attached keyboard) to a specific musical scale. This functionality has been added to Logic and other DAWs. In Logic it is the **Can't Go Wrong** setting of the **Transposer MIDI FX** plugin.

In describing how his original scale device could be expanded, Winkler points out how commercial software's feature creep can become a problem if these features "add confusion or [are] rarely used" (p. 199). But, alternatively, sometimes a feature might be useful in a way that may not have been intended. Practically speaking, the **Can't Go Wrong** setting ensures that if you are playing a MIDI keyboard into Logic, you can map all the keys to that scale, and you will never play a note outside of the scale: good for music that uses only one scale, but ultimately very restrictive. The setting, however, can be used to help us *learn* scales and might ultimately be more valuable for that purpose. In Chapter 3, I introduce another scale device— **Scale Generator**. **Scale Generator** is a **patcher** built with Max that plays scales starting on any note—a quick and easy scale dictionary.

Throughout this book, I provide examples of Max patchers that help us learn music theory. These patchers (self-contained computer programs made in Max) are similar to DAW plugins and components of commercial music theory software programs, but there is a big difference—we can reconfigure the Max patchers ourselves. Chapter 2's **Rhythm Generator** patcher, created to help students learn about rhythmic patterns, for example, might be modified to become an automatic drum machine. I'll also show how a patcher for playing chords (Chapter 4's **Triad Generator**) can be modified to quiz users on those chords.

I have provided descriptions of how the patchers are constructed, and what the components (**objects**) in each are doing. The reader might ask, "Do I need to learn how to program with Max to learn music theory?" The answer is, of course, no. For centuries, people have been learning music theory from teachers, and/or books, by playing instruments, and by listening to music.

Learning to program music theory, however, is an excellent way to learn and discover. Music theory and programming complement each other well. At their core, both are about logical systems for manipulating data. Learning to program music theory, furthermore, goes a long way to answer the question: How do music and math relate? For those with prior music theory knowledge, learning programming in this area can lead to new avenues of musical investigation and discovery.

At certain points, I will show how to modify patchers so that rather than being a music theory device, these patchers create music automatically. Chapter 6 introduces the **Diatonic Melody Generator**, which can be modified so that it creates its own melodies. These passages provide a foray into the basis of **algorithmic music**, showing how we can program the computer to make decisions in creating music that will follow the principles of music theory.

I hope this book will increase the reader's interest in both music theory and music programming. My message to DAW musicians who want to explore music theory and to music educators who want to explore how DAW and APLs can help music students is that music software and programming can greatly expand our musical understanding and abilities.

0.2 Transmitting MIDI between Programs

One common link among almost all types of music technology software is the use of MIDI (Musical Instrument Digital Interface), a protocol developed in the early 1980s to allow synthesizers and computers to easily communicate with each other. Despite some limitations, MIDI is the *lingua franca* of music technology software today, and it's used in Logic, Finale, and Max.

One of our learning modalities is to transmit MIDI data between programs. Apple's **IAC (Inter-Application Communication) Driver** and PC Drivers such as **MIDI Yoke** were designed for this purpose. To enable the Apple **IAC Driver**, navigate to **Applications** → **Utilities** → **Audio MIDI Setup** → **MIDI Studio**, then double-click the **IAC Driver icon**. In the **IAC Properties** window, click the **Device is online** box and add ports (**IAC Bus 1, IAC**

Bus 2, etc.) as necessary. We can also use Max's own virtual MIDI busses: **from Max 1**, **from Max 2**, **to Max 1**, and **to Max 2**.

The Max patcher (figure 0.1) allows us to play a note on the onscreen keyboard by clicking on a key, thus sending the note to another program. The **noteout** object is used to select a destination for the MIDI data. We can type in the destination, as shown in figure 0.1: **"from Max 1"** (the quotation marks are required in this context), or we could have selected a destination by double-clicking on the **noteout** object and selecting **from Max 1** in the drop-down menu when the patcher is locked, as shown on the right.

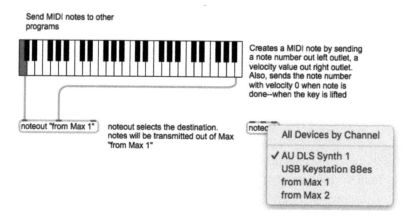

Figure 0.1: Max Patcher to send MIDI notes to Logic or Finale.

Creating this pathway for MIDI transmitting out of Max enables Logic or Finale to receive these MIDI notes. When set to record, Logic's **Software Instruments** receive MIDI data sent through all connected devices, so any Logic MIDI track that's record-enabled will receive this MIDI output from Max.

Finale requires us to specify where we receive MIDI data. From menu item **MIDI/Audio → Device Setup → MIDI/Internal Speaker Setup**, we get **MIDI Setup** (figure 0.2). When Max is on, we can select the **Input Device** as **from Max 1** for channels 1–16 (MIDI Port A). In this window we can also select the output device as **to Max 1** if the playback is set to **MIDI System**, and **Enable Inter-Application Ports** is checked. With Finale, however, we will transmit MIDI in only one direction at any time. We don't use both transmission pathways simultaneously.

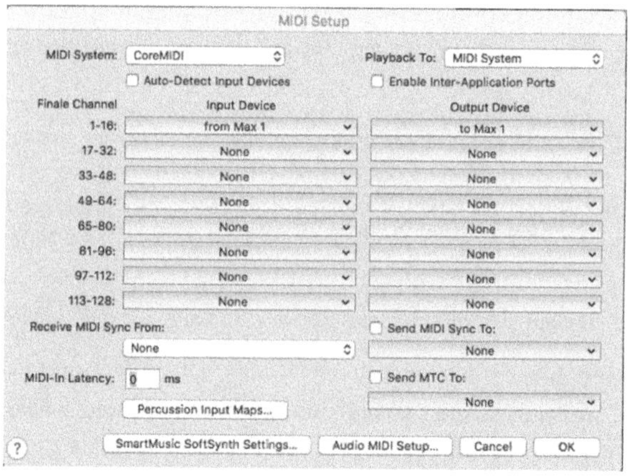

Figure 0.2: Specifying the Input and Output Device as Max in Finale.

We also will want to send MIDI data from Logic to Max. In Logic we can create an **External MIDI** track to send MIDI data to Max by specifying the destination for this track as **to Max 1**, as per figure 0.3—Max must be open for this output connection to be available. When clicked, the triangle to the right of each output destination displays (and allows us to select) MIDI channel numbers.

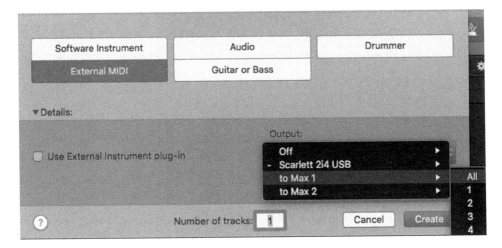

Figure 0.3: Selecting to Max 1 **output for** External MIDI **track in Logic.**

We should be aware of a potential problem if we have MIDI transmission happening in both directions. Simply put, we don't want to send MIDI data **from Max 1** to a *record-enabled* Logic track while also sending the output from this track **to Max 1**. This generates a MIDI loop which endlessly transmits MIDI back and forth between programs, possibly resulting in a computer crash and unpleasant sounds. MIDI transmits at about 1000 notes per second, so a MIDI loop can happen right away.

If we're using both **from Max 1** and **to Max 1** in Logic, we will want to make sure that the **to Max 1** track is *not* record-enabled so that it will not receive MIDI while transmitting MIDI. We can also use different channels to send and receive MIDI data. To get Logic to differentiate incoming MIDI channels, we select **File → Project Settings → Recording →** and from **MIDI → Auto demix by channel if multi-track recording**.

We can see how and why we might have MIDI notes transmitting in both directions between Max and Logic in **Send and Receive (*Max Patcher 0*)**, shown in figure 0.4. (Although this patcher is the *first* patcher discussed, we're numbering it *Patcher 0* because, by convention, computer programs often start counting with 0.) **Send and Receive** is to the right of the Logic screen. Both Logic and **Send and Receive** are sending and receiving MIDI (figure 0. 4). **Send and Receive** transmits the notes of an ascending and descending **chromatic scale** from C4 to C5 (see Chapter 3 for more on pitch names and the chromatic scale) when triggered by a MIDI message from Logic. This chromatic scale output of Max is recorded in Logic's track 2.

Logic starts the Max patcher by sending it MIDI note 60 from track 1, and stops it with MIDI note 61. These MIDI notes are functioning only as **triggers**. Track 1 is an **External MIDI** track set to transmit **to Max 1** on channel 16. In this case we are using two tracks in Logic for two different purposes: one to trigger Max, and the other to receive (and record) the output from Max. Looking at the Logic window on the left, we can see that **Send and Receive** starts and stops transmitting the chromatic scale twice. We can use this inter-application MIDI transmission in different music-theory related settings—for scales, melodies, chords, and harmonic progressions.

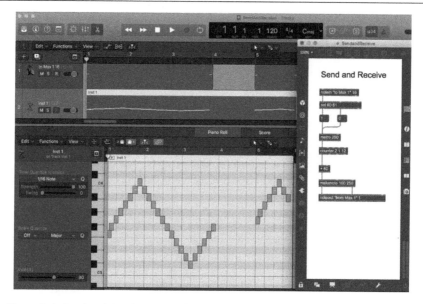

Figure 0.4: Send and Receive. **MIDI data sent from Logic to Max and Max to Logic.**

0.3 Max Patcher 0: *Send and Receive*

Patchers use objects, the rectangular boxes with words in them that are connected to other objects by virtual patch cables via their **inlet outlet** (figure 0.5). The patcher below has three objects. Some of the icons displayed in three of the side menus (top, right, and bottom) are identified for the reader as these will be used throughout the book. Max patchers, objects, and tools in Logic and Finale are identified in *bold* print throughout this book.

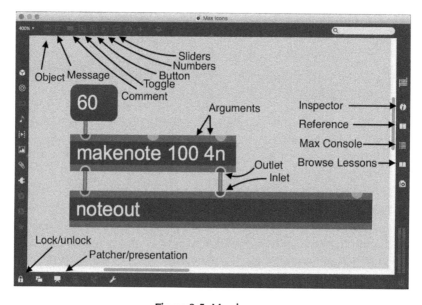

Figure 0.5: Max icons.

Send and Receive (fig 0.4) has nine objects and a **comment**. The objects start off with **notein** "**to Max 1**" **16** at the top. The name (**Send and Receive**) at the top is a comment. Comments are ignored by the patcher, but are useful for providing information to the user.

This **notein** "**to Max 1**" **16** object receives MIDI note-on messages transmitted via "**to Max 1**" on channel 16. MIDI note-on messages are how MIDI directs a synthesizer to play a note. The **notein** sends the note numbers received to a **sel** (or **select**) object. The **sel** listens for incoming numbers and sends out an impulse (a **bang**) when it receives a number matching one of its arguments. **Arguments** (used in many objects) are user-defined data inserted after an object's name. We can see that this **sel**'s arguments are 60 and 61. If **sel** receives a 60, it bangs out of the left outlet, and if it receives a 61, it bangs out of the middle outlet. A bang out of the left causes the **message 1** to go to **metro 250** to start it, while a bang out of the middle sends a **message 0** to **metro 250** to turn it off. When **messages** are banged in their left inlet, they send out their contents.

The **metro 250** object sends out continuous bangs at the rate of every 250 milliseconds (or a ¼ of a second). Each of these bangs from **metro 250** causes the **counter 2 1 12** object to output the numbers from 0 to 12 and back down to 0, a numerical palindrome that becomes an ascending and descending chromatic scale. This **counter** object arguments **2 1 12** create this pattern. We next add the value 60 to this output with a (**+ 60**) object so that it becomes 60, 61, 62 . . . 72, 71, 70. . . . These values are turned into MIDI notes by **makenote 100 250**, with durations of 250 and velocities of 100 (MIDI loudness values). The notes (starting on middle C) are then sent **from Max 1** to a MIDI destination—Logic's track 2—where they're recorded.

At the end of this book is a list of the patchers and objects discussed throughout. For each patcher, the objects introduced with that patcher are also listed.

CHAPTER 1

Rhythm: Tempo, Meter, Durations

1.1 Tempo

A good starting point in a discussion of rhythm is **tempo**, the pace of music, or how slow or fast a piece of music sounds. More specifically, the tempo is the rate of the **beat**. The beat is music's pulse, moving forward at regular intervals of time, and can often be heard in music's rhythmic elements. Tempos can be indicated by descriptive names, such as Fast, *Allegro* ("cheerful" in Italian), *Andante* ("walking speed"), Up-tempo, or Moderate. Tempo can also be set precisely as a **BPM** number (beats per minute), which is how tempos are set in DAWs. In Logic's **LCD Display** (figure 1.1), we see that the default setting is 120 BPM, meaning that there are 120 beats per minute or two beats per second. To change the BPM, click on the number and drag it up or down, or double-click on it and type in a new BPM. Tempo and the BPM can vary within a piece of music as well. BPMs and metronome-marking numbers are the same concept, and mechanical metronomes have been helping musicians keep a steady beat since their invention in 1816 by Johann Maezel.

Figure 1.1: LCD Display **with tempo set as BPM = 120 in Logic.**

The difference between BPM and tempo indications (such as *Allegro*) is significant, as the words allow for some flexibility and variation. A musician might play a piece of music with an *Allegro* tempo marking at a 140 BPM one day and 136 BPM the next. Additionally, even a steady-sounding human musical performance will have slight variations in the temporal distance between beats. A DAW music performance will remain precisely at the indicated BPM with exactly equal distances between beats, unless the user creates some differences. To give a DAW performance a human feel, large and small variations in tempo can be added.

Seen in figure 1.2 is a MIDI realization of *Greensleeves* with thirteen tempo (BPM) changes visible in Logic's **Tempo Global Track**—the top area's horizontal lines (figure 1.2). We can create tempo changes that occur within a piece of music by editing the **Tempo Global Track** with the **Pencil** tool. The initial tempo is 120 BPM, and these added BPM tempo changes create a more human quality to the performance. This *Greensleeves* MIDI realization could be played on the piano, but the written music would not include these tempo changes. Pianists and other performing musicians learn how to vary the tempo slightly in performance, while still sounding steady—part of creating an interpretation or styling.

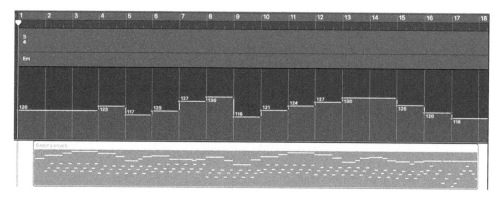

Figure 1.2: Changing BPM in Tempo Global Track **in Logic.**

To hear the beat and listen for changes in tempo in Logic, we can turn on the **metronome**. In measures 5–8 (hereafter mm. for measures and m. for measure) and mm. 9–13, we'll hear a gradual and slight speeding up of the tempo, an **accelerando (accel.)**. The BPM in mm. 14–17 gradually slows down, a **ritardando (rit.)**.

In Finale, the usual method of setting the tempo is with the **Expression** tool (from the main menu, choose the *mf* icon) with which we can put input a tempo indication such as Allegro, and a BPM such as quarter note equals 120. With the **Expression** tool selected, double-click in the score where you want to place the tempo indication. From the **Expression Selection** window, choose **Tempo Marks**, and select a tempo. To make sure the **Tempo Mark** will control the BPM, in the lower portion of the **Expression Selection** window click **Edit**, and from there → **Playback** → **Type** → **Tempo**. Then, type in a BPM value in the **Set to Value** box if there isn't a number there already. Some **Tempo Marks** have default BPMs, but others don't.

DAWs define time in two main ways: musical time and clock time. Musical time provides a connection to music theory concepts, and will thus be our main focus, but we should describe how clock time is represented to provide a context.

Seen in figure 1.3 are two displays in Logic (**Time** and **Beats**) showing these different versions of marking time. **Time**, the lower window, has clock time in the **SMPTE** (Society of Motion Pictures and Television Engineers) format which indicates hours, minutes, seconds, and frames (as in video frames), separated by colons. In keeping with film industry convention, the default SMPTE code starts with hour one as opposed to hour zero, although this can be changed. SMPTE time code can also display milliseconds instead of frames.

Beats (figure 1.3) displays musical time of **bars**, **beats**, **divisions**, and **ticks**. Performing musicians often use the terms bars (or measures), beats, and divisions (or subdivisions), but not ticks. Ticks (also known as **PPQN**—Parts or Pulses Per Quarter Note) are a smaller subdivision of a beat, and strictly a MIDI unit of time. Because they are so small, an individual tick is usually impossible to discern. A musician might say to a fellow performer, "I came in one beat late," but no one would say, "I played that note one tick too late."

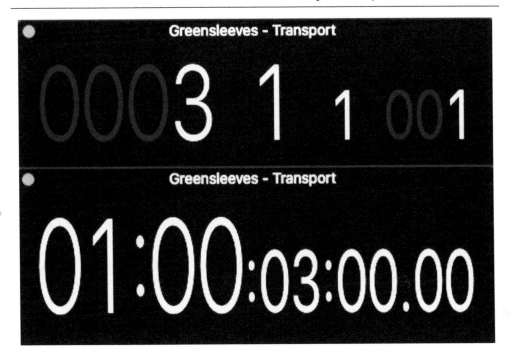

Figure 1.3: Two versions of time (Beat and Time) **in Logic.**

1.2 Meter

Logic's **LCD Display** in figure 1.1. also shows a **time signature** of $^4_4$. The term time signature is simplified to **TIME**. The time signature represents how the pulse is organized into groups of beats, or musical **meter**. One unit of a meter is a **measure** or **bar**. In music notation, measures are separated by the **bar line**. The most common meters consist of groups of two, three, or four beats, known as **duple**, **triple**, and **quadruple meter**. The most common type of quadruple meter is **common time**, which has a $^4_4$ time signature. The first beat of a metrical pattern is often the strongest felt, and is called the **downbeat**. The Logic session seen in figure 1.4 demonstrates these meters as expressed by time signatures and the beats played on the drums. In each measure the kick drum plays on the downbeat, and the last beat (or **upbeat**) is played by the Hi-Hat.

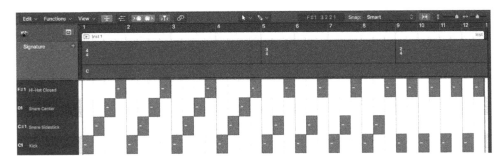

Figure 1.4: Simple meters played by a drum in Logic.

In figure 1.4, the first four measures are quadruple **simple meter** (common time), followed by four measures each of triple and duple simple meters. The designation "simple" means that usual beat subdivisions are based on multiples of two, and in simple meters, beats are regularly divided into two, four, or eight parts. Greater divisions are possible, and divisions in odd numbers are also possible. Listening to the Logic session one hears that in each measure each beat is heard as a drum hit, either the kick drum, snare, or hi-hat. Counting the beats out loud ("One, two, three, four" for quadruple; "One, two, three" for triple; and "One, two" for duple) as you listen to the Logic session helps you get the feel of the meters.

The lower number in the time signature indicates the **rhythmic value** of each beat. For these simple-meter time signatures, a four indicates a **quarter note**, a common rhythmic duration. In Logic, this beat value and the time signature can be changed by clicking on the time signature in the **LCD Display** and selecting a new time signature. Meters often remain the same throughout a piece of music, although changing meters are possible—we'll explore some other aspects of changing meters in Chapter 2. For now, we'll note that you can change the meter in a Logic session by positioning the playhead, clicking on the **Time** in the **LCD Display**, and selecting a different time signature from the drop-down menu.

The **compound** (as opposed to simple) meters have *three-part* beat subdivisions. Once again, two-, three-, and four-beat groupings (duple, triple, and quadruple meters) are common in compound meters, with the duple compound (such as $^6_8$) being the most common. Simple meters are more common overall, but one hears compound meters in many contexts, including the rock **shuffle**, such as *Crazy*, written by Steven Tyler, Joe Perry, and Desmond Child (Aerosmith). The example in figure 1.5 demonstrates four measures each of duple, triple, and quadruple compound meters with $^6_8$, $^9_8$, and $^{12}_8$ time signatures.

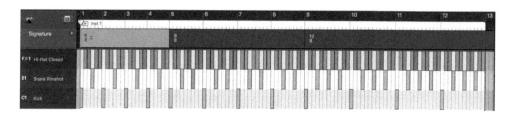

Figure 1.5: Compound meters in Logic.

An important difference between simple and compound meters is how the basic beat value is represented in the time signature. If the top number of a time signature is greater than *and* divisible by three, then (1) it's a compound meter; and (2) a three-times multiple of the rhythm value represented by the time signature's lower number is the beat in most cases (the rhythmic value shown can also possibly equal the beat). The time signatures in the Logic session in figure 1.5 have a beat value of a dotted quarter note, or three eighth notes as one unit.

1.3 Note Values

Basic rhythmic note values or durations are **whole, half, quarter, eighth, sixteenth, thirty-second, sixty-fourth**, etc. Musical notation represents rhythmic durations proportionally—a half note is half the length of a whole note. A quarter note lasts half as long as a half note, and twice as long as an eighth note. To know the time duration for a rhythmic value, one must also know the BPM. A quarter note at 60 BPM lasts one second, but a quarter note at 120 BPM lasts ½ a second.

In addition to the piano-roll format, Logic also displays MIDI notes in musical notation. In the Logic session shown in figure 1.6, the basic rhythmic durations are arranged to show all of the proportions of each value, both in terms of the spacing in traditional notation (in the **Score Editor**), and in the **Piano Roll Editor**, where one sees the notes laid out from left to right as lines of different lengths. Listening to the session shows us how the notes relate proportionally to each other, and how these proportions stay consistent when the tempo, or BPM, is changed. Changing the BPM does not alter the proportions: eighth notes always last ½ the duration of quarter notes, and double the duration of sixteenth notes. We can also notice that groups of eighth and sixteenth notes can be beamed together by horizontal lines, but quarters and half notes cannot be beamed.

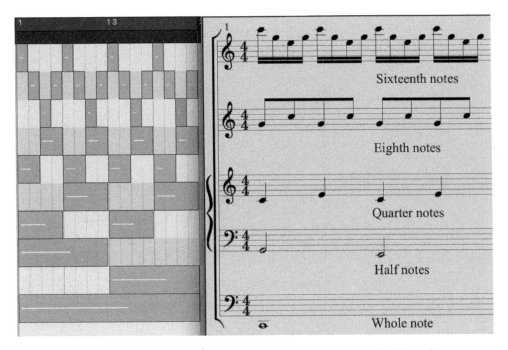

Figure 1.6: Durations shown in Piano Roll Editor and Score Editor in Logic.

Where an instrument or voice doesn't play or sing in written music is indicated as a **rest** (figure 1.7). The rests are shown directly before the corresponding note values.

Figure 1.7: Rests and notes.

Understanding rhythm durations is helpful for using DAWs, as the tools we use in DAWs often rely on traditional rhythmic values. Logic Pro X's **Echo** plugin, for example, creates an echo effect based on rhythmic durations. In order to determine the actual time of the echo, we also need to know the BPM, just as we need to know the BPM to know the clock-time duration of note values. **Echo** links durations to the beat, called **syncing**. When a quarter-note value is selected in **Echo**, the plugin is synchronized (or "synced") to the 120 BPM tempo, and echoes are heard at ½-second intervals (figure 1.8). If the BPM is set to 60, the echoes are heard at one-second intervals. If the BPM is at 120, the echoes are heard every half-second.

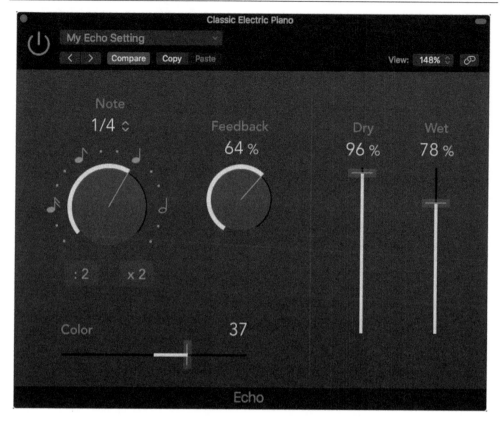

Figure 1.8: Echo **in Logic.**

1.4 *Dotted Rhythms and Pickup*

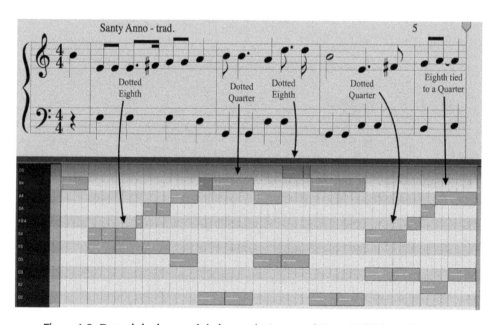

Figure 1.9: Dotted rhythms and tied notes in Score **and** Piano Roll Editors **in Logic.**

To create note values that are halfway in duration between the basic note values, we use the **dotted rhythms** as shown in figure 1.9. A dot extends the duration (of a note or a rest) by half its original value. A dotted eighth is equal to 1½ eighths or three sixteenth notes combined, as seen in figure 1.9 in m. 1 of the song *Santy Anno*. A dotted quarter (m. 2) is equal 1½ quarters, or three eighth notes combined. Dotted half notes are equal to three quarters, and a dotted whole note is equal to three half notes. Less common, but also possible, is a double-dotted rhythmic value, which adds both a half and a quarter of its duration (½ + ¼). We also see the **tie** in m. 5 joining two rhythmic values together as one. Here an eighth and a quarter are tied together, creating a duration that equals a dotted quarter. The tie can be used to join durations over the bar line.

In addition to dotted rhythms, *Santy Anno* also has a **pickup** (or **anacrusis**), the single quarter note in the incomplete measure at the beginning. Pickups are common and are not counted in musical scores as the first measure, but rather as a lead-in to the first downbeat.

1.5 Triplets

In simple meters, dividing notes into three parts is done with a **triplet**. Triplets of any basic note value are possible. In figure 1.10 we see half, quarter, eighth, and sixteenth triplets and their durations (whole, half, quarter, and eighth respectively). In Chapter 2 we'll discuss dividing durations into larger odd numbered amounts, known as **tuplets**.

Figure 1.10: Triplet halves, quarters, eighths, and sixteenths.

Triplets, such as eighth-note triplets, can have different values within them, and triplet note values can also be tied. In the example in figure 1.11 we see two tied eighth-note triplets between beats 1 and 2, and a quarter note taking the place of two triplet eighths on the third beat (fig 1.11).

Figure 1.11: Tied triplet and quarter note in triplet eighths.

1.6 Quantization

Logic uses rhythmic values in its **quantization** settings. These determine the resolution used for aligning events to Logic's **grid**. In the quantization setting shown in figure 1.12 (in **Classic Quantize** mode), the sixteenth note is selected and is therefore the smallest possible note value for **Score Editor** rhythms. The quantization setting must be at least as short as the shortest note value in order for the rhythms to be correctly displayed in musical notation. Quantization has other uses and meanings as well, such as correcting rhythmic imperfections in a performance, or imbuing a MIDI performance with a rhythmic feel, such as the types of **Swing** quantization settings in figure 1.12.

Figure 1.12: MIDI quantization settings in Logic.

1.7 Inputting Rhythm in Logic

To record MIDI input in Logic: (1) attach a MIDI device to the computer, (2) open a software instrument track, (3) make sure the MIDI data is coming to the software instrument track, and (4) press the record button and play notes on the device. As we see in figure 1.13, what's recorded can be viewed in the **Piano Roll Editor** or in the **Score Editor** as notation. Whole, half, quarter, eighth, and sixteenth notes were played and recorded in the track.

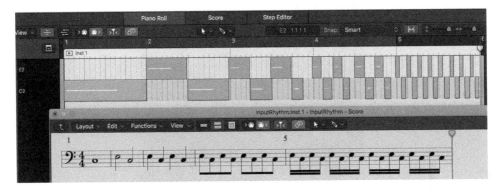

Figure 1.13: MIDI notes input in Piano Roll and Score Editors in Logic.

If we look at the **Piano Roll Editor** carefully, we'll see that the notes are not perfectly aligned to the **Grid**, the vertical lines that represent beats and subdivisions. Although the **Metronome** was used so that we heard the beat out loud (**Metronome** and **Count-ins** enable buttons shown in figure 1.14), the notes are just a bit off the **Grid** lines. The **Count-in** button, also enabled, creates a number of beats that are heard before the recording starts, to provide a reference for the performer.

Figure 1.14: Metronome and Count-in enabled in Logic.

Because Logic's quantization is in this case set to sixteenth notes, these slight errors are corrected (or quantized) in the notation. If the performance errors had been significant enough for the notes to be incorrectly positioned, we could quantize the track in the **Piano Roll Editor** to align the notes by selecting them and pressing the **Q** in **Time Quantize**.

For exact rhythmic durations, we can input MIDI notes with the **Step Input Keyboard**, as shown in figure 1.15, available in Logic's **Window** menu.

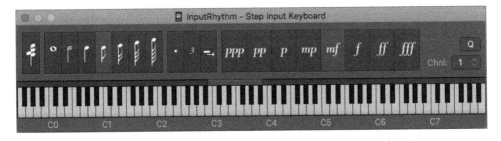

Figure 1.15: Step Input Keyboard in Logic.

If a MIDI track is record-enabled, we can select the note values and play notes from an attached keyboard, or click on the keys in the **Step Input Keyboard**. An eighth note is selected above, and to the right of the rhythmic values we see the tabs to select dotted rhythms or triplets and to select dynamic levels for setting the notes' loudness.

We can also drag the rhythmic values in the **Score Editor** into a score staff to create MIDI notes, although this is more time-consuming than the methods mentioned previously. The top row has values from a whole note to 128th note, the middle row has triplet values, and the lower row has dotted rhythms (figure 1.16).

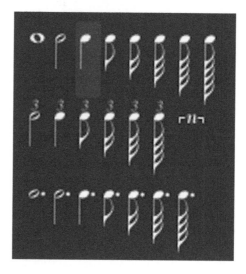

Figure 1.16: Score Editor **note values in Logic.**

1.8 Meter, Time Signatures, and Rhythmic Durations in Finale

Finale's **Document Setup Wizard** takes the user through several steps for choosing the style of music notation and page set-up, naming the piece and composer, and selecting the instruments, and then takes the user to the **Score Settings** window (figure 1.17), where we can choose the time signature, key signature (see Chapter 3), and tempo marking with BPM, pickup measure, and overall length.

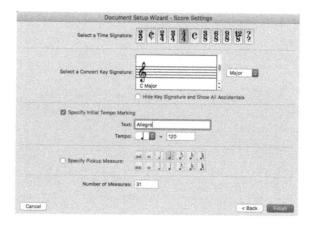

Figure 1.17: Score Settings **in** Document Setup Wizard **in Finale.**

In the **Score Settings** one can specify the tempo with a BPM number and what the beat will equal as a rhythmic duration, as well as a tempo indication. In this case, we've written in *Allegro* and set the quarter note equal to 120 BPM.

In the top section one selects the initial time signature. The C stands for common time ($^4_4$), and the C with a slash through it stands for **Cut Time** (or $^2_2$), typically a fast duple meter. We can see additional examples of simple time signatures ($^2_2$, $^2_4$, $^3_4$, $^4_4$, $^3_8$), and compound time signatures ($^6_8$, $^9_8$, $^{12}_8$). We can also create less common time signatures with the $^?_?$ button, which brings up the **Time Signature** tool (figure 1.18). The **Time Signature** tool has a selection for the **Number of Beats** and for **Beat Duration** in rhythmic durations. The **Beat Duration** sets the time signature's lower number as a standard rhythmic duration number, such as 1=whole note, 2=half note, 4=quarter note, 8=eighth note, 16=sixteenth note, etc.

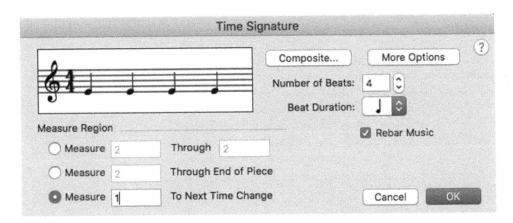

Figure 1.18: Time Signature **tool in Finale.**

In the example in figure 1.19, each measure has a new time signature, and we've also included a pickup or anacrusis.

Figure 1.19: Six time signatures.

For each of these measures' time signatures, the rhythmic durations shown are equal to the beat. In measures 5 and 6, the dotted quarter note (equal to three eighth notes) is the beat values of $^9_8$ and $^{12}_8$. The quarter note is the beat value for $^4_4$, $^3_4$, and $^2_4$, and the eighth note is the beat value of $^2_8$.

Finale has two primary methods for inputting rhythmic durations and pitches into a score: **Simple** and **Speedy Entry**. With **Simple Entry** the user can choose either a note or rest value from the **Simple** or **Rests** windows and click and drag it into a staff (figure 1.20). The **Simple Entry** note window also includes an eraser and a tool for changing the pitch. Dotted rhythms are created by selecting a note value and the dot, then click dragging it into the music. Triplets are created by selecting a note value and **Triplet** icon.

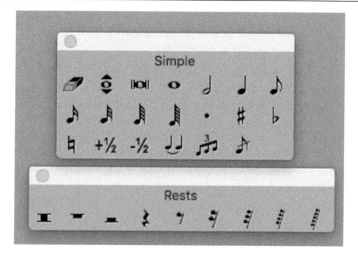

Figure 1.20: Simple Entry **rhythmic durations in Finale.**

Simple and **Speedy Entry** allows users to input notes by playing the note on an attached MIDI controller. With **Speedy Entry** the duration can be selected with the numeric keypad so that rhythmic values can be easily changed. The numbers on the numeric keypad correspond to rhythmic durations, as shown in figure 1.21, and this diagram also shows which keys to use to create triplets, dotted rhythms, and ties (figure 1.21).

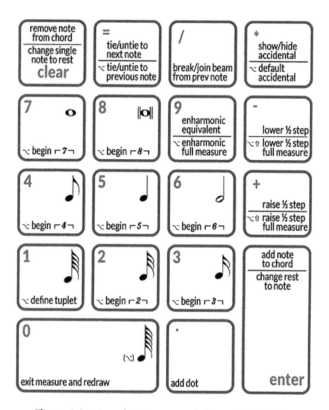

Figure 1.21: Speedy Entry **numeric keypad in Finale.**

Individual rhythmic durations can be edited via either **Simple** or **Speedy Entry** tools. To change a group of note values we can use the **Change Note Durations** tool (**Utilities** → **Change** → **Note Durations**). We can change selected note values to another value, or a group of notes can be changed by a percentage (figure 1.22). In figure 1.22 the first measure's note values were cut in half or changed by 50% in the second measure.

Figure 1.22: Change Note Durations **in Finale.**

1.9 Max Patcher I: *Drum Pattern*

To demonstrate tempo, BPM, and meter, we'll make a MIDI-based drum machine in Max that plays one measure of a common-time pattern with kick, snare, and hi-hat. Our goal is to be able to change the BPM or tempo of the patcher, something we've seen how to do with Logic and Finale.

Max patchers use **objects**, which represent bits of code that do common computing tasks. Max is thus described as an *object-oriented* programming environment. Objects mostly appear as rectangular box shapes and can be used and arranged in limitless ways. Objects sometimes appear as icons, such as the speaker icon for the **EZ DAC** object, an object that routes audio to the computer's sound output. Objects connect to one another by **patch cables**—the term and concept come from modular analog synthesizers, such as the early Moog synthesizers, which used actual cables to connect a synthesizer's modules or units. Depending on its particular attributes, an object has a certain number of inlets (on top) and outlets (on bottom). Outlets connect to inlets. Data, messages, or impulses (called **bangs**) flow downward and from right to left on the computer screen, from one object's outlets to another's inlets.

To begin our patcher, we'll make a single kick-drum sound. We drag an **object** (a blank object, ready to be named) from the top part of the patcher window onto the edit area and type "noteout" as one word in the object (figure 1.23). The **noteout** object we have created (or instantiated, to use the programming term) has three inlets to receive MIDI note number, velocity, and channel data, but no outlets. If you mistakenly type "note out" with a space between the words, the box will turn a faded color, letting you know that it isn't an object in Max. Max only understands correctly named objects, and object names are always continuous text or single words. Objects may have words, numbers, or symbols after their name. This text might be the name of that specific instance of the object, or it might be **arguments** used by the object, such as values that control how the object does its task.

At the top right of the patcher window, next to **object**, is **message**. We drag a **message** into the edit area and place it above the right inlet of our **noteout**, typing the number 10 in the message and connecting its outlet to **noteout**'s right inlet by click-dragging from the outlet to the inlet. When we click on the **10 message**, we send that number to **noteout**'s channel number. This sets the MIDI channel as 10, the channel designated for drum or percussion sounds.

Next, we drag another object above **noteout** and type in **makenote 100 4n** with spaces between the word "makenote" and the numbers. The object name is **makenote**, and 100 and 4n are **arguments**. These arguments for **makenote** represent a MIDI note's *velocity* value and its *duration* as a note value. We'll connect the outlets of **makenote** to the first two inlets of **noteout** so that all three of **noteout**'s inlets have connections.

We drag another **message** above **makenote** and type in 35, which will function as a MIDI note number to play a kick-drum sound. We'll connect this **message** to the left inlet of **makenote**. Our screen now looks like figure 1.23. Before listening to our kick, we need to lock the patch by clicking on the **Edit lock/unlock** icon at the lower left of the window, and click on the **10**. Clicking on the **35** produces a kick-drum sound. To continue working, we need to unlock it to get back to edit mode.

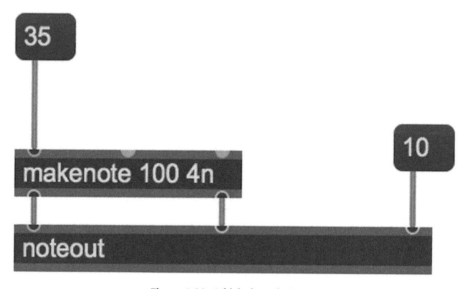

Figure 1.23: A kick drum in Max.

Next, we'll create snare and hi-hat sounds. To do this, we'll create two more messages boxes with numbers 40 (snare) and 42 (hi-hat) that also connect with **makenote**'s left inlet. Our one-measure pattern's notation is as per figure 1.24, a single measure in common time with a drum-hit on each of the four quarter-note beats. The hi-hat notes have the X-shaped **note-heads**.

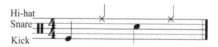

Figure 1.24: The drum pattern.

We want the pattern to repeat continuously, with each drum sounding on the four beats as per figure 1.24. To set up the timing we'll use the **metro**, **delay**, and **transport** objects. The **metro** object sends out steady bangs. The **delay** object delays a bang, and the **transport** object controls time-related objects and allows us to change the tempo. First, we create a **transport** object and connect its left inlet to a **toggle** above it so that it can be turned on and off.

Next, we create two **metro** objects. In the first **metro** object we type in the argument **1n** for whole note, and in the second we type in **2n** for half note. We connect the toggle outlet to the two **metros**' left inlets and connect the **metro 1n** to the **35 message**. This will play the kick drum once every measure on the downbeat. Next, we create a **delay 2n** and connect its output to the snare (**40** message) and connect its inlet to **metro 1n**. This will play the snare every measure, but with a half-note delay from the downbeat, meaning that it will play on the third beat of every measure.

To play the hi-hat at double speed and shifted over from the downbeat by one quarter note, we connect the **metro 2n** to a **delay 4n** (for quarter note) and connect this to the **42 message**. We connect the **metro 2n** to the toggle so that we can turn the hi-hat on and off. Finally, to simplify the patcher we remove the **10 message** going into **noteout** and replace it with an argument (10) in the object itself. All these connections should be made through the left inlets and outlets as shown in figure 1.25. We can also see the **Global Transport** window, which we open by double-clicking on the **Transport** object (figure 1.25), when the patcher is locked.

In addition to the **1n**, **2n**, and **4n** note values in Max, eighth notes are **8n** and sixteenth notes are **16n**. Triplets are created by adding the letter *t*, so that triplet eighth notes are **8nt**. Dotted rhythms are created by adding the letter *d*, so that a dotted eighth note is **8nd**.

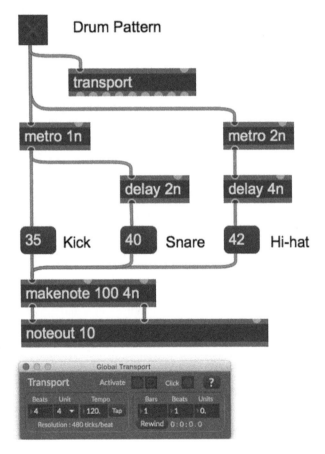

Figure 1.25: Drum Pattern **in Max.**

In the **Global Transport** we can see a 120 BMP number under **Tempo**. Dragging this number up or down will change the tempo. The **Global Transport** also keeps track of how long it has been playing by **Bars**, **Beats**, and **Units** (ticks) with the three number boxes in the lower right section, and the real-time counter below that. As we're in common time, the **Bars** number advances after four **Beats** have elapsed.

Drum Pattern demonstrates that changing the tempo alters note durations, but it doesn't change patterns' internal structure. In other words, the pattern sounds the same at different tempos (equally spaced kick, hi-hat, snare, hi-hat, etc.). We hear patterns that maintain their structure speeding up or slowing down all the time in music (accelerando and ritardando). The timing objects **metro** and **delay** can also accept arguments in milliseconds, but using note values (as we have done) allows us to change the tempo in **Drum Pattern**.

1.10 Exercises

1.10.1 Exercise 1: Rhythmic Values in Measures

In a measure with a $^2_4$ time signature (a duple meter in which each beat is equal to a quarter note) and using only quarter- and eighth-note rhythmic values, we can create five different rhythmic patterns that complete one full measure (figure 1.26):

Figure 1.26: Combining quarters and eighths in $^2_4$ measures.

Using the **Simple Entry** tool in Finale or **Step Input** in Logic, create examples of all the different combinations possible of these rhythmic values in these time signatures:

1. Combine quarter and eighth notes in $^3_4$, $^4_4$, and $^5_4$ time signatures.
2. Combine half, quarter, and eighth notes in $^3_4$, $^4_4$, and $^5_4$ time signatures.

As an example, thirteen different combinations of quarters and eighths are possible in a single measure in $^3_4$ time. After figuring out all the combinations, (1) listen to all the measures and (2) practice each measure's rhythm by speaking each note as a "Ta" while you listen. More advanced exercises can be created by incorporating different note values (including triplets and dotted rhythms) and using different time signatures ($^6_4$, $^7_4$, $^3_8$, $^4_8$, $^4_8$, $^2_2$, $^3_2$, $^4_2$, etc.).

1.10.2 Exercise 2: Practice Rhythm with Logic and Finale

Developing rhythm skills takes practice, and we can use Logic and Finale to create useful drills. In the Logic session in figure 1.27, we've taken several of the measures from figure 1.26 to create a four-measure rhythmic exercise.

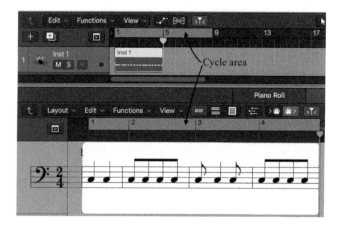

Figure 1.27: Practicing a rhythm exercise in Logic.

Figure 1.28: The Cycle **button (at right) in Logic.**

When the **Cycle Area** is activated (by clicking the **Cycle** button shown in Figure 1.28) and positioned as per figure 1.27, mm. 1–8 will continuously repeat when we press play. First, we hear the four-measure rhythmic phrase, then we can practice the rhythms by speaking them during the four empty measures (with or without the Metronome–a Logic tool). If we speak the rhythms in correct time, we will be in sync as the **Cycle Area** brings us back to the downbeat. We can use a "Ta" for the quarter notes and "Tee" for eighth notes: "Ta Ta, Tee Tee Tee Tee, Tee Ta Tee, Tee Tee Tee Tee." Using these syllables is one approach; other rhythm syllabification systems include the **Takadimi** or **Kodaly**. We can play this track back at faster BPM to increase the challenge.

We could also use the solutions to *Exercise 1: Rhythmic Values in Measures* to create rhythm exercises. The thirteen possible rhythmic patterns in $^3_4$ time using only quarter and eighth notes are challenging because every measure is different (figure 1.29):

Figure 1.29: Rhythmic exercise.

Finale also includes a library of exercises (including rhythmic exercises) that students and teachers can assemble with the **Exercise Wizard**. These exercises can be used in conjunction with MakeMusic's **SmartMusic** program, which allows for interaction between students and teachers. The exercises can also be edited in Finale, and the edited versions imported into the **SmartMusic** platform or into a Logic session as a MIDI file. The exercises range from beginner to advanced levels.

1.10.3 Exercise 3: Modifying Drum Pattern

Modify the **Drum Pattern** so that it plays the rhythmic patterns (A and B). Patching solutions are shown in figure 1.30:

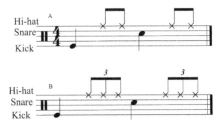

Figure 1.30: Modifying Drum Pattern **in Max.**

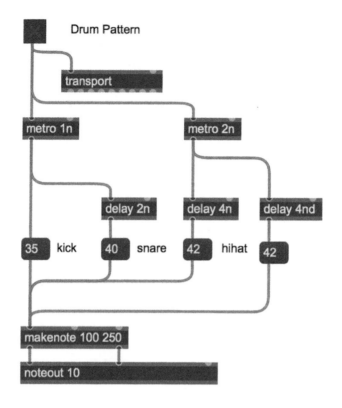

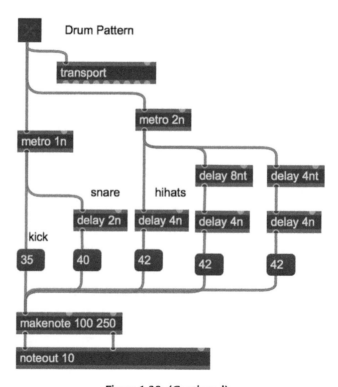

Figure 1.30: (Continued)

1.10.4 Exercise 4: Add Tempo Changes in Logic or Finale

Find a **Standard MIDI File** (SMF) of a favorite piece of music by searching online. Many websites contain free MIDI files of public-domain works—created by music technologists who want to share their work! After downloading the file, import the file into Logic and open the **Tempo Global Track**. Many SMFs will already contain tempo changes. To clear them, select all the tempo changes in the **Tempo Global Track** and delete them. Then, add your own tempo changes by editing the **Tempo Global Track** with the Pencil–a Logic tool. The piece in figure 1.31 is Henry Purcell's *Rondeau*, with small tempo changes added to create a less mechanical quality of playback. We can hear a slight ritardando in m. 8, for instance; a tempo change that pianists might incorporate for expressive reasons.

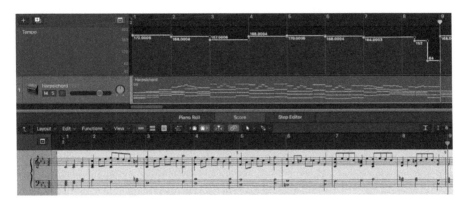

Figure 1.31: Tempo Global Track **above the track and** Score Editor **in Logic.**
Henry Purcell's *Rondeau*

In Finale, tempo changes can be inserted with the **Expression Tool** as described on page 2. Another way to create tempo changes in Finale is the **Tempo Tap**. To use Finale's **Tempo Tap**, first set the **View** to **Studio**, then open the **MIDI Tool** by clicking on the **Edit** button in the top right part of the screen. In this edit window, we can set tempo changes by selecting a portion of the screen and then from the **MIDI Tool** drop-down menu select a tool such as **Set to . . ., Scale . . ., Add . . ., Percent Alter . . ., Limit . . ., or Clear** to create or change MIDI tempo data. In figure 1.32 we see a gradual increase (accelerando) then decrease (ritardando) in tempo in the **MIDI Tool Tempo** data window in this MIDI realization of Johann Sebastian Bach's *Invention No. 1*.

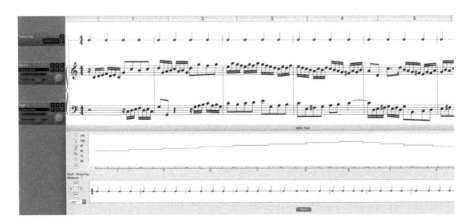

Figure 1.32: MIDI Tool **tempo data in Finale. John Sebastian Bach's** *Invention No. 1.*

CHAPTER 2

Rhythm: Loops and Advanced Rhythm

2.1 Loops in Logic

Repeated patterns are heard in all kinds of music, from the baroque ground and classical Alberti bass patterns to the loops in DAWs. In earlier days of music technology, the tape loop was developed by attaching the ends of a piece of reel-to-reel magnetic tape together so that it would play continuously. Composers such as Karlheinz Stockhausen and Steve Reich used tape loops to great effect in their 1960s electronic music. In the digital realm, the tape loop has become just a **loop**, a repeatable segment of audio (or MIDI). Starting in 1998, **Acid Pro** was one of the first DAWs to incorporate loops, and now most DAWs provide ready-made loops. Logic has over 21,000 loops of various kinds, including drum loops. Finale's **Drum Groove** has twenty-nine MIDI-based drum loops, and Max has one example. What can we learn from loops? How can we incorporate them into the music learning process? And finally, what can we learn from making our own loops? In figure 2.1 are five **Apple Loop Beats** from Logic:

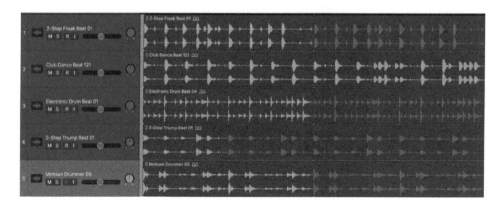

Figure 2.1: Apple Loop Beats **in Logic.**

All of these loops are audio files with tempo at 130 BPM and in quadruple meter. To listen to each loop in turn, we press the **S** button (for "solo") on a track to listen to only that track. Which note values are used in the loops, and how are they organized? The four-measure *Club Dance Beat 121* emphasizes all quarter notes, but with a little more weight on beats 2 and 4. The two-measure *Electronic Drum Beat* includes more sixteenth notes between beats. The two-measure *Motown Drummer 05* emphasizes beats 1, 2, and 4. Notating these drum loops is a worthwhile challenge, as is deciding how to use them in musical projects. An understanding of whether loops work well in specific contexts might be developed from the sort of rhythmic analysis described here, and creating one's own loops can be rewarding in its own right. Algorithmically generated drum loops can also be part of this process, and have become important components in EDM (electronic dance music) and other musical genres.

The **2-Step Freak Beat** is shown in figure 2.2 in transcribed musical notation. To create a notated score for an audio file, we first transform it to MIDI. (1) Select a region and enable **Flex Pitch** from **Flex** time, then (2) select **Create MIDI Track from Flex Pitch Data**. Once we have a MIDI track region, we can open the score window for the notation. The kick is notated on the first space, the snare on the third space, and the hi-hat on the top line (figure 2.2):

Figure 2.2: 2-Step Freak Beat **notated.**

2.2 Drum Loops in Finale

Finale has a selection of twenty-nine drum patterns in **Plugins → Scoring and Arranging → Drum Groove**. Seven of these patterns are shown in figure 2.3 as musical notation, and can also be played via MIDI in Finale. The **Drum Groove** style window has the list of patterns (figure 2.4).

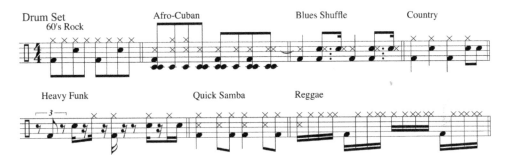

Figure 2.3: **Seven drum patterns in** Drum Groove **in Finale.**

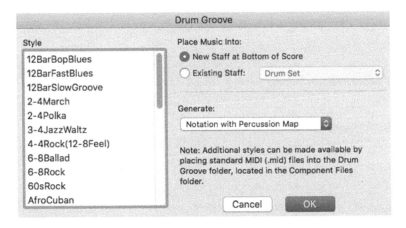

Figure 2.4: Drum Groove **in Finale.**

Basic drum patterns tend to use three or four different drum components. **60's Rock**, for instance, has a kick drum, snare, and hi-hat. Some of the patterns in Finale's **Drum Groove** have more components than one sees in the notation, however, because various elements share a line or space in the notation (placed in different layers) or are indicated by alternate notation, such as the X-shaped note-head, or the double note-head, or even the double-X-shaped note-head. If one places these patterns over a stretch of measures in a Finale piece, alternate patterns are sometimes included. When spread over many measures, **Drum Groove** mainly uses the basic patterns shown in figure 2.3, but sometimes includes alternate measures to make the percussion part sound less static and more like an actual drummer mixing things up and inserting different patterns. Skilled drummers regularly add and subtract elements in patterns to provide interest and a dynamic quality, and structural points in music are often marked in the drum part with substantially different patterns, such as drum fills or techniques such as stop-time. In figure 2.5 we see a drum fill replace the basic **60's Rock** Drum Groove at the sixteenth measure of a stretch of music, while m. 15 is the same as m. 1 in figure 2.3.

Figure 2.5: Drum Groove 60's Rock **fill in Finale.**

Finale inserts the alternate measures in **Drum Groove** automatically, but we can move measures around by hand by selecting and dragging them to new locations. Users can also add their own patterns to the **Drum Groove** tool.

2.3 Tuplets in Logic

The beat subdivisions discussed in Chapter 1 are based on ratios of 2:1 (quarters subdivided into eighths, for example) and 3:2 (triplets). To create more varied rhythms, we can use odd-numbered subdivisions greater than 3, which are called **tuplets**. These include the five-part quintuplet or seven-part septuplet. Logic can create tuplets in both MIDI and notation. Shown in figure 2.6 are **Score Editor** and **Piano Roll Editors** with quintuplets and septuplets based on various note values.

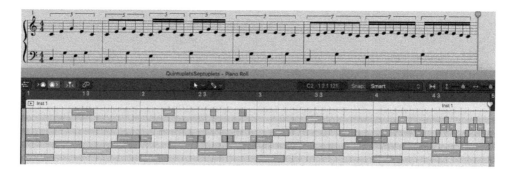

Figure 2.6: Quintuplets and septuplets in Logic.

These quintuplet and septuplet figures span different amounts of time. Quarter-note quintuplets and septuplets span a whole measure in common time (first and third measures above), whereas eighth-note quintuplets and septuplets span two beats, and sixteenth-note quintuplets and septuplets span just one beat. Keeping quintuplets and septuplets even and equal is a challenge for human performers, but DAWs can perform them perfectly, which provides a good aural reference.

Creating larger tuplets in Logic requires more steps than triplets. To create a quintuplet or larger tuplet, one first creates the number of notes required of equal duration, such as five quarter notes for a quintuplet. In the Logic session in figure 2.7, we can see the five quarter notes laid out horizontally. To ensure that the notes are perfectly equal in duration, we can use the **Step Input Keyboard** with the quarter note selected.

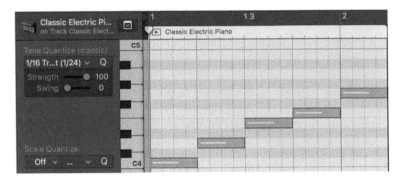

Figure 2.7: Five quarter notes in Piano Roll Editor **in Logic.**

A quintuplet is five equally proportioned durations which subdivide some other duration by five. To make a quintuplet that is equal to one quarter note (a sixteenth-note quintuplet), we need to shorten the quarter notes equally into sixteenth notes, and ensure that the positions of the sixteenth notes are aligned to five subdivisions of a quarter-note beat. We can do this in the **Piano Roll Editor** with **Time Handles** (figure 2.8), which can be enabled in the **Functions** menu.

Figure 2.8: Time Handles **in** Piano Roll Editor Functions **in Logic.**

First, we select all five notes. With **Time Handles** active, we'll see the two handles on either side of the notes we've selected, and we drag the right handle to the position which creates a quarter-note length for the five notes (figure 2.9). Each note gets shortened, but retains its relative position as an equal value to the other notes.

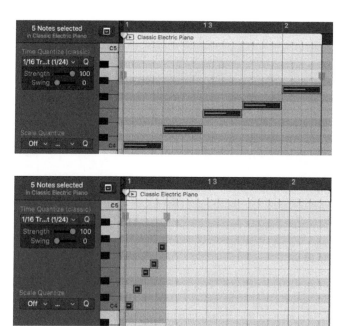

Figure 2.9: Moving Time Handles to create sixteenth note quintuplets in Logic.

These quintuplets sound correct, but they will appear in the score window as sixteenth-note triplets (figure 2.10). In order to make them appear as sixteenth-note quintuplets, we drag the **Tuplet** tool onto the first note, as seen in figure 2.10. From the **Tuplet** window we can specify the quintuplet notation of five sixteenth notes in place of four (figure 2.11), and the result will appear as below.

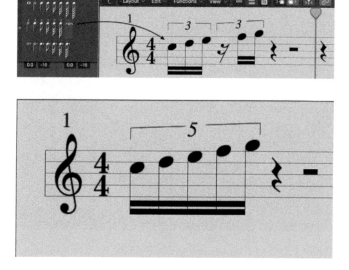

Figure 2.10: Quintuplets as sixteenth triplets, and adjusted with Tuplet tool in Logic.

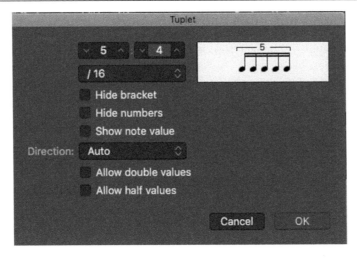

Figure 2.11: The Tuplet **tool in Logic.**

If we need a quarter-note quintuplet, we drag the right **Time Handle** to the entire bar line, so that the five quarter notes span the duration of four quarter notes. If, on the other hand, we need an eighth-note quintuplet, we drag the right **Time Handle** to the middle of the measure to create five eighth notes in the time of four eighth notes.

2.4 Tuplets in Finale

Tuplets can be created in Finale using its **Tuplet Definition** tool (figure 2.12). With this tool we can add helpful details for the musical notation, such as ratio symbols or brackets. **Tuplet Definition** also has parameters for placement of the tuplets. We can also create common tuplets in Finale using the **Speedy Entry** tool by holding down the Option-key and typing a number for the tuplet. The number then defines the tuplet. For tuplets of seven or greater, however, we need to use the **Tuplet Definition** tool.

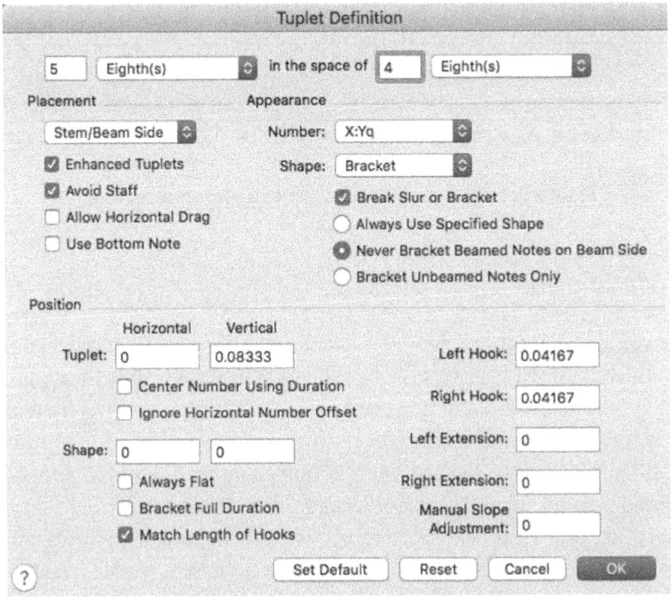

Figure 2.12: Tuplet Definition **in Finale.**

In the example in figure 2.13, the colons between notes mean "equal to." In m. 1, the quintuplet eighth notes (the five eighth notes together) are equal in duration to four eighth notes, hence 5:4. Similarly, the septuplet eighth notes (seven) are equal in duration to four eighth notes. It is possible, although less common, for a septuplet to be equal to eight notes. In this case the ratio symbol would be 7:8. The next three measures divide entire measures into nine, eleven, and twenty-seven equal parts respectively. Incorporating such rhythmic subdivisions allows for great possibilities. Tuplet figures with large values, like that in the fourth measure, are sometimes found in the orchestral music of the late romantic composers, such as Nikolai Rimsky-Korsakov or Richard Strauss, among others:

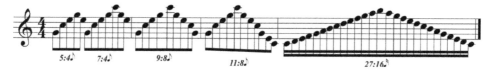

Figure 2.13: Larger tuplets.

2.5 Nested Tuplets

Twentieth-century composers such as Elliott Carter, Pierre Boulez, and others expanded the rhythmic repertoire and performance limits with increasingly complex rhythms, such as **nested tuplets**. In the first measure in the music in figure 2.14, the first nested tuplet is within a half-note triplet. The middle half note is itself a quarter-note triplet. Creating nested tuplet rhythms is possible in Finale, and we can export Finale files as SMF into DAWs. The Finale example in figure 2.14 shows nested triplets and a nested quintuplet within larger triplets and a quintuplet. The eighth note in the bass provides a reference beat. Perfectly accurate when performed by the computer, complex nested tuplets are challenging to perform live.

Figure 2.14: Nested tuplets: triplets and quintuplets.

2.6 Metric Modulation

Meters often remain the same throughout a musical work, but they can also change as the music proceeds. In some music, meters change at every measure. Igor Stravinsky's *The Rite of Spring* is a famous example of a musical work with fast changing meters. Changing meters at a fast tempo can be challenging for performing musicians and requires advanced skills. DAWs and notation programs can provide musicians with audible versions of changing meters, which can be useful for reference or as exercises. In figure 2.15 we see music which changes time signature and meter every measure. With these nine measures, we have changes in the beat value from half notes in mm. 1–3 to quarter-note beat values in mm. 4–6 and to eighth-note beat values in mm. 7–9. The meters are also changing every measure, from duple to triple to quadruple, and repeating those changes.

Figure 2.15: Changing meters.

Music with changing meters sometimes sounds as if it is the *tempo* that is changing rather than the meter. In the example in figure 2.15, the quarter notes starting in m. 4 are half the duration of the preceding measure's half notes, and we might hear this as a doubling of the tempo, especially as the pitches are repeating. Likewise the eighth notes starting in m. 7 have half the duration of the quarter notes, and we might hear this either as the note values having been cut in half, or as the tempo having been doubled again. The challenge presented to the performer by the notation is that the meter's beat value changes three times, from half note to quarter to eighth.

Putting this example of changing meters into a Logic session can demonstrate the concept of **metric modulation** (sometimes known as **proportional tempi**). If we begin this Logic session at 240 BPM, switch to 120 BPM at m. 4, and then switch to 60 BPM at m. 7 (figure 2.16), then all the notes will have the same actual duration. There will be no *perceived* change in tempo, although we know that there were two *actual* changes in tempo, demonstrating the relationship between tempo and beat durations in metric modulation. Examples of metric modulation occur throughout music history, and many twentieth-century composers have incorporated the practice in their music.

Figure 2.16: Metric modulation (changing tempo and time signature) in Logic.

Metric modulations can be notated in music by two beat durations on either side of an equal sign, leaving it to the performer to figure out the changes in tempo. In our example in figure 2.16 with changing time signatures and tempi, we could also have indicated the tempo changes at measures 4 and 7, showing that the durations would be of equal length (figure 2.17):

Figure 2.17: Metric modulation symbols in Finale.

To work this out in performance, the players would have to change the tempos by slowing them down by half for each metric modulation.

Another kind of metric modulation is where a quarter-note beat duration becomes equivalent to a dotted quarter note, or vice versa. In the music in figure 2.18, the beat subdivision changes from two to three based on the metric modulation. All of the notes are the same duration, but a triplet feel is implied by the compound duple meter of the $^6_8$ measures. This provides a change in rhythmic quality (figure 2.18).

Figure 2.18: Metric Modulation, dotted quarter equals quarter.

2.7 Rhythm Generator

One way we can develop rhythm skills with our programs is to generate music for practice or study. Max, for example, can also generate rhythmic patterns on its own. When we program computers to generate music we use specific instructions or *algorithms*, and the result is **algorithmic** music. Algorithmic music can be used both in the study of music theory and as a compositional tool. Traditional music theory instruction typically demonstrates music theory concepts with examples from the "great" composers. Algorithmically created music doesn't have this mark of greatness, perhaps making it less intimidating. Algorithmic music often encourages us to ask the question "how can this music be better?" It's a good question for the creative musician who is learning music theory.

The **Rhythm Generator** (figure 2.19) creates continuous and varying rhythms, based on a set of rhythmic units. The two-part algorithmic basis is: (1) combine one-, two-, three-, or four-note durations to create a rhythmic unit with a quarter-note duration; (2) continuously and randomly vary the nine rhythm units. The nine rhythmic units are seen along the lower part of the patcher.

Rhythm Generator has an on/off **toggle** for the patcher which also turns **Transport** object on and off. The **Transport** controls a master clock which allows us to change the tempo while keeping Max's **Note Values** in sync. As we saw with **Drum Pattern**, the **Note Values** are Max's alphanumeric representations of rhythmic durations—4n for quarter note, 8n for eighth note, etc. If one double-clicks on the **Transport** object, the **Global Transport** window opens, and here we can change the tempo and also rewind the counter.

We can also change the tempo by selecting from three BPM settings: 120, 60, and 30. The controls on the left side are for MIDI input and output. We can listen with an internal synth, or we can send the MIDI data out to Logic or Finale for recording. We can change the **Drum Sound**; this number corresponds to the drum sounds in **General MIDI Percussion Key Map**. In figure 2.19, we can see that rhythm 4 (sixteenth note, dotted eighth) is being played on a snare drum (#40).

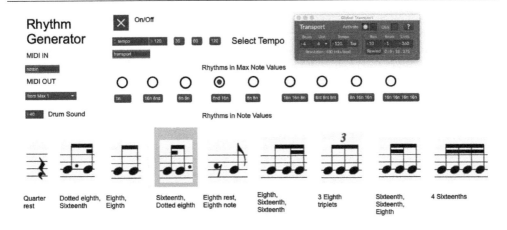

Figure 2.19: Rhythm Generator **(Max).**

To send **Rhythm Generator**'s output to Logic, we set the **MIDI OUT** to **from Max 1**, as shown in figure 2.19. When we're recording in Logic, we want to start and stop **Rhythm Generator** according to Logic's beat. In order to do this, we trigger the **Rhythm Generator** with MIDI notes sent from Logic. In a Logic **External MIDI** track set to transmit **to Max 1,** we'll put a C4 (MIDI note 60) where we want **Rhythm Generator** to start, and a C#4 (MIDI note 61) to end. These notes should be as short as possible (one tick) to ensure that the synchronization is exact.

With **Rhythm Generator** set up to transmit to Logic, we can record its output. Both programs' tempi are set at 120 BPM for the example in figure 2.20, which shows the Logic session with the MIDI triggers in Track 1 (an **External MIDI** track) and the recorded output from the **Rhythm Generator** in Track 2. The session recorded the rhythms in $^4_4$, $^3_4$, and $^2_4$ time signatures (quadruple, triple, and duple meters) (figure 2.20). With the score, we have an advanced rhythm exercise with changing meters! The **clef** for drums, as seen in the **Score Editor** in figure 2.20, can be selected from the **Score Inspector – Region – Style** drop-down menu → **#drums**. See Chapter 3 for more on clefs.

Figure 2.20: Rhythm Generator **output recorded in Logic.**

The next demonstration stays in common time ($^4_4$), and we record three segments of output at each of the **Rhythm Generator**'s three BPM settings (30, 60, 120) while keeping Logic at a 120 BPM, and arranging them in tracks 1, 2, and 3. The result is three levels of rhythmic activity: slow, medium, and fast rhythms (figure 2.21). The interplay between levels of rhythmic activity often happens in music with multiple parts. In Logic, we can set up the playback so that **Inst 1** is a kick drum, **Inst 2** a snare, and **Inst 3** hi-hats, creating our own algorithmic drummer.

Figure 2.21: **Eight measures of** Rhythm Generator **output at 120, 60, and 30 BPM.**

2.8 Max Patcher 2: *Rhythm Generator*

The view of **Rhythm Generator** (figure 2.19) is in **presentation mode**. Many objects and connections (virtual patch cables) are hidden in this mode to simplify the screen and make it easier to use. Most of the patchers in the chapters ahead will be introduced in presentation mode. Displaying **patcher mode**, however, with all the objects visible, allows us to explain how patchers work (figure 2.22).

In Chapter 1's **Drum Pattern**, we saw that the objects **metro** and **delay** with **1n**, **2n**, and **4n** values (whole, half, and quarter notes) produce steady but staggered pulses to trigger drum hits. For **Rhythm Generator**, we'll use a **metro 4n** to produce a quarter-note pulse which will trigger various combinations of rhythmic values or short patterns. This **metro 4n** sends bangs to a **random 9** object which outputs values between zero and eight randomly at the rate of **metro 4n**, a rate that is determined by the **Global Transport** BPM. The random numbers then enter the **sel 0 1 2 3 4 5 6 7 8** object, which selects a rhythmic unit to play—implementing the second algorithm: continuously vary the rhythm units (figure 2.22). When a **sel** object receives a value, it sends out a bang from the outlet that corresponds to that value, based on its arguments (in this case a number between 0 and 8).

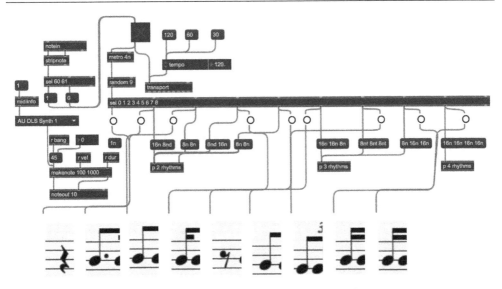

Figure 2.22: Rhythm Generator **in patcher mode in Max.**

The rhythm patterns are represented by note values in nine **messages**, visible in figure 2.22 directly below the circles (buttons which flash when the patterns to which they're connected are heard).

When any of these note-values messages is banged, a bang is also sent to the frame around the musical notation—these are along the bottom of the screen in the patcher mode. In this way, we see the rhythms as they're playing. The picture of the notation is brought into the program by reading a **.png** file into an **fpic** object, and the frame (which also lights up when the rhythm is heard) is an otherwise invisible **ubutton** object. You can see the **ubutton** activated on the sixteenth-note, dotted eighth-note rhythm in the **Rhythm Generator** presentation view (figure 2.19).

With this patcher, we'll introduce the **subpatcher**, portions of programming encapsulated into an object—named as *"p" something*. There are three subpatchers in Rhythm Generator—**p 2 rhythms, p 3 rhythms**, and **p 4 rhythms**. To create a subpatcher, we select all the objects we want to be in the subpatcher and choose **encapsulate** from the edit window. We can name it by typing in the object after the "p." These subpatchers create patterns of either two, three, or four notes.

To explain how we turn lists of note values into sequences of drum hits with the specified rhythms, we'll look at the subpatcher's inner workings, which we can access by doubling-clicking on the object name in the locked mode. We'll start with **p 2 rhythms** (figure 2.23).

In the **p 2 rhythms** subpatcher we can see on the left side that after the elements of the two-part lists enter via inlet 1, they are separated into two items by **unjoin 2**, and then the second note value is delayed by the first note value amount with **pipe** (figure 2.23). Both note values are used to create **bangs** to trigger the notes and **makenote** durations. The **t i (trigger integer)** object takes multiple integer inputs in succession and sends them out via the same pathway. We send both durations to an **s dur** (send durations) object that is connected to **makenote**. Max objects can send and receive data to and from multiple locations without patch cable connections by using pairs of **send** (or **s**) and **receive** (or **r**) objects. Our **r dur** object will receive note durations, and our **r bang** object will receive a bang to trigger notes.

On the right side of the p2 rhythms subpatcher, we see the eighth rest—eighth-note rhythm programming, which is created by sending a 0 velocity for the first note, then resuming the 100 velocity for the second note—a velocity which is used by all the other notes.

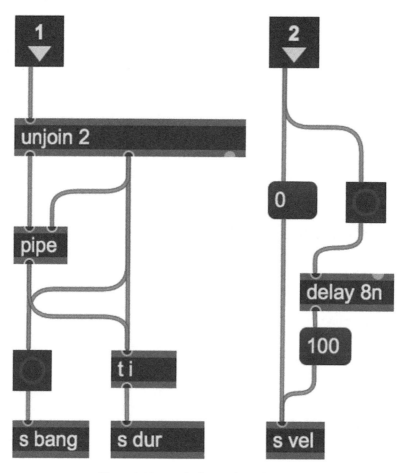

Figure 2.23: p 2 rhythms **subpatcher in Max.**

The process is expanded in the **p 3 rhythms** and **p 4 rhythms** subpatchers, but here we run into an issue concerning the **note values** used as a time delay (figure 2.24). The rhythm messages enter in inlet 1. Then, we delay the second note in the list by the first duration, and the third item in the list by the sum of the first two durations. The actual durations of Max **note values** are variable depending on the tempo, however, so adding **note values** is not possible. While 4n + 4n = 2n (a quarter note plus a quarter note equals a half note) is true in terms of rhythmic values, without knowing the BPM, we don't know these note values' actual durations, and thus we can't add them together. We can, however, translate the **note values** to durations in milliseconds with **translate notevalues ms** to add them together. As we are using **note values** elsewhere in the patcher to allow for tempo changes using the **transport**, we'll need to translate the milliseconds back into **note values** with **translate ms notevalues** after adding them together.

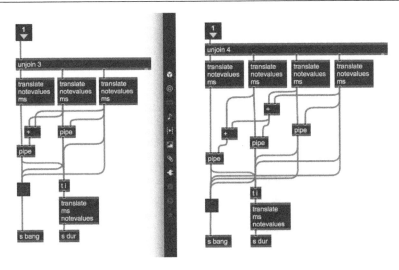

Figure 2.24: p 3 rhythms **and** p 4 rhythms **subpatchers in Max.**

We continue using this same process for the four-item list, using an **unjoin 4** object, four **translate notevalues ms** objects, and the required processing objects (**pipe**, **+**, **ti**, and **translate ms notevalues**).

All of the **s bang** and **s dur** messages are received by each of the **r bang** and **r dur** objects. (When using **send** (**s**) and **receive** (**r**) objects, make sure they are named exactly the same wherever they appear, as any variations will not be understood by Max.) These bangs and durations are then sent into a **makenote** object to set each note's duration and to start each new note. The note number corresponds to a percussion instrument as we have set the channel to ten, the MIDI percussion channel. For the list of percussion instruments in the General MIDI specifications, we can reference the official MIDI website (www.MIDI.org).

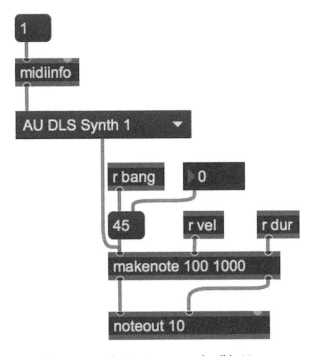

Figure 2.25: Rhythm Generator **detail in Max.**

The **noteout 10**'s MIDI output destination (as shown in figure 2.25) can be set by a **umenu** object's output going to the left inlet. Here the **AU DLS Synth 1** is selected so that we'll hear Apple's internal MIDI synth, but we could set the output to **from MIDI 1** to transmit the output to Logic or Finale.

The patcher mode view of **Rhythm Generator** reveals a few more programming details. In the top right, we notice a **note in**, **stripnote**, **sel 60 61**, and **1** and **0 messages**. This part of the patcher is listening for incoming MIDI notes C4 and C#4, which turn the patcher on and off—so that Logic's **External Instrument** track can stop and start the patcher.

Finally, the **transport** object has an **attrui** (attributes) object, a drop-down menu with two parts. When attached to certain objects, **attrui**'s menu becomes automatically populated with that object's attributes. Being attached to **transport**, the **attrui** object includes a tempo-setting parameter. We can change the tempo in the **Global Transport** itself, but clicking on the messages 120, 60, or 30 avoids some extra noise.

2.9 *Mouse Click Melody*

Rhythmic skills are an essential part of musicianship, and developing musicianship is an integral aspect of learning music theory. With the **Mouse Click Melody** patcher (figure 2.26), we can practice performing rhythms using computer-mouse clicks—a bit like the *Guitar Hero* game without the graphics.

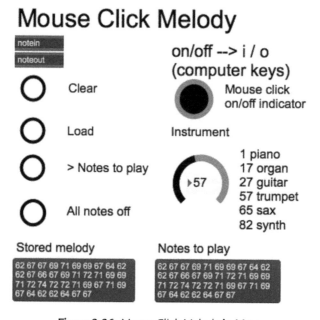

Figure 2.26: Mouse Click Melody **in Max.**

With **Mouse Click Melody** we can store the pitches of a melody by: (1) clearing any previously stored melody (**Clear** button); (2) playing a melody on an attached MIDI keyboard; (3) pressing the **Load** button. Only the pitches (as note numbers of the melody) are input. Next, (4) we click on **> Notes to play** to make these notes playable by mouse click. (5) To turn on mouse-click playing, we press the **i** key on the computer keyboard. Any mouse click will now play a melody note for as long as the mouse click is down, releasing the note when the mouse is up, and a new click will play the next note. (6) We turn off mouse-click playing by pressing **o** on the computer keyboard, returning the mouse to its usual functions.

When we finish playing a melody, we can reload it by clicking the **> Notes to play** button. We can try different instrument sounds with the **Instrument** dial. We can also send the MIDI data to Logic to use any of their software instrument sounds by setting the MIDI output destination to **from Max 1** with the **noteout** object.

It's possible that MIDI notes would not turn off properly. This might happen if you turn off mouse-click playing (**o**) before releasing the mouse click. These are known as **MIDI stuck notes**, and clicking the **All notes off** button will turn them off.

To practice rhythms with **Mouse Click Melody**, we can input a song such as the traditional *The Water is Wide* (fig 2.27). The song contains eight two-measure phrases with similar rhythmic qualities. Each first measure of each phrase consists of quarters and eighths. Each phrase has a second measure with whole notes.

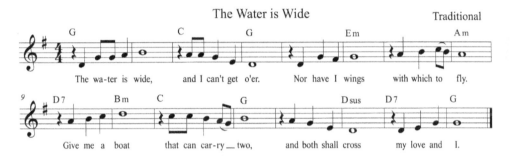

Figure 2.27: *The Water is Wide.*

The tempo is not indicated, but the song is usually at a relaxed tempo, but not too slow considering all of the whole notes. We can practice the rhythms of the song's melody on its own, or we could practice performing the melody in the context of a Logic session (figure 2.28). A drum part (track 2) and an accompaniment (track 3) are added. In the exercise section of this chapter are two suggested melodies, but any melody can be used.

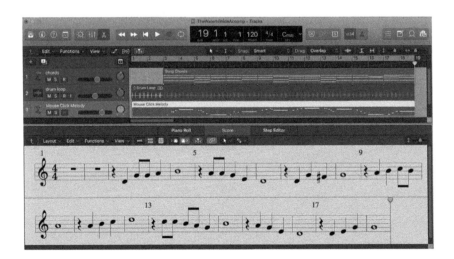

Figure 2.28: Mouse Click Melody **recorded in Logic.**

2.10 Max Patcher 3: *Mouse Click Melody*

Mouse Click Melody collects a melody's pitches as a list of MIDI note numbers. The user can play the melody by clicking the mouse for each note. A **notein** object to receive incoming MIDI is in the upper middle portion shown in patcher mode (figure 2.29) and is connected to both **stripnote** and **noteout** objects. The **noteout** object sends these incoming MIDI notes to an internal synthesizer (**AU DLS Synth 1**) so we can hear them as they're played. The **stripnote** object removes all **note-on** messages with the velocity 0 value and sends the note numbers out the left outlet. A **note-on** message with 0 velocity tells a MIDI synthesizer to stop playing a note.

From the **stripnote** object, these incoming MIDI notes are sent to **capture** and **zl.group** objects, which are patch-cabled together. The **capture** object stores values to list or edit, and the **zl.group** object creates a list of incoming values. The **capture** object also responds to two essential commands, **count** and **dump**. **Count** reports the number of items, and **dump** sends out the items and resets the **capture** object.

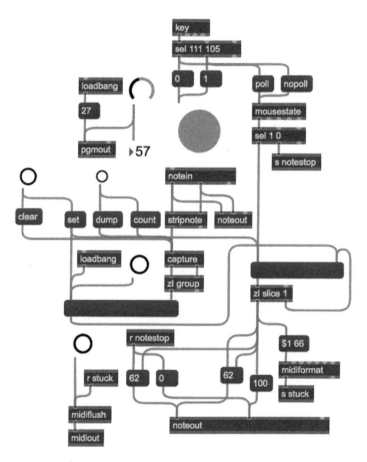

Figure 2.29: Mouse Click Melody **patcher in Max.**

The **capture** and **zl.group** objects create the list of melody notes. The list is stored in a **message** on the left side of the patcher, visible in both patcher and presentation mode with its right inlet connected to the output of **zl.group**. A **button** is attached to this **message** to bang its contents into the second **message** box on the right side (also visible in both modes).

A **set message** clears the contents of both messages when needed, and a **loadbang** bangs the left **message** so that the contents will be sent over to the right **message** when the program is loaded. The right-side message box is used to play the melody notes. The **capture** object is also cleared by the **clear message** before inputting a new melody.

This right-side **message** outputs to a **zl.slice**, an object which slices off the leftmost item in a list and sends the remainder of the list out the right outlet. As each note is sliced off, the remaining list of notes (minus one note) is sent back to the message. The result is that the list steadily gets smaller by one as we slice off each note of the melody in turn. The sliced-off note numbers go to two **messages**. These two messages are sent to a **noteout** object, one of them to play the note and the other to stop it.

Looking at the top part of the patcher, we see the **key** object connected to a **sel 111 105** object. **Key** reports computer keyboard keystrokes as ACSCII values, and the **o** and **i** keys are values 111 and 105 respectively. Thus, when the letters **o** and **i** are typed, **sel 111 105** sends out bangs through its left and right outlets respectively. These bangs do two things: (1) they turn **mousestate** on and off (the message **poll** turns **mousestate** on, and **nopoll** turns it off), and (2) they turn a **led** object on and off (1 turns it on, 0 turns it off). The **led** object is the grey circle below the 1 and 0. When **mousestate** is on, the **led** turns black, indicating the patcher is ready to play.

The **mousestate** object sends out a 1 when the mouse is down and a 0 when it's up. Clicking the mouse down starts a new note by sending the note number and velocity (100) to the **noteout** object. Releasing the mouse (mouse up) ends the note by sending **r notestop** a bang, which in turn sends the note number paired with a 0 velocity to the **noteout** playing the note to stop it playing.

Two other functions in the patcher are the selection of a program number and the ending of stuck notes. The **loadbang** and **27 message** in the upper left part of **Mouse Click Melody** send a 27 to a **pgmout** object. The **pgmout** object sets the program number (the instrument sound) from the list of 128 instrument sounds in the **General MIDI** specification. Six instrument types and their numbers are shown in the presentation view for quick reference. Program 27 is a guitar sound; we can change to any of the other instruments (such as the trumpet sound "57" seen in figure 2.26) with the **dial** object. The ending of stuck notes is achieved with the **midiflush** object.

2.11 Exercises

2.11.1 Exercise 1: Rhythm Generator Drum Loops

To use the **Rhythm Generator** to create a drum pattern for looping, we first consider that many basic patterns include three or four drum components. The kick drum, snare, and the hi-hats will work for a two-measure loop. We can record the output of **Rhythm Generator** three times for the kick, snare, and hi-hat, as we did for the music in figure 2.21 with BPM's 30, 60, and 120. From that eight-measure phrase, for example, mm. 6–7 might work well as a drum loop (figure 2.30). As the **Rhythm Generator** can produce an unlimited quantity of output, however, we could keep recording and searching for as long as we want.

Figure 2.30: Two measures selected for looping.

Drummers usually read from one staff. To make a single staff from the three tracks in Logic, we select the three regions in the tracks, and from the **Edit** menu choose **Join → Regions**. The exercise of creating drum loops **Rhythm Generator** and Logic helps develop a sense of rhythmic interplay.

2.11.2 Exercise 2: Rhythm Generator for Rhythmic Exercises (Performance and Dictation)

We've seen that **Rhythm Generator** can create rhythmic exercises for practicing speaking rhythms, such as with the "Ta" and "Tee" syllables, by recording its output in Logic or Finale and viewing it as musical notation. Another kind of exercise is rhythmic dictation, which is where one listens to a musical example, then notates the music's rhythms based on just the listening. As this skill can be challenging to acquire, it makes sense to start with short examples at moderate tempos.

To make a short rhythm-dictation exercise, record two measure of **Rhythm Generator**. In this case, the note that turns the patcher on (middle C) will be at the beginning of measure 1, and the note that turns it off (C#4) will be at the end of measure 2.

After you've recorded the two measures, but before doubling-clicking on the newly recorded region to reveal the notation in the **Score Editor** (in Logic), notate the rhythms. Listen to the measures as you count the beats, and determine which rhythmic values are used in which order. Make sure to turn **record enable** off on the track before listening, or you might inadvertently add more rhythms to the measures. After you've notated the rhythms, double-click on the region and select **Score** to open the **Score Editor** to see the notation.

2.11.3 Exercise 3: Melodies for Mouse Click Melody

Here are two melodies for **Mouse Click Melody** practice, first in musical notation (figures 2.31 and 2.32), and showing the note numbers for these two melodies (figure 2.33). Any melody can be used, however, as long as we can input the notes via a MIDI keyboard.

Figure 2.31: *Fanfare* **should sound important!**

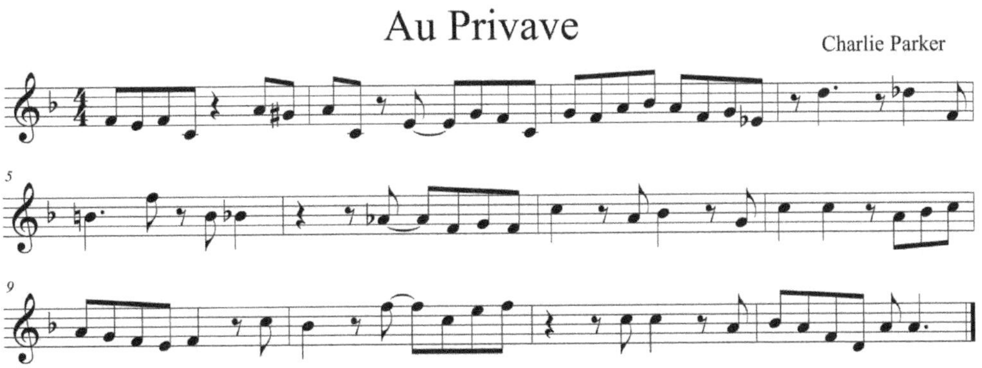
Au Privave
Charlie Parker
5
9

Figure 2.32: *Au Privave* is fast bebop and quite challenging because of the rests.

76 74 72 67 72 74 76 77 76 74
72 74 76 77 79 79 79 79 81 79
77 76 76 77 79 84 79 79 77 76
74 76 77 79 76 77 74 67 74 74
74 74 76 74 72 67 72 74 76 77
76 74 72 74 76 77 79 79 79 79
81 79 77 76 76 77 79 84 79 79
77 76 74 76 77 79 76 77 74 79
77 76 74 72 72

65 64 65 60 69 68 69 60 64 67
65 60 67 65 69 70 69 65 67 63
74 73 65 71 77 71 70 68 65 67
65 72 69 70 67 72 72 69 70 72
69 67 65 64 65 72 70 77 72 76
77 72 72 69 70 69 65 62 69 69

Figure 2.33: (a) *Fanfare* and (b) *Au Privave* note numbers in Max.

CHAPTER 3

Pitch, Intervals, Scales

3.1 Pitch Notation

Pitch is the quality of how high or low musical tones sound, and pitch notation ranges vertically on musical **staves** (**staff**, singular) corresponding to the high or low quality, just as we see pitches arranged in a piano roll. In figure 3.1, we see **Score Editor** and **Piano Roll Editor** in Logic, two ways to represent pitch. The **Score Editor** shows a series of ascending whole notes in the two **staves**. These two staves together, the **grand staff**, are used primarily for keyboard music. The top staff has the **treble** (or G) **clef** (to the left of the time signature), and the bottom staff has the **bass** (or F) **clef.** The treble clef has higher pitches than the bass clef, but the C in the first measure of the treble clef is the same pitch as the C in the last measure of the bass clef. Other clefs exist, such as the percussion clef we encountered in Chapter 1, but the treble and bass clefs are the most commonly used.

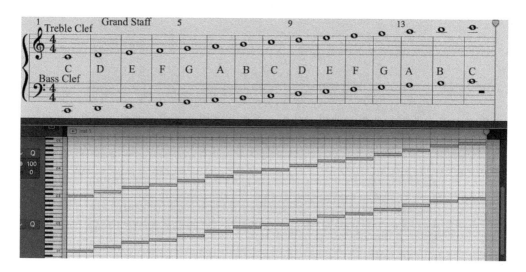

Figure 3.1: C Major scale pitches in Score Editor (top) and Piano Roll Editor (below) in Logic.

The **C major scale**, which contains the pitches named by alphabet letters C, D, E, F, G, A, B, is shown in the grand staff repeated four times—twice in the bass clef staff and twice in the treble clef staff. The C major scale can also be played by striking just the white keys on a keyboard—from C to C. The pitches of the C major scale ascend as **scale degrees 1 to 7** and are named: (1) **tonic**; (2) **supertonic**; (3) **mediant**; (4) **subdominant**; (5) **dominant**; (6) **submediant**; (7) **leading tone**. These names are also used for the chords built on those scale degrees, as we'll see in Chapter 4.

Starting in m. 8, the scale is repeated in both staves. Looking at the left side of the lower window, we see that the first scale in the bass clef starts on C2, then repeats at C3, whereas the first scale in the treble clef starts on C4 (**middle C**) and repeats at C5. The 4 in C4 indicates the **octave register**. Pitches with the same name can occur in different **octaves**—they sound similar to our ears and can be used interchangeably in many contexts. There are differing standards for octave register numbers; sometimes middle C is referred to as C3, but we'll use the C4 standard. To set **Logic** for middle C as C4, go to **Preferences** → **Display** → **Display Middle C as C4 (Roland)**. Mm. 1–3 in the bass clef use **ledger lines** to extend the staff below, and mm. 13–15 use ledger lines to extend the staff above. C4 is the *fourth* C on an eighty-eight-key piano, and it's *middle* C because it lies in the middle of the keyboard.

In the **Piano Roll Editor**'s keyboard on the left, we see that some scale degrees have pitches in between them, and some are directly adjacent on the keyboard. These pairs of notes: C–D, D–E, F–G, G–A, and A–B have one pitch between them, but there are no pitches between E–F and B–C. The pairs of notes with a pitch in between are **whole steps**, and the pairs without a pitch are **half steps** or **semitones**. Ascending or descending by two half steps is equal to a whole step. Each of the twelve major scales follows the same pattern of whole steps (W) and half steps (h): W, W, h, W, W, W, h.

To name all of the notes on the keyboard, including those located in between the whole steps of the C major scale, we use **accidentals**. The accidentals are **sharp** (#), **flat** (♭), **natural** (♮), **double-sharp** (𝄪), **and double-flat** (♭♭). A sharp raises a pitch one half step. A flat lowers a pitch one half step. The natural sign simply tells us that there's no sharp or flat, and often comes after a sharp or a flat to let us know that the note is no longer sharped or flatted.

In figure 3.2, accidentals are notated before pitches to raise or lower them by one half step, and here we have a **chromatic scale**. The chromatic scale ascends or descends by half steps and contains all the pitches in our musical system. The C# is one half step higher than the C, just as the F# is one half step higher than the F. Likewise, the E♭ is one half step lower than the E, just as the A♭ and B♭ are one half step lower than the A and B, respectively. Any pitch letter name can have any accidental, and because of the ways that accidentals can be applied, every pitch has multiple names. In figure 3.3, we can see some examples of the same pitch with different pitch names; these are **enharmonic equivalents**. The double-flat lowers the pitch by two half steps, and the double-sharp raises the pitch by two half steps. These double accidentals can provide even more ways to name pitches—although they are less commonly used than sharps, flats, or naturals.

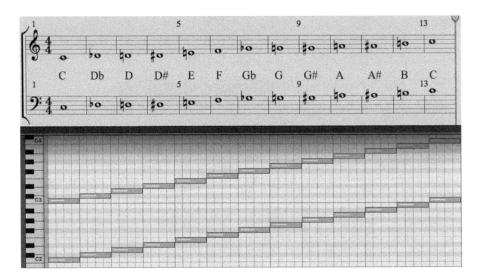

Figure 3.2: Chromatic scale and accidentals in Logic.

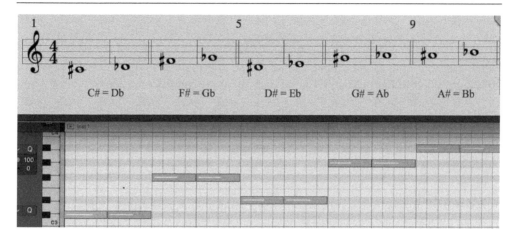

Figure 3.3: Enharmonic spellings of the same pitch in Logic.

Spelling the same pitch with different names becomes helpful when we have a piece of music with different types of scales and chords within it. Even though each pitch is represented in the **Piano Roll Editor** only once, it's important to know they can have different names.

3.2 Pitch Generator

At the end of the chapter are exercises for practicing reading pitches on the grand staff with Logic and Finale. The Max patcher **Pitch Generator**, shown in figure 3.4, provides another way to practice reading pitches. The button **Click for new note** creates a new pitch on the grand staff, and **Click for note name** displays where the pitch is on a piano keyboard and its name.

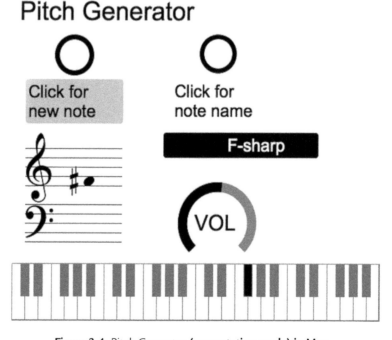

Figure 3.4: Pitch Generator (presentation mode) in Max.

3.3 Max Patcher 4: *Pitch Generator*

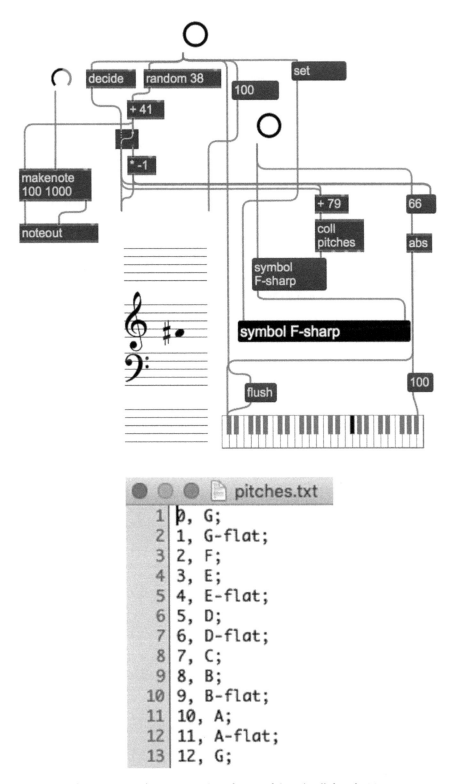

Figure 3.5: Pitch Generator **(patcher mode)** and coll **data in Max.**

The basic function of **Pitch Generator** is to create new pitches to display on a **nslider** object—the object that shows a grand staff—then to display its name and position on a keyboard. The patcher displays pitches from F2, or note number 41 (the space below the bass clef), to G5, or note number 79 (the space above the treble clef) in the grand staff. The **random 38** object produces numbers between 0 and 37, and to each of these numbers we add 41 with the **add two numbers** object (**+ 41**) The result is random numbers in the desired range between 41 and 79. The output of the **+ 41** object is also sent to **makenote 100 1000** and **noteout** objects to play a one-second MIDI note at the pitch. The volume can be controlled with the **dial**, which sends values from 0–127 into the middle inlet of **makenote 100 1000**. The 0–127 range corresponds to the range of MIDI velocities. The duration of the notes is controlled by the second argument, which here is 1000 milliseconds, or one second.

The **nslider** object displays sharps by default for any note number requiring an accidental. For pitches without an accidental, **nslider** accepts both negative and positive values, but if a note requires a flat, it must be negative. Note 61, for instance, displays as C#, but −61 will be displayed as the enharmonic spelling of D♭. So, to include flats in our output, we send roughly 50% of the numbers to a *** −01** object to make them flatted. The **decide** object randomly outputs a 0 or 1, thus flipping a **ggate** object back and forth so that some numbers are left positive (these will be sharps or naturals), and some become negative (these will be flats or naturals).

The negative numbers entering the **nslider** object are in the range of −41 to −79, and the positive numbers are from 41 to 79. Because being a negative number is used only to indicate that the note is flatted if an accidental is required, −78 and 78 are actually the same pitch in the two enharmonic spellings (F#5 or G♭5). This aspect of negative values as pitches in Max also means that −79 is a higher pitch than −41, even though it's a lower number.

We will translate MIDI note numbers (either positive or negative) into pitch names with the **coll** object. The **coll** object index numbers must be positive numbers. To translate the entering **note** numbers to pitch names using a **coll** object (a collection of indexed data), we make all the numbers positive by adding 79 to each value with the **+ 79** object. We link them to pitch names in the **coll pitches** object. The index numbers for the flats (or naturals that were negative) are thirty-eight to zero, from lowest to highest pitches on the grand staff—again counting down even though the pitches are going up. The index numbers of the sharps or naturals group is from 120 to 158—in this case counting up from the lowest to highest. Table 3.1 shows the correspondence between the note numbers and the pitches.

Table 3.1: Pitch Generator note numbers, coll values, and note names.

	Note Numbers for nslider	Coll index values	Note names
Flats or naturals	−41 to −79	38 to 0	F2 to G5
Sharps or naturals	41 to 79	120 to 158	F2 to G5

The output of the **coll** objects is sent to a **message** box not included in the presentation mode. The content of this **message** box (visible in patcher view) can be sent to the second message box (visible in presentation mode) by clicking the button connected to the message and thereby sending its contents into the next message box. This action allows us to test our pitch reading by providing the correct answer on demand.

The **coll** object adds the word "symbol" to various kinds of data. As this word is not required for the note name and would just be confusing for the user, it is covered up in the presentation mode. The **message** box viewable in presentation mode is cleared every time a new note is generated by a **set message**.

The notes are also sent to a **kslider** object, an onscreen piano keyboard. Because the flat notes are represented by negative numbers, we take the absolute value of these numbers with the **abs** object before sending it to the **kslider**. We also send a 100 velocity value to **kslider** as it requires both the note number and a velocity to display the note. Finally, when we select a new note, we send **flush** and **set messages** to the **kslider** and the pitch name **message** to erase previously displayed content. The **Pitch Generator** creates notes randomly, and the pitch name, notation, and the location on a keyboard are all displayed, helping us become fluent with pitch names and their musical notation.

3.4 Intervals

An **interval** is the distance between two pitches, as determined by the number of half steps between them. Intervals can be (1) **harmonic**—two notes sounding at the same time, as with chords, or (2) **melodic**—two notes heard one after the other, as in melodies. In figure 3.6, we see the **Score** and **Piano Roll Editors** showing the intervals we can create between the first scale degree (C) and the rest of the scale degrees of C major. These intervals formed by notes in a scale are **natural intervals** (or **diatonic intervals**).

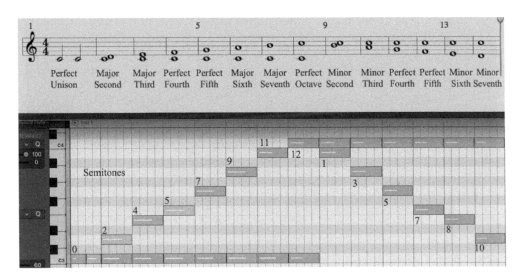

Figure 3.6: C major natural intervals in Logic.

In the **Score Editor**, we see the notes in a treble staff with the interval names for each pair of notes. Each interval name has two parts: the **quality** is given first and the **ordinal number** (sometimes just the number) follows the quality. The interval qualities we see here are **perfect**, **major**, and **minor**. Two other qualities not shown here are **diminished** and **augmented**. Minor intervals are smaller than major by one half step, and diminished intervals are smaller than perfect or minor intervals by a half step. Augmented intervals are larger than perfect or major intervals by a half step (figure 3.7).

Diminished ⟵→ Minor ⟵ → Major ⟵→Augmented

Diminished ⟵→ Perfect ⟵→ Augmented

(each double arrow represents one half step)

Figure 3.7: Interval quality half step differences.

Ordinal numbers are another part of intervals' names. The ordinal numbers **unison, second, third, fourth, fifth, sixth, seventh,** and **octave** are smaller than or equal to one octave and are thus called **simple. Compound intervals** larger than one octave are **ninths, tenths, elevenths,** etc. We'll focus on **simple** intervals.

Ordinal numbers are based on music notation, specifically on how many lines and spaces the interval spans in the staff. Unisons are on one line or space. Seconds span a space and a line, or a line and a space in either direction. Thirds span a space-line-space or line-space-line, and so forth. The quality added to ordinal numbers further defines how many half steps (or semitones) are between the two pitches. In figure 3.6, the **Piano Roll Editor** shows the number of half steps for the ascending intervals: 0, 2, 4, 5, 7, 9, 11, 12 and 1, 3, 5, 7, 8, 10, 0 for the descending intervals. Not all qualities can be used with all the ordinal numbers. Unisons, fourths, fifths, and octaves can be perfect, diminished, or augmented. Second, thirds, sixths, and sevenths can be major, minor, diminished, or augmented. Certain combinations of quality and ordinal number don't exist, such as major fifths and perfect thirds. Natural intervals are always either perfect, major, or minor, regardless of which scale they are in.

In figure 3.8 we see the same pitch-name pairs forming different intervals as the distance between them is changed. The C/D pair in m.2 is a major second first, then appears as a minor seventh. The minor seventh C/D and the major second C/D are **inversions** of one another, and below we see pairs of natural intervals from the C major scale that are inversions of one another (figure 3.8). The first B/C minor second **inverts** into a C/B major seventh when we move the C down one octave.

Figure 3.8: Intervals related by inversion from C major scale.

Each musical interval has its own distinct sound—but identifying them by ear is a challenge. This skill is often a component of musicianship or ear training. Certain intervals such as perfect octaves and fifths that have a restful sound are **consonant**, and intervals that sound agitated (such as the minor second) are **dissonant**. These qualities have a foundation in the acoustical properties of intervals—something we'll touch on in Chapter 10. Most people listening to consonant and dissonant intervals side by side would tend to describe the consonant intervals as more pleasing, but dissonance provides music with interest and vitality. Eliminate dissonant intervals in any well-loved piece of music, and it will likely ruin the music. For the natural intervals found in the major scale, the table in table 3.2 lists the intervals with gradations of consonance and dissonance. The perfect fourth is in the consonant column, but in certain contexts it is considered dissonant.

Table 3.2: Consonant and dissonant intervals.

Consonant	Dissonant
Perfect Octaves	Major/Minor Sevenths
Perfect Fifths	Major/Minor Seconds
Perfect Fourths	
Major/Minor Sixths	
Major/Minor Thirds	

3.5 Creating Intervals in Logic and Finale

The primary purpose of Logic's **Chord Trigger MIDI FX** (effects plugin) is to create chords of three of four notes, but it can also create ascending intervals (pairs of notes) based on a note input via keyboard or in a MIDI region. As shown in figure 3.9, from the top left drop-down menu, you can select any simple interval by **Single → Interval →** (choose from list). **Chord Trigger** will play the interval on that track and display the notes on the **Output Keyboard**. Using the **Chord Transpose**, you can also transpose the interval (both pitches simultaneously) up or down by semitone amounts.

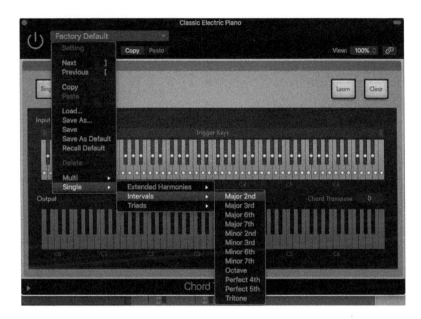

Figure 3.9: Chord Trigger **can create intervals in Logic.**

In Finale we can create intervals with the **Transposition** tool. After entering single notes in a musical staff, we select a measure and can add notes at specific intervals by opening **Transpose** tool in the **Utilities** menu item, checking **Preserve Original Notes**, and clicking **OK**. Both notes will be displayed, and the new note will be at the selected interval. From the **Transposition** tool (figure 3.10) we can choose the new note forming the interval to be either ascending or descending, simple or compound (for creating compound intervals we use **Plus # octave(s)**), or diatonic or chromatic. The diatonic intervals are restricted to notes in the scale, resulting in natural intervals. Chromatic intervals include all possibilities, including augmented and diminished intervals. Starting in m. 2 in figure 3.10, the following intervals were created with the transposition tool: major second, augmented second, diminished third, minor third, and major third. The intervals connected by arrows are enharmonically equivalent: major seconds and diminished thirds sound the same, as do augmented seconds and minor thirds.

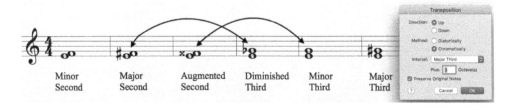

Figure 3.10: Transposition **tool creates ascending chromatic intervals from E4 in Finale.**

3.6 Inverting Intervals with Finale and Logic

The inversions we are describing here are **harmonic inversions**—as opposed to **melodic inversions** (see Chapter 6), and we can use Finale's **Canonic Utilities** to create them. Harmonic inversions of intervals are created by transposing one of the pitches one octave above or below its current octave position. In the Finale example in figure 3.11, the first-measure interval is a C4/D4 major second. To get the harmonic inversion, we select the interval, choose **Chord Inversion Up** from **Canonic Utilities**, then **Apply**. The C4 pitch is transposed up one octave, resulting in the interval inversion—a D4/C5 minor seventh. If we choose **Chord Inversion Down** with the same interval, the D4 is transposed down one octave, and the D3/C4 minor seventh interval is transposed down one octave and in bass clef (figure 3.11).

Figure 3.11: Canonic Utilities Chord Inversion Down **on a major second interval in Finale.**

As we are transposing pitches by octaves, the interval inversion has the same two pitches in both the up and down mode, and the same pitches as the original—C and D. The intervals, however, change from major second to minor seventh. Harmonic inversions are used with chords as well, as we'll see in Chapters 3 and 4.

With Logic's **MIDI Transform Transposition** preset we can create harmonic inversions of intervals. For any interval less than one octave, we first select the lower of the two pitches, then with the **Transposition Pitch** set to **Add** (add 12 semitones), we choose **Operate Only** (figure 3.12). This will transpose the lower pitch up one octave, creating the harmonic inversion. In this case, we don't want to choose **Select Only** or **Select and Operate**, as these commands will select *all* the pitches for transposition—leaving us with the same interval as before, but now transposed. We could also select the upper pitch and set the transposition value to **Sub 12** (subtract 12 semitones) to get a descending interval inversion.

Figure 3.12: MIDI Transform Transposition **preset creating harmonic interval inversions in Logic.**

3.7 Major Scales and Keys

So far, we've worked with the C major and chromatic scales. We can build major scales on any of the twelve pitches in the chromatic scale. To make things a little simpler, we choose only one of the enharmonic names for pitches with sharps or flats, except for the pair of G♭/F#. Major scales are built on: C, D♭, D, E♭, E, F, F# or G♭, G, A♭, A, B♭, B. In other words, we won't create major scales on C#, D#, G#, or A#, but they are possible.

The scale creates a foundation for a piece of music, and when music is built from a scale it's in the **key** of that scale. Music in the key of G major, for instance, uses the G major scale as its raw material, both melodically and harmonically.

With Logic we can construct all major scales starting with a single instance of a C major scale by using basic copy and paste functions (Command C and Command V) and **MIDI Transform**. **Key signatures** (a group of accidentals directly to the right of a clef) show the accidentals needed for a scale, and they also tell us what key we are in. To create the key signatures for each scale, we'll also use the **Key** function in the **LCD** display. The process of creating all twelve major scales has a number of steps which are outlined in the following list; the end result is shown in figure 3.13.

Figure 3.13: Major scales in Logic.

1. Open a Logic session and create a **Software Instrument Track** using any instrument sound.
2. In a two-measure region, input quarter notes of the ascending C major scale from C4 to C5. These are the white notes on the keyboard from middle C to one octave above. (C4 – D4 – E4- F4 – G4 – A4 – B4 – C5.)
3. Select the measures, hold the **option** key down, and drag/copy it forward to mm. 3–4.
4. Select mm. 3–4, and open **MIDI Transform (⌘ 9) Presets → Transposition; Pitch → Add 7**; then **Select and Operate**.
5. An F# appears as the second-to-last note as the major scale pattern was shifted up seven semitones.
6. Place the **playhead** at the start of m. 3, click the **Cmaj** in the **KEY** area of the **LCD Display** and select **G major** from the drop-down menu.
7. Select all four measures in the **Edit** window. From the menu item **Window** choose **Open Score Editor**. In the **Score** window, you no longer see the sharp next to the last F, because there is a single F# key signature now—the key signature for G major. We see the first two measures of C major scale, then two measures of G major scale with its key signature.
8. Continuing this process, option-drag mm. 3–4 to mm. 5–6. Select mm. 5–6 and transpose them down a perfect fourth (five semitones) by **MIDI Transform (⌘ 9) → Presets → Transposition → Pitch → Sub 5**; then **Select and Operate**.

9. We will now see a C# as the second-to-last note. Move the **Playhead** to the start of m. 5. To get a key signature with both the F# and C#, click in the **Key** area and choose **Dmaj.**

10. Repeat the above steps so that mm. 7–8 is transposed up seven semitones to A major; mm. 9–10 down five semitones to E major; mm. 11–12 up seven semitones to B major; and mm. 13–14 down five semitones to F# major. Change the key signatures every two measures for each new scale.

11. Copy mm. 13–14 onto 15–16, but don't transpose them. Instead, just change **F#maj** to **Gb-maj** in the **KEY** square of the display. This Gb major scale is enharmonically equivalent to F# major, so now we have two different versions of the same scale, and we've shifted from sharps to flats. From this point forward, the keys will have flats.

12. Continue the process for another ten measures: mm. 17–18 transpose down five semitones to Db Major; mm. 19–20 up seven semitones to Ab major; mm. 21–22 down five semitones to Eb major, mm. 23–24 up seven semitones to Bb major and mm. 25–26 down five semitones to F major. Notice that we always transpose the scale by a perfect fifth up or a perfect fourth down. Finally, change all the key signatures to the keys listed above.

We have created all the major scales and put them in order by ascending perfect fifths or descending perfect fourths. This sequence of keys is the **circle of fifths**, and it's often used to show key signatures and the arrangement of accidentals in each key (figure 3.14). In our Logic session, we can see the keys displayed in the **Global Tracks** area directly below the **Ruler**. **Global Tracks** include several track types, such as **Arrangement**, **Marker**, or **Movie**. To see key signatures displayed in the **Global Tracks**, we click on the **Show/Hide Global Tracks** button—it turns blue. We can make sure key signatures will be displayed by control-clicking in the track header to the left of the **Show/Hide Global Tracks** button and selecting **Signature** (figure 3.15).

Just as we have enharmonic spellings for pitches, we can have enharmonic spellings for key centers as well, which we see in the circle of fifths chart (figure 3.14) for Gb/F#. The Gb/F# key has either six sharps or six flats. On either side of this key in the circle we have Db major and B major, and these keys could be spelled at C# major and Cb major with seven sharps and seven flats respectively. These keys are possible, but less common.

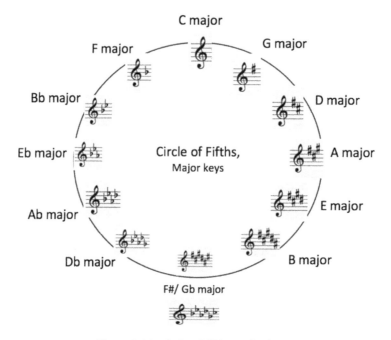

Figure 3.14: Circle of fifths, major keys.

Figure 3.15: Displaying key signatures with Signature **in** Global Tracks **in Logic.**

3.8 *Minor Scales and Keys*

The counterpart to the major scale is the **minor** scale, which has three forms: **natural, harmonic,** and **melodic**. We can build minor scales on any of the twelve pitches, and we will choose these spellings to create minor scales: C, C#, D, D#, Eb, E, F, F#, G, G#, A, Bb, and B. Notice that we have both a C#, F#, G#, and Bb minor scales, but do not use the Db, Gb minor scales. The Ab or A# minor scales with seven flats and sharps respectively are possible but quite rare.

Two important connections between major and minor scales (or keys) are: (1) major and minor scales that start on the same pitch are **parallel** and have different key signatures, and (2) major and minor scales that have the same key signature are called **relative**, but have different starting or tonic notes. The relative minor is always a minor third below its relative major. C major and C minor are parallel major/minor keys and have different key signatures, and C major and A minor are relative major/minor keys and have the same key signature.

The **natural minor scale** has this ascending pattern of whole steps (W) and half steps (h): W h W W h W W. As we did for the major scales, we can create all the natural minor scales in Logic by taking the minor scale with no sharps or flats (A minor) and copying, pasting, and transposing it multiple times. The end result appears in figure 3.16. After making enough copies, we transpose each copy of the two-measure scale by a series of ascending perfect fifths (seven semitones) or descending perfect fourths (five semitones). This series is A → E → B → F# → C# → G# → D#/Eb → Bb → F → C → G → D. The enharmonic pair of scales D# and Eb minor have six accidentals (either sharps or flats) in their key signatures. The key signatures for the minor scales can be added by placing the playhead in the correct position and choosing the key with the **LCD's Key** display.

Placing the minor keys next to their relative majors (with the same key signatures), we add the minor keys to our circle of fifths to display all twenty-four major and minor keys (figure 3.17).

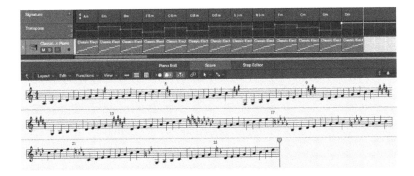

Figure 3.16: Natural minor scales in Logic.

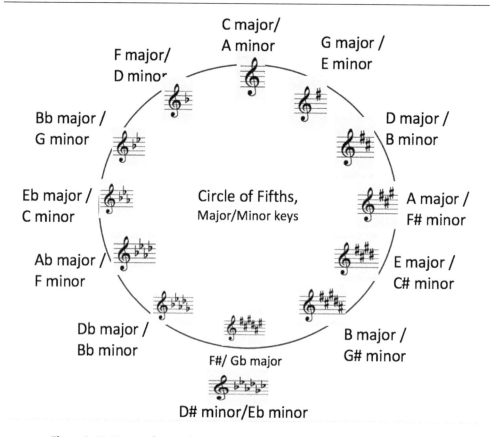

Figure 3.17: Twenty-four major and minor keys (with F#/Gb major and D#/Eb minor enharmonic spellings).

3.9 Intervals in Minor Scales

The natural intervals formed between the root and successive scale degrees of the three minor scale forms are all a bit different. We can use the **Key Signature** and **Scale Quantize** in Logic to see and hear the differences. We start with a MIDI region with the natural intervals in C major scale (see figure 3.6). We then create two additional tracks (for the harmonic minor and melodic minor) and option-drag the region into tracks 2 and 3 to create three copies in all. First, making sure the **playhead** is at measure 1, we change the **Key Signature** to **Cmin**, which will change all the scales to C natural minor. Then, in the **Piano Roll Editor** of tracks 2 and 3, we can use **Scale Quantize** on these specific regions to change them to C harmonic minor and C melodic minor. In track 3 we see that Logic quantizes the melodic minor to the ascending form, although traditionally the descending portion of the scale reverts to natural minor. To use the descending melodic minor scale, we can select the intervals from the descending scale portion (mm. 9–10) and scale-quantize these two measures alone to C natural minor (figure 3.18). Courtesy accidentals (see page 57) were added to these measures of the melodic minor scale to remind us that these notes are flatted.

Scale Quantize has nineteen scale forms in all, including the **modern modes** (**Ionian, Dorian, Phrygian, Lydian, Mixolydian, Aeolian,** and **Locrian**) (figure 3.19). Any musical passage (including scales) can be quantized into any scale or mode, a feature of Logic that holds vast potential for experimentation and learning.

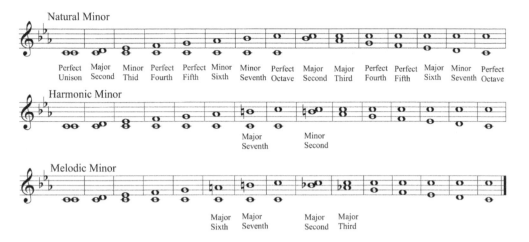

Figure 3.18: Intervals from the three C minor scale forms.

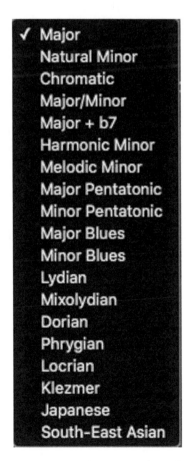

Figure 3.19: Scale Quantize in Logic.

3.10 Creating Major and Minor Scales in Finale

Starting with a C major scale as two measures of quarter notes, we can create any major or minor scale with the **Key Signature** tool in Finale. First copy and paste the scale into new measures, then with **Key Signature** and the two measures selected, double-click in the measures to bring up the **Key Signature** dialog window. Here we can choose any key and either major or minor. The scale will be transposed up or down depending on the **Transposition Options**, and the key signature will change as well. In figure 3.20, C major is transposed into G major (one sharp is added), and then transposed to its parallel C minor (three flats added).

Figure 3.20: Transposing scales with Key Signature **in Finale.**

3.11 Scale Generator

Play any note on the keyboard in **Scale Generator**, and it plays the selected ascending and descending scale forms starting on that pitch, using the major scale (as shown in figure 3.21) or one of the three minor-scale forms (**natural minor, harmonic minor,** or **melodic minor**). The harmonic minor pattern is W h W W h (W+ h) h. Notice that the second-to-last step is a whole and half step *combined*, an augmented second. The melodic minor scale has an ascending pattern W h W W W W h, but its descending pattern W W h W W h W is the same as the natural minor.

We can use Logic to record the **Scale Generator**'s output and see the scales in a **Score Editor** as we listen to them. **Scale Generator** creates any of the forty-eight possible scales (four scales starting on twelve pitches).

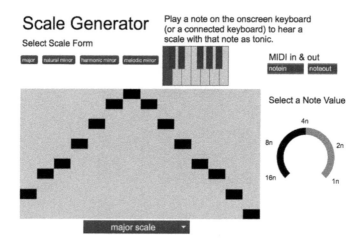

Figure 3.21: Scale Generator **in Max.**

We can follow the same method we used for **Rhythm Generator** to send the scales to Logic by selecting **from Max 1** from **noteout** and recording in Logic (figure 3.22). In the following is a Logic session that has recorded output from **Scale Generator**. The scales played are the C major and the three forms of the C minor. In m. 5 of the Logic session the key signature changes from C major (no sharps or flats) to C minor (three flats—B♭, E♭, A♭). We use the same key signature (based on the natural minor scale) for all forms of the minor scales, and include accidentals to create the harmonic and melodic forms.

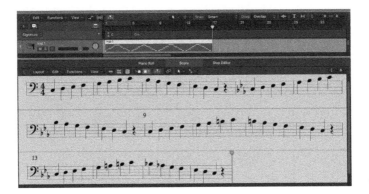

Figure 3.22: Scale Generator **recorded in Logic.**

Added accidentals (those not included in the key signature) only affect notes within one measure and are canceled by a bar line. Looking at the C melodic minor scale in the last line, we see A♮ and B♮ in the ascending form, but B♭ and A♭ in the descending. As (1) accidentals in the key signature apply to all notes, and (2) accidentals added in a measure are canceled by a subsequent bar line, the B♭ and A♭ in m. 9 don't require accidentals—they are flatted by the key signature. But adding these **courtesy accidentals** as reminders makes it easier to read. To create courtesy accidentals in Logic, select notes that need them, then from the **Score Editor** select **Functions** → **Note Attributes** → **Accidentals** → **Force Accidental**. To make courtesy accidentals in Finale, select the note(s) and press the Shift 8 (*) to force the accidental to be displayed.

3.12 Max Patcher 5: *Scale Generator*

The **Scale Generator** in patcher mode (figure 3.23) shows the objects and connections.

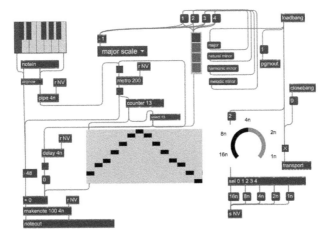

Figure 3.23: Scale Generator **in patcher mode in Max.**

Some objects (such as **kslider** (keyboard), **dial** to choose a note value, **messages** to choose scale form, etc.) are included in presentation mode, but many objects that aren't necessary for using the patcher are left out. **Scale Generator** includes objects we have used in earlier patchers (**notein, noteout, makenote, stripnote, metro, sel, delay, pipe, toggle, button, message, addition**) and some objects which we haven't yet used, such as **itable** and **presets**.

To create the ascending and descending scales, we add interval amounts in a timed sequence to the note input by an attached MIDI controller, and then output these as the notes of the selected scale. These interval amounts (in semitones) for the different scale degrees are listed in figure 3.24, and we can store multiple sets of these values with the **itable** object (figure 3.23) with a **preset** object.

Index	0	1	2	3	4	5	6	7	8	9	10	11	12	13
Major	2	4	5	7	9	11	12	11	9	7	5	4	2	0
Natural	2	3	5	7	8	10	12	10	8	7	5	3	2	0
Harmonic	2	3	5	7	8	11	12	11	8	7	5	3	2	0
Melodic	2	3	5	7	9	11	12	10	8	7	5	3	2	0

Figure 3.24: itable **values for intervals above the tonic note.**

The **itable** object is a data table editor to store, retrieve, and display values. To create **itable**, we create a new object and type "**itable**" in the object box. When we click elsewhere on the screen, it becomes a gray box. Selecting this gray box, we click on the **Inspector** to open the **itable** inspector. The inspector icon is the circled **i** in Max's right side panel. At the bottom of the **Inspector** are the **Table Range** and **Size** attributes, and the default values for both are 128. Because the range and size are too large for our purposes, we set **Range** to 13 to span one octave (giving us values 0–12), and **Size** to 14 (values 0–13) to have ascending and descending scales (figure 3.25).

When the patcher is locked, we can click inside the **itable** to set values for each index number. Once we have clicked-in a scale in **itable**, we save the values for each scale so that we can retrieve them with a **preset** object. We'll also modify the **preset** object from its default so that it has four slots (one for each scale). To save the values in **itable** with **preset**, we shift-click a **preset** slot when the patcher is locked—this slot will then retrieve those values when clicked. We stored four scale types (the major and the three minor scale forms) in the four slots of our **preset**.

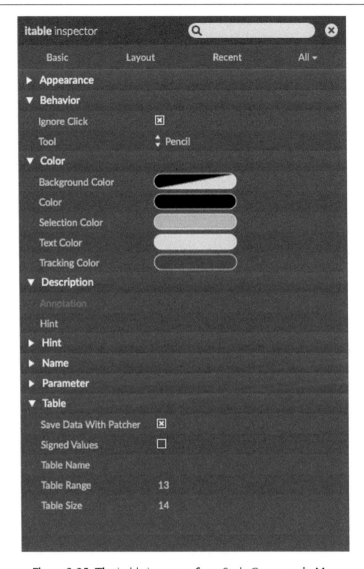

Figure 3.25: The itable inspector **from** Scale Generator **in Max.**

To make sure the **itable** is only controlled by the preset once it has stored the four scales, we can check **Ignore Click** in the **Behavior** tab of its inspector. In the **Color** tab of our **itable**'s **inspector** we also modified the colors from the default mode.

To read through the **itable** from index numbers 0 to 13, we can send the output of a **counter 13** object (counting from 0 to 13—corresponding to the index numbers) to send out the semitone amounts stored at each index number. Once turned on by the **toggle**, the **metro** object bangs the **counter** object at the note-value rate, and it sends out numbers in order from 0 to 13. When the **counter** reaches 13, the connected **select 13** object bangs the **toggle**, which turns off **metro**. Both **itable** and **counter** start at 0. Each interval amount is added to the tonic note in turn by the addition object, and the scale is output to **noteout**.

As an example, if we play C4 or MIDI note number 60 the scale produced would be [60, 60+2, 60+4, 60+5, 60+7, 60+9, 60+11, 60+12, 60+11, 60+9, 60+7, 60+5, 60+4, 60+2, 60+0], or [60,

62, 64, 65, 67, 69, 71, 72, 71, 69, 67, 65, 64, 62, 60], which is the ascending and descending C major scale starting on middle C. Playing a D4 produces 62, and then the **itable** values will produce a D major scale. As we are adding values to any input note number, we can create a scale on any pitch.

When the counter reaches 13, in addition to turning **metro** off, the number 0 is sent to the **add two numbers** object (+0) after a quarter note. This ensures that when the scale starts again, it will start on the pitch played and that no value is added to the first note.

To select note durations for **Scale Generator** notes, we've created a **Select Note Value** section in the lower right part of the patcher. The **dial** displays note values (4n=quarter note, 8n=eighth note, 2n=half note, etc.), but sends out simple integer values (0, 1, 2, 3, 4). This **dial** was modified in the inspector, and its output is sent to a **sel** (select) object which causes one of the messages with the actual note values to be sent to **s NV** (which stands for **send** note values). Additionally, the **loadbang** turns on the **transport** and sets the initial note value to quarter note (the **2 message** input to **dial**). We'll use **Select Note Value** in other patchers as well.

We send this note value to several places to make sure that the note durations and delays are all the same length. **Scale Generator** can be modified to play any scale or **modern mode** (see page 67 in the exercises), and the **counter** object can be controlled to read through the **itable** in different ways. One might, for instance, read through only certain sections of the table to hear different portions of the scale.

3.13 Chromatic Intervals

In addition to the natural intervals (those formed using only one scale) are the **chromatic intervals** formed between any pitches with any accidentals by using the chromatic scale. The following Logic session with **Score** and **Piano Roll Editors** shows the intervals formed between middle C and a chromatic scale from C4 to C5 (figure 3.26). Some of these intervals are also natural intervals in C major, but others are not. Given the possibility of enharmonic spellings, we could come up with more, but as a general rule we use intervals with the simpler spellings. Rather than considering the interval between C4 and E#4 an augmented third, for instance, we are more likely to call it a perfect fourth by spelling it as C4 to F4. Likewise, intervals with double-sharps and double-flats can be, and in most cases should be, spelled in simpler terms, although sometimes these uncommon spellings are required.

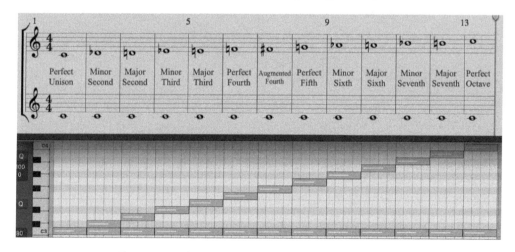

Figure 3.26: Chromatic intervals from C4 to C5 in Logic.

A significant challenge in the music theory/music technology area is that musical notation and the MIDI format don't record pitch information in the same way. Musical notation uses multiple names for enharmonic equivalents, while MIDI pitches are simply numbers (**note numbers**). MIDI note number 61 could be a C# or it could be a D♭. The situation with intervals is similar. From MIDI note 60 to 66 is six semitones, but it can be either an augmented fourth or a diminished fifth. In pitch notations, C4 to F#4 is an augmented fourth, but from C4 to G♭4 is a diminished fifth. Both versions of the interval are used; the C–F# interval occurs in G major, and the C–G♭ interval occurs in D♭ major.The augmented fourth/diminished fifth interval is also known as the **tritone.**

3.14 Interval Identifier

To help us recognize chromatic intervals and the different names we can use for them, we can use **Interval Identifier** (figure 3.27). Play an interval of one octave or less from an attached MIDI keyboard, then click on the **NOTATE** button to view two possible interval names and notation. We see in figure 3.27, for instance, that the interval with four semitones from E to G# is a major third, but it could also be a diminished fourth (E to A♭). If the interval is larger than an octave, the notes themselves and the semitones amount will be displayed, but the interval name reads "Larger than Octave."

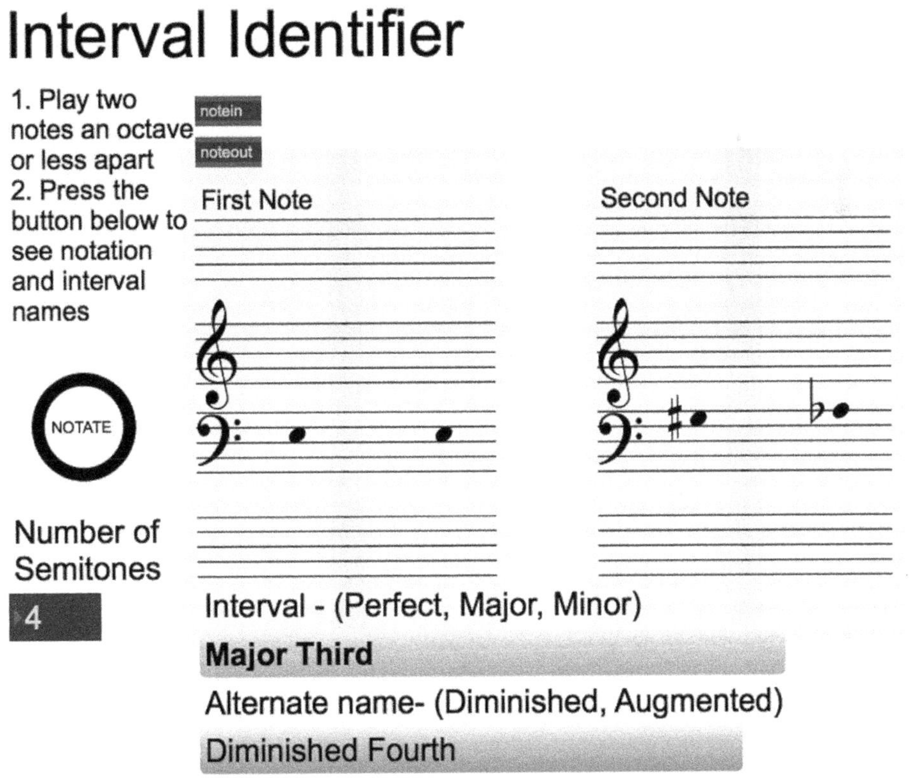

Figure 3.27: Interval Identifier **in Max.**

3.15 Max Patcher 6: *Interval Identifier*

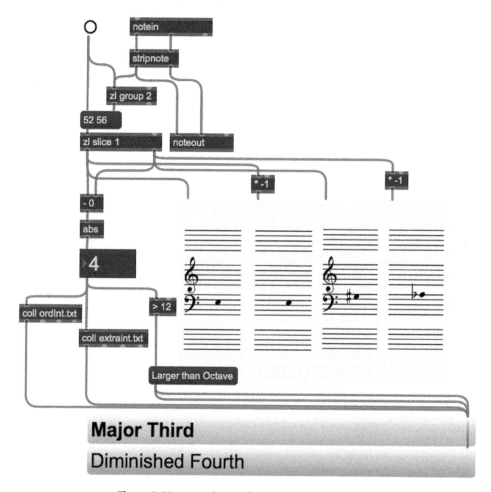

Figure 3.28: Interval Identifier **(patcher mode) in Max.**

The **Interval Identifier** receives two notes played on a MIDI keyboard with **notein**, then uses the semitone interval number between the two notes to provide two possible interval names. The patcher is shown in patcher mode in figure 3.28.

When two notes are played from a MIDI keyboard into **Interval Identifier**, the **stripnote** object deletes the incoming **noteon** message with a 0 velocity. This **noteon** message is generated when we release the key on a MIDI keyboard. It is used by MIDI synthesizers to end notes, but we don't need it to figure out the interval.

The note numbers are sent to the **zl group 2** object to join them together as a **list** of two elements. The **zl slice 1** object then splits the numbers up so that we can subtract one from the other with the **subtract two numbers** object (− **0**). If the first number is larger than the second (which happens when the interval descends), a positive value is produced, but if the second number is larger (as happens with ascending intervals), a negative value is produced. The **abs (absolute value)** object turns any negative value positive. This value, the interval as number of semitones, is then sent to two **coll (collection)** objects which match the semitone number with interval names.

The **coll** object stores data with index numbers. In our patcher, **coll ordint.txt** stores the more common names for intervals, and **coll extraint.txt** stores the less common ones (figure 3.29). The **coll** objects have index numbers which correspond to the semitone values. For example, when **coll ordint.txt** receives a 7, it outputs the data at index 7, which is the text "Perfect Fifth." The **coll extraind.txt**, on the other hand, outputs a less common alternative for an interval of seven semitones—the text "Diminished Sixth." The contents of the two **coll** objects follow a required format: index number—comma—data—semicolon. The outputs of the **coll** objects are connected to **messages**, and when the messages receive the interval name they display this output, the interval name.

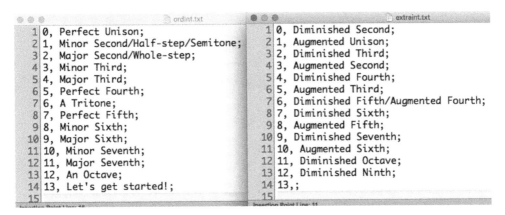

Figure 3.29: Two colls **of interval names as data stored by index number in Max.**

If the interval is larger than twelve, then the message "Larger than Octave" is banged out by the **Compare numbers for greater than condition** object (> 12). The **coll** objects could be expanded to include compound intervals, but here they are limited to simple intervals (an octave or less).

The note numbers are also sent to four **nslider** objects, which display the notes on a grand staff. Positive MIDI note numbers are displayed as notes with sharps or no accidentals by **nslider**, and negative MIDI note numbers are displayed with flats or no accidentals. For instance, MIDI note 61 is C# and −61 is D♭—enharmonic equivalents. By showing every note in both sharp and flat or natural form, we can see two possible spellings for certain intervals, such as (60, 68) being both a minor sixth (−60, −68 as C–A♭), and an augmented fifth (60, 68 as C–G#).

3.16 Modern Modes

When using the **Scale Quantize** function in Logic to create the three forms of the minor scale (natural, harmonic, and melodic), we saw that it can quantize music to any one of nineteen scale forms (figure 3.25). In addition to the major and minor scale forms, we can use this function to learn about other scale forms, such as the **modern modes**. The modern modes (**Ionian, Dorian, Phrygian, Lydian, Mixolydian, Aeolian**, and **Locrian**) are based on historical antecedents and are used today in many musical contexts. As the Ionian and Aeolian are the mode names for the major and natural minor scales, respectively, we'll focus on the other five.

We can create each modern mode by using only the notes of the C major scale, but starting and ending on different scale steps. Starting on D and ascending with only C major notes to the D an octave higher creates the D Dorian mode. The E Phrygian mode starts and ends on E with C major notes, the F Lydian on F, G Mixolydian on G, and the B Locrian on B. This is a good way to introduce the modern modes. Modern modes, however, can start on any pitch.

To create all the modes starting on C4 with the help of Logic's **Scale Quantize**, we start with a C major scale in eighth notes in one measure and then option-drag it six times forward to create the seven measures in all. Selecting each measure in turn, we can **Scale Quantize** them to each of the modern modes (figure 3.30).

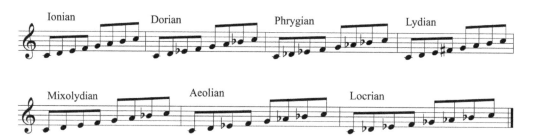

Figure 3.30: The modern modes on C4.

Any music material can be made modal in this same way using **Scale Quantize**. As we view the modes as in figure 3.30, we notice that each one uses a different number of accidentals, with one sharp for the Lydian mode, and two flats for Dorian, etc.

This means we can change the mode by changing the key signature. The C major scale becomes the C Dorian scale if we add the B♭ major key signature (B♭ and E♭) and flatten all B and E pitches. The C major scale can become the C Phrygian mode if we add the A♭ major key signature (B♭, E♭, A♭, and D♭) and flatten all the B, E, A, and D pitches.

With Finale, we can turn any major-scale material into a modal passage by changing the key signature: (1) select the **Key Signature** tool; (2) select the material that we want to change into a mode; (3) select the appropriate key signature for the change of mode desired (such as B♭ major to change C major into C Dorian); (4) select **Hold Notes to Same Staff Lines (Modally)**; (5) press OK. In figure 3.31 is a two-measure phrase in C major that has been transposed into C Dorian (measures 3–4), and C Lydian (measures 5–6) with Finale's **Key Signature** tool.

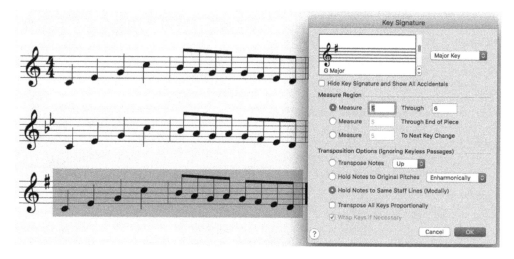

Figure 3.31: Transposing materials modally with Key Signature in Finale.

This method of transposing material modally works in all keys, and we can think of shifting scales to modes as the change of key signatures by certain amounts on the circle of fifths (see figure 3.32). We can extrapolate that for any key to shift from major to Lydian, the key signature moves once clockwise. Similarly, to change a key from major to Mixolydian, we shift one place on the circle counterclockwise, or from major to Dorian, we shift two places on the circle counterclockwise. The shifts from minor to modes are also possible with changes in key signature.

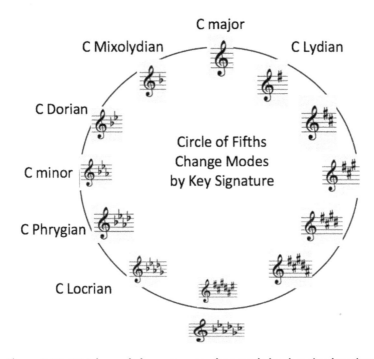

Figure 3.32: C Major scale becomes a modern mode by changing key signatures.

If you change the key signature of a C major scale in Logic, on the other hand, the scale remains intact, and accidentals are added. When you change the **LCD Display Key** of a C major scale to the B♭ major key signature to create a C Dorian scale the E and B will remain natural. To make these notes conform to C Dorian, select the notes and **Scale Quantize** them to C Dorian. The key signature is now two flats (B♭ major), and there are no accidentals, so we have a C Dorian scale. We can transform any major and minor scale-based material to modal music in Logic with key signatures in this way.

3.17 Exercises

3.17.1 Exercise 1: Reading Pitches in Logic

We can use Logic to practice reading pitches. First, open a Logic session and create a **Software Instrument** track. Insert a series of whole notes in a measure in the track (any notes will work), and with the region selected, open the **MIDI Transform (command ⌘-9)** (figure 3.33). From **MIDI Transform**, choose **Random Pitch** from the **Presets** and select the range of pitches. All notes in this range will be randomly changed to other pitches.

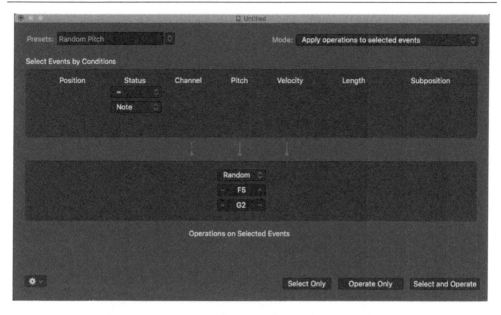

Figure 3.33: MIDI Transform, Random Pitch Preset **in Logic.**

In this case, we've chosen G2 to F5 for the range, the entire span of pitches in the grand staff. Click on **Select and Operate** button in the lower right, and twelve new and different notes replace ones previously entered. Name the notes that are generated, then click on each note to create a pop-up window which displays note position, length, and pitch name to check your answer (figure 3.34). Every time you press **Select and Operate**, new notes are created, so the reading practice can continue for as long as needed.

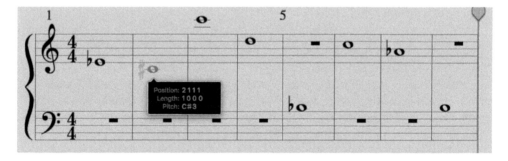

Figure 3.34: Clicking on notes gives you pitch information in Logic.

3.17.2 Exercise 2: Reading Natural Intervals in Finale

We can use Finale to practice reading natural intervals or intervals from diatonic scales. First, we create two treble-clef staves, with the **Document Setup Wizard** (add two blank staves). Two screens later we choose a key by selecting a tonic pitch and either major or minor (we can also choose the key with the **Key Signature** tool). For the following example, we chose A major.

With **Simple Entry**, randomly enter notes in all ten measures in each staff by selecting a whole note and clicking somewhere once in each measure. The result should look something like this figure 3.35.

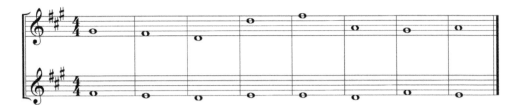

Figure 3.35: Notes in A major in two staves in Finale.

Next, we select all ten measures in both staves, and choose **Utilities → Implode Music** as shown in figure 3.36, then select **Place Music Into: Top Staff of Selection** before pressing **OK**. We now have intervals in the top staff and one note from the interval below.

Figure 3.36: Imploding Music **joins the material of staves together in Finale.**

To practice reading the intervals formed, we can select single notes in the lower staff, then choose **Utilities → Transpose**, either **Up** or **Down** and **Chromatically**, and then find the correct interval, which gets us to the second note. In the first measure above, the G# is a major second above the F#, so we'll choose transpose by a major second to match the pitches (figure 3.37). Make sure **Preserve Original Notes** is checked, then press **OK**. If we selected the correct interval, the upper and lower measures will be identical.

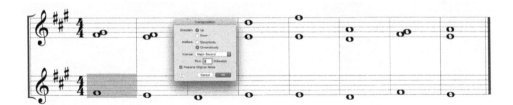

Figure 3.37: Using Transposition **to determine intervals in Finale.**

3.17.3 Exercise 3: Scale Practice

Logic can help us practice scales on a MIDI keyboard. Let's say we want to practice playing the G major scale on a MIDI keyboard and have Logic identify any wrong notes we play. We record enable two **Software Instrument** tracks by clicking on the **R** button in both tracks' name fields. With track 2 selected, open the **Inspector** for this track, then open the **Transposer** tool from the **MIDI FX** drop-down menu (figure 3.38).

Then, select the **Can't Go Wrong** preset and select the key and scale in the drop-down **Root** and **Scale** menus. If we play an incorrect note (a note which is not in the selected scale), we'll hear two different pitches at that moment because the **Can't Go Wrong MIDI FX** will play the correct note along with the note we played (figure 3.38). As we practice the scales or other exercises, we should always hear only one pitch when the scales are played correctly.

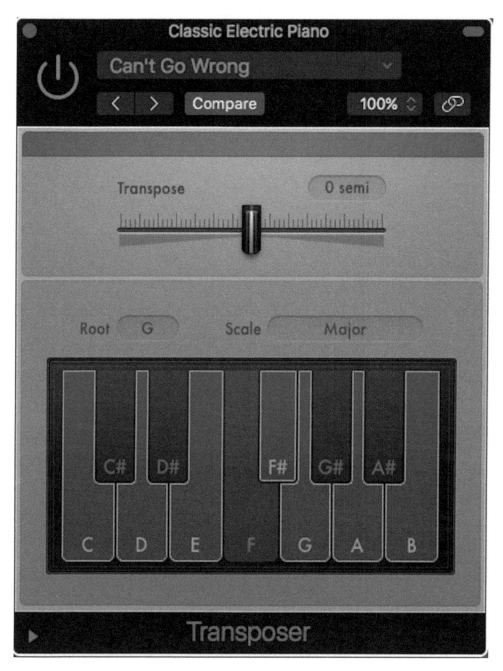

Figure 3.38: Transposer **MIDI FX with** Can't Go Wrong **setting in Logic.**

After working on all the scales (D major is shown in figure 3.39), we can practice chord patterns, such as the B♭ pattern, and transpose the patterns to all the keys (figure 3.39). The **Can't Go Wrong** preset of the **Transpose MIDI FX**, like **Scale Quantize**, also has settings for the modern modes, blues scales, and other scale forms, so we can use it to practice any of the scales. The following example includes **keyboard fingerings** for the scale and B♭ major pattern—the numbers above the staves.

Figure 3.39: D major scale and B♭ major pattern with right-hand fingerings.

To read the fingerings in the previous exercise, we use the numbers to tell us which finger to use in the right hand: 1=thumb, 2=index finger, 3=middle finger, 4=ring finger, and 5=pinky. Playing scales on a keyboard proficiently requires correct fingerings—that is, fingerings that help us play the passages easily. Keep in mind that the best fingerings in one key may not work well in another key. The D major scale fingering in figure 3.39, for example, would not work for F major. Doing piano exercises with awkward fingering patterns can even be counterproductive. Piano teachers and keyboard instruction texts are both good resources to learn how to create good fingerings.

3.17.4 Exercise 4: Change Scale Generator into Mode Generator

We can make a copy of the **Scale Generator** and turn it into **Mode Generator** so that it plays the modern modes (Dorian, Phrygian, Lydian, Mixolydian, and Locrian) (see figure 3.30). First, we should change the number of **Select Scale Form messages**, **presets**, and the number boxes to select **presets** from four to five. We can also change the content of the **umenu** to the modes in its **inspector** and rename the **messages** to the mode names.

To input different pitches for the modes, we'll need to uncheck **Ignore Click** in the **itable inspector**. Then we can input all the different modes' pitches in the **itable**, remembering that each **itable** represents a semitone as the positions in the table's Y axis. We save each mode to a **preset** by shift-clicking. Our new **Mode Generator** will play the five modes on any pitch.

3.17.5 Exercise 5: Interval Quiz

We can modify **Interval Identifier** to be **Interval Quiz** to test our aural recognition of intervals (fig 3.40), a useful skill for musicians and one best learned with individualized practice.

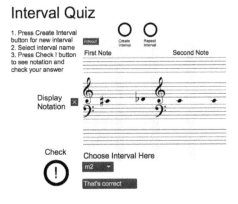

Figure 3.40: Interval Quiz

The new tasks in **Interval Quiz** are: (1) randomly generate an interval, and (2) allow the user to match their answer with the actual interval. These tasks are accomplished by the **p create interval** subpatcher and several added objects visible in the patcher view of **Interval Quiz** (figure 3.41). The left **button** entering **p create interval** subpatcher's inlet 1 (fig 3.42) bangs two **random** objects which create the two notes of the interval. The range of pitches is determined by the arguments of the **random** objects and by the **addition** and **subtraction** objects—these objects limit the ascending or descending intervals to one octave or less, centered around middle C. The second inlet allows the user to play the interval again, which can be helpful.

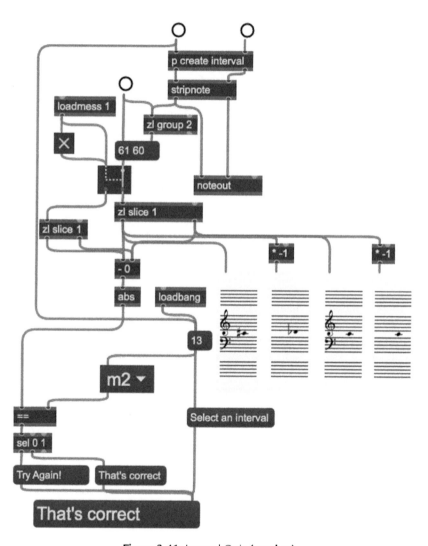

Figure 3.41: Interval Quiz **(patcher).**

The process whereby the user matches their answer to the actual interval is accomplished by a **umenu** with a list of intervals being compared to the interval semitone size. The **umenu** contains the simplest interval names, each has an index number corresponding to the interval. If correctly identified, the **== (compare numbers for equal to condition)** object sends out a 1 which bangs the "That's correct" to the user. If incorrect, this object sends out a 0 which bangs the "Try Again!" message.

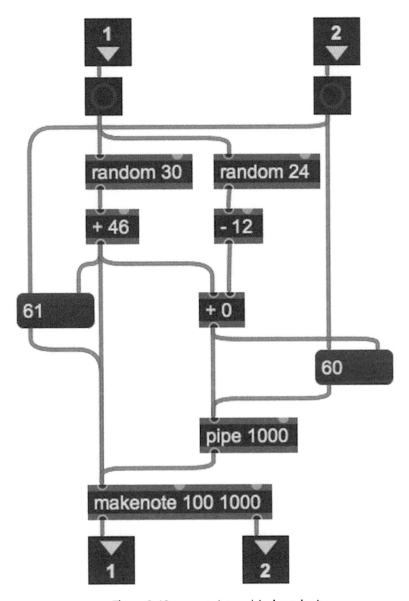

Figure 3.42: p create interval **(subpatcher).**

CHAPTER 4

Triads

4.1 Constructing Triads

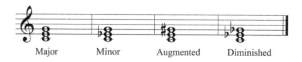

Figure 4.1: The four triad qualities.

The four chords that provide the basis for harmony are the **major**, **minor**, **augmented**, and **diminished triads** (figure 4.1), with the major and minor triads being the most common. The triad names, as with interval names, refer to their **qualities**. Each of the four triads shown in figure 4.1 is built on middle C, which is the **root chord tone** (or just **root**) for these triads. The triads' upper notes are the **third** and the **fifth** chord tones, respectively. Every triad has three different chord tones, and all triads are built with major or minor thirds. The interval from the root to the fifth is either perfect, augmented, or diminished. Table 4.1 shows which thirds are found between chord tones, and which fifths exists between the root and the fifth.

Table 4.1: Triads and their intervals.

Triad Type →	Major	Minor	Augmented	Diminished
Between root and fifth	Perfect fifth	Perfect fifth	Augmented fifth	Diminished fifth
Between third and fifth	Minor third	Major third	Major third	Minor third
Between root and third	Major third	Minor third	Major third	Minor third

The triads in figure 4.1 are all in **root position**, meaning that the root of the chord is the lowest pitch. They are also all in **closed voicing**, which means that the notes are all less than one octave apart. If we transpose just the root of the triad up an octave, the third becomes the lowest pitch, and the triad is now in **first inversion**. If we transpose both the root and the third up an octave, the fifth becomes the lowest pitch, and the triad is in **second inversion** (figure 4.2). When the triad is spread out larger than an octave, we say it's in **open voicing**. In figure 4.2 we see each of the four triads on C in root position and in first and second inversion. All together, we have twelve closed voicing triad types. These triad types can be created on any pitch, which means that for twelve notes in the chromatic scale, the total number of triads is 144 (12 x 12).

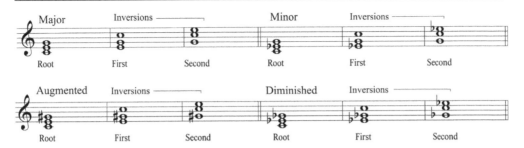

Figure 4.2: Each of the four triads in root position and in the two inversions.

4.2 Logic's Chord Trigger

We can use Logic's **Chord Trigger** to help us learn about triads. When we create a new software instrument track, we'll see a **MIDI FX** drop-down menu in the track's **Inspector**. Among the **MIDI FX** is **Chord Trigger** (figure 4.3), which plays chords based on single notes (triggers). Triggers can be input from the **Trigger Keys**, a connected MIDI keyboard, or can be played on the track itself. When opened, **Chord Trigger** plays **minor seventh** chords, a four-note chord we'll learn about in Chapter 5. **Chord Trigger** can also play triads, harmonic intervals, and can be programmed to play chords that the user inputs.

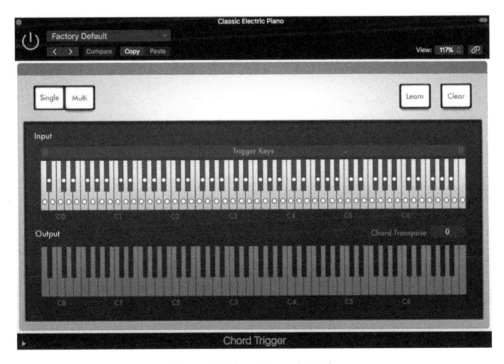

Figure 4.3: Chord Trigger **in Logic.**

To get **Chord Trigger** to play one of the basic triads, we click on the top left drop-down menu (**Factory Default**) and navigate **Single** → **Triads** → and select from this list: **Augmented, Diminished, Major, Minor, Sus2,** or **Sus4** (figure 4.4). In addition to the four triads, **Sus2** and **Sus4** are useful three-note chords, although technically not triads because they're not built with thirds. We can toggle through the list of chords with the Left and Right arrows directly under the drop-down menu, which is helpful for moving quickly through the chords.

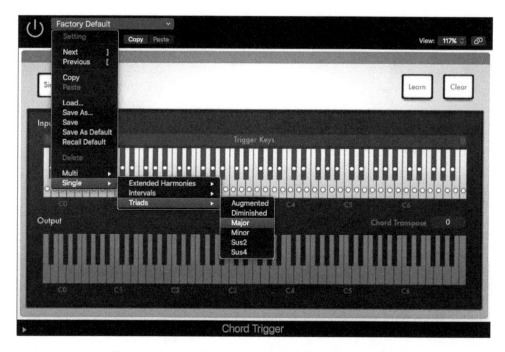

Figure 4.4: Chord Trigger: **choosing triad quality in Logic.**

When **Chord Trigger** is active on a software instrument track, it outputs audible chords, but when recording on that track, only the trigger notes are recorded. To see the chords created by **Chord Trigger** as MIDI notes or in musical notation, we must record the output of **Chord Trigger** to another track using the **IAC** driver, as described next.

Recording **Chord Trigger**'s output with the **IAC** (Inter-Application Communication Driver) requires that the **IAC** be activated before opening Logic. To do this: (1) Open **Applications** → **Utilities** → **Audio MIDI Setup**. From this set-up window, (2) double-click on the **IAC** driver icon and (3) make sure the **Device is Online** box is checked. At that point, the **IAC** driver icon should be bold (not grayed out).

With **Chord Trigger** active on software instrument/track 1, we'll record the trigger notes. Next, we create a new instrument track by clicking on the + sign above the track header area, or clicking **Option-Command-N**. We can use any polyphonic instrument, such as a keyboard, for this track. In track 1's **Inspector** (the track with **Chord Trigger** playing the chords), we locate the instrument name's drop-down menu. In this drop-down menu, we select **Utility** → **External Instrument** → and **Stereo** or **Mono** (figure 4.5). Instead of having a software instrument play the track, we set the track **Instrument** to **External Instrument** to send MIDI output to an external destination, such as a connected MIDI synthesizer or a virtual **bus**. When you choose **External Instrument**, an **Output Destination** window appears (figure 4.6). We'll choose the **IAC Driver IAC Bus 1** so that track 1's MIDI output can be virtually routed to (and thus recorded on) another track—track 2. This **Bus 1** is an internal routing pathway for MIDI data, and we're using it to send the chords from track 1 to track 2.

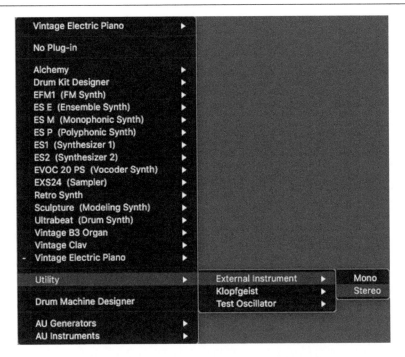

Figure 4.5: **Choosing** External Instrument **in Logic.**

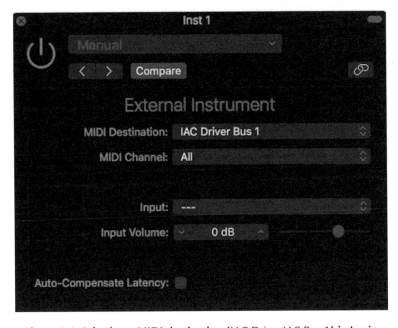

Figure 4.6: **Selecting a MIDI destination** (IAC Driver IAC Bus 1) **in Logic.**

Track 2 will now be receiving the MIDI notes from **Chord Trigger**, and we'll record this output onto track 2. Make sure that track 1 is *not* set to record, as only track 2 should be record-enabled. If track 1 is recording MIDI in this situation, then a MIDI feedback loop will occur and cause problems.

To hear each one of the four different types of triads, we'll need to adjust the chord-type, selecting from major, minor, augmented, and diminished. If we record each of the four triads, we can see them notated in the **Score Editor** (figure 4.7). We will use this method of displaying **Chord Trigger** output in the **Score Editor** in upcoming chapters as well.

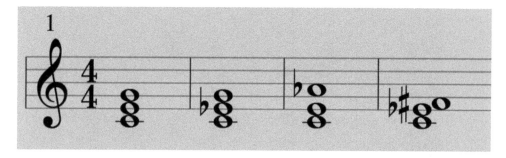

Figure 4.7: Chord Trigger **triads (major, minor, diminished, augmented) built on C4 in Logic.**

Chord Trigger is a MIDI-based device, so triads are output as three MIDI note numbers, and sometimes may not be spelled correctly. The C augmented triad should have a G# as the top note to create a major third between its third and fifth: E–G#. The chord sounds correct, because G#4 and A♭4 are the same pitch (they are enharmonic equivalents), but C–E–G# and C–E–A♭ are actually two different chords: the first is a C augmented triad and the second an A♭ augmented triad in first inversion. To correct the spelling in the **Score Editor**, we can change individual accidentals in Logic by selecting them, then navigating to **Functions → Note Attributes → Accidentals → Enharmonic Shift #** (⇧3) or **Enharmonic Shift b** (⇧B) (figure 4.8).

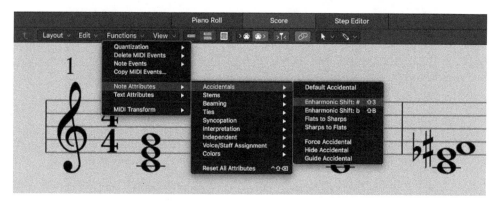

Figure 4.8: **Adjusting accidentals in a** Score Editor **in Logic.**

The C diminished chord should also be adjusted from C–E♭–F# to C–E♭–G♭. The interval between E♭ and F# is an augmented second, whereas the interval required is the minor third E♭–G♭. We can create any of the four triad types on any pitch with **Chord Trigger**.

4.3 Finale's Chord Tool

With Finale's **Chord** tool we can create triads by typing in chord symbols. To see the notation, however, we have some extra steps. To begin, we create a Finale file, choose the **Chord** tool, set it to **Manual Input**, and type in the chord symbols above the staff for the triads we want. Instead of triads built on C, we'll build four triad types on F by typing F, Fm, Fdim, and Faug (no spaces between the letters) for our major, minor, diminished, and augmented triads, respectively (figure 4.9). Even though the measures are blank, we'll hear these chords in playback if the **Enable Chord Playback** setting is checked in the **Chord** tool menu (figure 4.10).

Figure 4.9: Chord tool's four triad symbols in Finale.

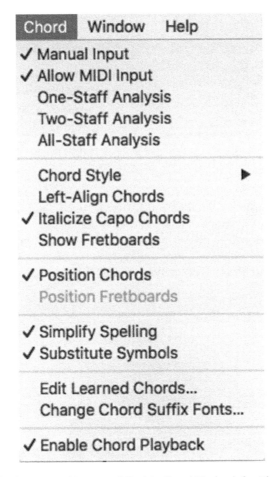

Figure 4.10: Selecting Manual Input **and** Enable Chord Playback **for** Chord **tool in Finale.**

To see the notation of these triads, we can export the file as a **Standard MIDI file (SMF)**: **File → Export → MIDI File** (figure 4.11), then bring the file back into Finale by opening the SMF file we've created by **File → Open** and then locating the SMF. The SMF will have a **.mid** extension instead of Finale's **.musx** extension.

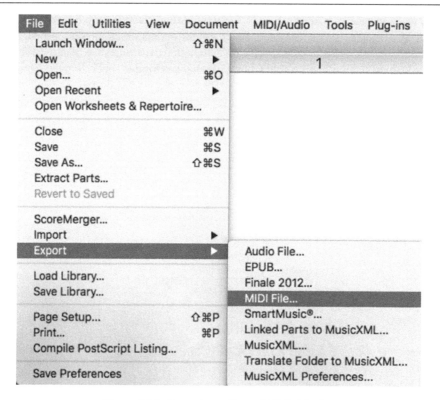

Figure 4.11: Exporting a file as SMF in Finale.

Before importing the SMF back into Finale, we can set the spelling preferences in Finale to correct problems that translating MIDI note numbers into pitches can create. Specifically, we should make sure the fifth of the diminished triad is diminished, and that the fifth of an augmented triad is augmented. To do this, we set the key to F major with the **Key Signature** tool. Then, from the Finale menu, we select **Enharmonic Spelling** → **Use Spelling Tables**, and open **Edit Major and Minor Key Spellings** (figure 4.12).

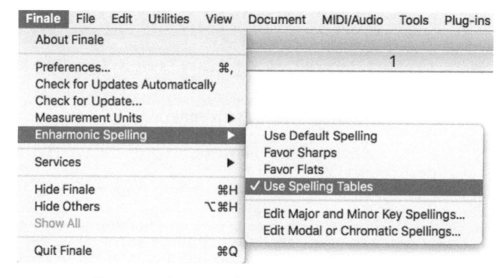

Figure 4.12: Enharmonic Spelling → Use Spelling Tables **in Finale.**

In **Edit Major and Minor Key Spellings**, we choose a flat spelling for the note between the fourth and fifth scale degrees (the diminished fifth), and a sharp for the note between the fifth and sixth scale degrees (the augmented fifth) in **Major Keys**. This setting will ensure that when we import the SMF of the four triads, they are spelled with a diminished and augmented fifth where needed. We set the key to F so that the **Altered Scale Steps** will affect the pitches six and eight semitones above F, but the **Spelling Table** will apply to all keys.

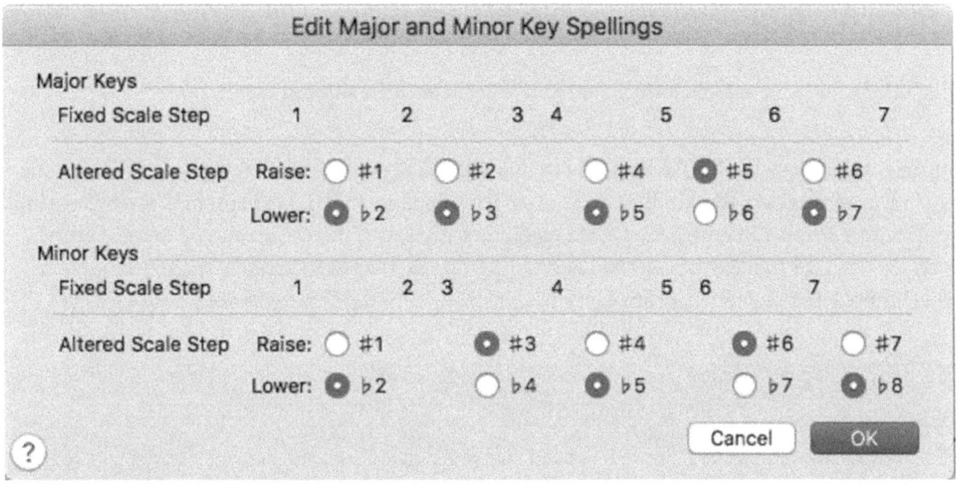

Figure 4.13: Edit Major and Minor Key Spellings **in Finale.**

The triads will be notated correctly when the SMF is opened in Finale (figure 4.14).

F Major   F Minor   F Diminished   F Augmented

Figure 4.14: Triads imported back into Finale.

When opening an SMF, a window for **Import Settings** appears. The default settings should work fine, so no changes are required. We can also change spellings in Finale by other means. To make a B into a C♭, for instance (as might have appeared with the F diminished chord), we select the note and, with the **Transposition** tool, transpose it up by a diminished second. To turn a D♭ into a C# we can similarly transpose the note down by a diminished second. We can also erase notes, and replace them by inputting new notes.

4.4 Inverting Triads in Finale and Logic

We can invert triads in Finale by selecting the triad and in **Canonic Utilities** selecting **Chord Inversion Up**. In figure 4.15, a D major chord was copied from the first measure to the next two measures. In the second measure, clicking once on **Apply** from the **Chord Inversion Up** created a first-inversion triad, and in the third measure clicking the **Apply** button twice created a second-inversion triad (figure 4.15). With a root-position triad the **Chord Inversion**

Down setting creates a second-inversion triad by moving the fifth down one octave, essentially inverting the chord in the opposite direction. With **Chord Inversion Down** applied twice, we would get a first-inversion triad.

Figure 4.15: Canonic Utilities **triad inversions in Finale.**

In Logic we can use the **MIDI Transform** to achieve the same effect. In figure 4.16, the same D major triad was copied into three measures. By selecting **MIDI Transform's Transposition** preset with a **Pitch** value of **Add 12**, we can either transpose the D4 up one octave for a first-inversion triad, or transpose both the D4 and F#4 up one octave to create a second-inversion triad (figure 4.16). Select **Operate Only** to transpose only the selected notes.

Figure 4.16: MIDI Transform Transposition **triad inversions in Logic.**

4.5 Diatonic Collection of Triads

Triads are the building blocks of harmony. Each key has its own set of triads, known as the **diatonic collection**, created entirely from the pitches of that key's scale. Harmony in C major is based on the triads built using the C major scale, whereas harmonies in D major are based on triads built from the D major scale, and so on. To understand this concept better, we can use **Chord Trigger** to build triads based on scales, starting with C major and proceeding to other keys.

So far, we have been using **Chord Trigger** in **Single** mode, as indicated by the rectangular button in the top left (figure 4.3). In **Single** mode, **Chord Trigger** produces only the currently selected type of chord and duplicates that chord on any input trigger note. The diatonic triads built on the C major scale, however, are not all the same quality, and the triad quality changes based on the input note. To create the triads that are based on a scale (the diatonic collection), switch **Chord Trigger** from **Single** to **Multi** mode. Then to create the diatonic set of triads, we'll choose **Multi → Parallel Chords → Triads** from the drop-down menu in **Chord Trigger** (figure 4.17).

Figure 4.17: Chord Trigger: **selecting** Multi → Parallel Chords → Triads **in Logic.**

The triads we'll hear when we play the C major scale from C4 to B4 with this setting of **Chord Trigger** make up the **C major diatonic collection**, shown in figure 4.18. Each chord has a name as well as a **Roman numeral** used for **harmonic analysis**. These chord names are the same ones used for the scale degrees (see page 40).

I	ii	iii	IV	V	vi	vii°
Tonic	Supertonic	Mediant	Subdominant	Dominant	Submediant	Leading Tone

Figure 4.18: Triads in C major with names and Roman numerals.

Capital Roman numerals indicate major chords, and lowercase Roman numerals indicate minor chords. Augmented chords add a + sign to capital Roman numerals, and diminished chords add a ° sign to lowercase ones.

The three major triads (**I-Tonic**, **IV-Subdominant**, and **V-Dominant**) are the **primary chords**. Primary chords occur frequently in harmonic progressions, and the harmony in some songs is limited to just these chords. The minor-quality **ii-Supertonic**, **iii-Mediant**, and **vi-Submediant** chords, and the diminished-quality **vii°-Leading Tone** chord are the **secondary chords**. The augmented triad does not occur in this major-key diatonic set, but does occur elsewhere in music.

To record the output of **Chord Trigger** (and to see the musical notation), we'll follow the technique outlined on page 72 for routing **Chord Trigger**'s output to a Software Instrument track via **External Instrument IAC Bus 1**. Now we have **Chord Trigger** playing chords based on trigger notes on track 1, and track 2 recording the chords where we can see them notated in the **Score Editor**. The resulting recording is shown in figure 4.19.

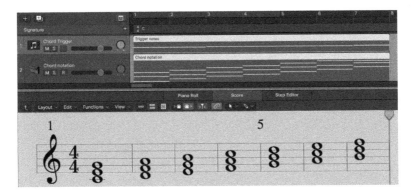

Figure 4.19: Chord Trigger **C major chords in Logic.**

4.6 Triads in Major Keys

Chord Trigger includes a **Chord Transpose** feature on the lower right that we can use to transpose its output. To hear all of the triads from every key, we transpose **Chord Trigger**'s output by twelve different semitone amounts, progressing through all of the keys and moving key centers up by a perfect fifth (seven semitones), or down a perfect fourth (five semitones), as per table 4.2.

Table 4.2: Semitone transpositions for Chord Trigger's output to all keys.

Key	C	G	D	A	E	B	F#	Db(C#)	Ab	Eb	Bb	F
Semitones	0	+7	+2	−3	+4	−1	+6	+1	−4	+3	−2	+5

We can copy the trigger-note region, paste it eleven times in the track, and make the **Chord Transpose** changes listed in table 4.2 using **track automation**. To see the automation on a track, click on the **Show/Hide Automation** button. Automation is often used for creating real-time changes in track volume, but it can control many parameters in audio and MIDI devices. In this case, we'll use it to change the transposition amounts before recording the triads from each key (figure 4.20).

Figure 4.20: Chord Trigger's Chord Transpose **with automated transpositions in Logic.**

The resulting **Score Editor** shows all the triads of all the major keys (figure 4.21). We have also inserted **Key Signatures** for every new collection of triads, which corrects the spellings for each. We can change the **Key Signature** in Logic by positioning the **playhead** where we want the change, then selecting a new key from the **Key signature display** in the **LCD display**, as described in the previous chapter. These key changes add the key signature in a **Score Editor** and add key-change markers in the **Signature** track.

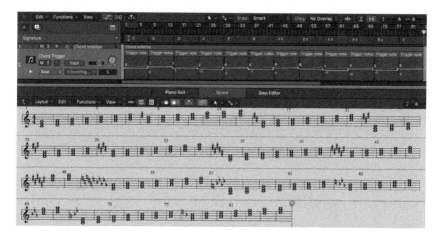

Figure 4.21: Diatonic collections of triads in all twelve major keys in Logic.

4.7 Triads in Minor Keys

Minor scales are likewise the basis for the diatonic collection of triads in minor keys. In
A natural minor we see major, minor, and diminished triads, and we have a new triad name,
the **Subtonic (VII)**, for the seventh scale degree triad (figure 4.22).

Figure 4.22: Triads from the A natural minor scale.

The most commonly used triads in minor keys, however, include the major-triad dominant
(V) on the fifth scale degree and the diminished-triad leading tone (vii°) on the raised seventh
scale degree. This common collection of triads uses the scale degrees of the harmonic minor
scale (figure 4.23), with the exception of the mediant triad (III), which has the lowered
seventh scale degree from the natural minor. The table with the names and qualities is in
table 4.3.

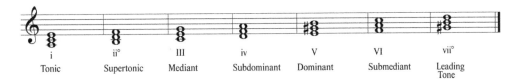

Figure 4.23: Triads using the harmonic and natural minor scales.

Table 4.3: Diatonic collection of triads in natural minor.

Roman Numeral & Name	Quality
i – Tonic	Minor
ii° – Supertonic	Diminished
III – Mediant	Major
iv – Subdominant	Minor
V – Dominant	Major
VI – Submediant	Major
vii° – Leading Tone	Diminished

As the melodic minor scale form has both raised and lowered sixth and seventh scale degrees,
there are more possible minor-scale triads (figure 4.24). The enclosed chords are the less usual
ones, and some are only rarely used, such as the submediant diminished triad (#vi°), which
includes the raised sixth scale degree from the ascending melodic minor. Let's also note that
the mediant chord can be an augmented triad.

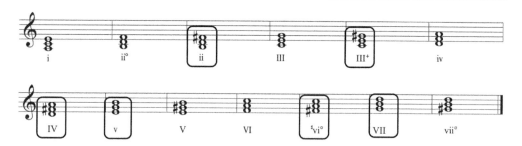

Figure 4.24: All possible triads in minor scales. Less common chords are enclosed.

The **Multi → Parallel Chords → Triads** setting we used for the major keys won't work in minor, because of the differences in triad types that come about with the addition of the raised seventh scale degree in V and vii°. But we can create our own custom-made A minor **Chord Trigger Multi**, and use it to generate all the triads in the minor keys. We can copy and paste the trigger notes to play its chords eleven times, and automate the **Chord Transpose** function to go through all the keys, just as we did for the major-key triads.

Chord Trigger's Factory Default Multi setting has two trigger notes (A3, B3), which play an A major and a B diminished triad (figure 4.25). Before making our own **Multi** set, we need to remove these two existing triggers. To remove a trigger, select the **Clear** button, then click on the trigger note in the **Input Trigger Keys** keyboard. Each note is cleared separately, and we will clear both A3 and B3.

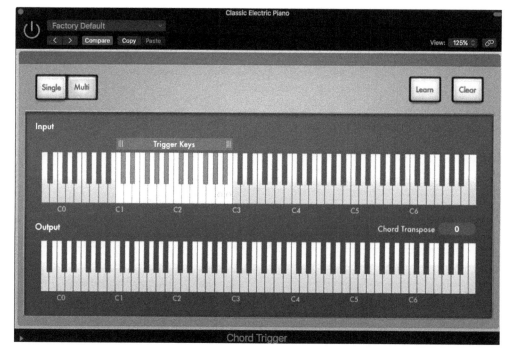

Figure 4.25: Chord Trigger Multi **default in Logic.**

Next, we set the **Trigger Keys** range from A2 to G#3. At this point, we can create our own custom **Multi** set by inputting triads. First, click on the **Learn** button at the top right. In the **Input** keyboard we click on notes of the A harmonic minor scale, and for each trigger note we'll play the corresponding chord shown in figure 4.23 on an attached MIDI keyboard. Once we have our seven triads, we can save and name this **Multi** set "**Minor Triads**" from the top drop-down menu (figure 4.26).

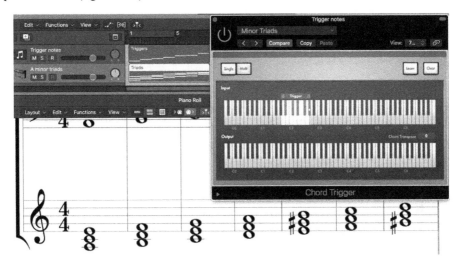

Figure 4.26: Chord Trigger Multi **triads in A minor in Logic.**

Repeating the process we used for major diatonic collections, we can copy and paste the trigger notes region eleven times, then automate the **Chord Transpose** feature to cycle through all twelve keys using the transpositions as per table 4.4.

Table 4.4: Chord Transpose semitone amounts for automation settings.

Minor Keys	A	E	B	F#	C#	G#	E♭	B♭	F	C	G	D
Semitones	0	+7	+2	−3	+4	−1	+6	+1	−4	+3	−2	+5

We can insert new key signatures for each new minor key, so that the correct accidentals for each minor key will be applied. In figure 4.27, we see all the triads in minor keys.

Figure 4.27: Chord Trigger: **triads from all twelve minor keys in Logic.**

4.8 Triad Generator

With Logic's **Chord Trigger** and Finale's **Chord** tool we can create all the diatonic triads in major and minor keys. The triads created will be in root and closed-position triads, however, unless we alter them with additional processes (such as with Finale's **Canonic Utilities Chord Inversion** or Logic's **MIDI Transform Transposition**). To have ready access to triads (major, minor, diminished, or augmented) in all positions (root, first, and second inversions) and different open voicings of the triads, we can use the Max patcher **Triad Generator** (figure 4.28).

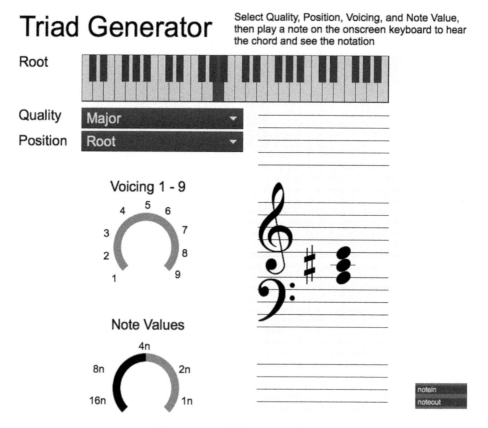

Figure 4.28: Triad Generator **in Max.**

Triad inversions are indicated in harmonic analysis by **figures** which are added to the Roman numerals. These figures indicate whether the triad is inverted or in root position, as shown in table 4.5. The figure for root-position triads ($^5_3$) is usually not included—which means that if there's no figure, then we know the triad is in root position. Figures for triad inversions ($^6_3$, ^{6}, and $^6_4$) are a convenient way to indicate the inversion.

Table 4.5: Triad figures.

Root Position		1st Inversion		2nd Inversion
Complete	Used	Complete	Used	Used
5	(no figure)	6	6	6
3		3		4

When first opened, **Triad Generator** will produce a major triad in root position on any played note on the keyboard diagram or on a connected MIDI keyboard. The user can select between any of the four qualities (the **Quality** drop-down menu shows: Diminished, Minor, Major, and Augmented) and three positions (the **Position** drop-down menu shows: Root, First Inversion (⁶), Second Inversion (⁶₄)). To hear a chord and see its notation, select the quality and inversion and then play the root note. The triads appear in the grand staff, and a chord is played. When first inversion is selected for the position the lowest note is the third, and for second inversion it's the fifth. As an example, setting the **Triad Generator** to play a C major triad in second inversion will make G natural the lowest note.

To hear different voicings of a triad, we can select one of nine possible voicings with the **Voicing dial**. Logic's **Chord Trigger** has named some sets of chord voicings in the **Keyboard Voicings** preset, such as **Blues Left Hand**, **Jazz Ballad Right Hand**, or **Songwriter Left Hand**. These names are specific to Logic's **Chord Trigger**, and not universally recognized, just as our numberings in **Triad Generator**'s **Voicing 1–9** are specific to the patcher. There are so many ways to voice a chord that creating names for voicings would be impractical, but in the context of programmed chord generation, naming or numbering them allow us to distinguish one voicing from another.

For harmonic analysis, changing a chord voicing doesn't change the Roman numeral or figure, but the different voicings certainly sound different. With the **Voicing 1–9** parameter we can select from among nine specific voicings. Voicing 1 is always closed position, whereas the rest of the voicings are all in open position. Displayed in figure 4.29 we see these nine possible voicings of the A major triad in root position based on A3.

Figure 4.29: Triad Generator's nine voicings for A major triad.

Triad Generator spells most triads correctly by determining whether sharps or flats are needed in the notation, depending on the root note and chord quality. Certain chords will always be spelled in a certain way; for instance, the major triad on F#/G♭ is always F# major, and a minor triad on G#/A♭ is always a G# minor triad. Just as F# can be enharmonically respelled as G♭, the F# major triad can be enharmonically respelled as G♭ major. **Triad Generator** incorrectly spells a F diminished triad with a B natural instead of a C♭, and also misspells these augmented triads: E, A, B♭, and B, as shown in figure 4.30. These spelling errors are more-or-less inevitable because we're using the number-based MIDI system which doesn't distinguish enharmonics, and also because Max's **nslider** object does not represent some musical pitches, such as double-sharp pitches.

Figure 4.30: Triad Generator's misspelled chords.

When sending **Triad Generator**'s output to Logic or Finale, however, we can see triads spelled correctly if we also select a key (in Logic or Finale) in which the triad would occur.

For example, the key E♭ minor has an F diminished triad (ii°), and if we send an F diminished triad from **Triad Generator** to Logic and specify the key as E♭ minor, it is spelled correctly (F, A♭, C♭). Likewise, the misspelled augmented chords will be spelled correctly in the right key context, as per table 4.6.

Table 4.6: Four minor key augmented triads (III+).

	E aug.	A aug.	B aug.	B♭ aug.
III+ →	C# min.	F# min.	G# min.	G min.

4.9 Max Patcher 7: *Triad Generator*

Triad Generator receives a MIDI note from an attached or onscreen keyboard and outputs a triad based on the selections. The user chooses the quality (major, minor, diminished, or augmented), position (root, first, or second inversion), and a voicing (how the upper two pitches are positioned by octaves above the bass note). The bass note is determined by both the note input and the inversion.

Creating triads is broken into tasks corresponding to the triad's attributes. In the patcher view of **Triad Generator** we see several subpatchers (figure 4.31). Each subpatcher accomplishes a specific task. The **p quality** subpatcher creates the triads with one of the four qualities as specified by the **Quality umenu** ("Major" appears in figure 4.31). The **p position** subpatcher inverts triads as specified by the **Position umenu** ("Root" appears in figure 4.31). The **p voicing** subpatcher moves around the two upper notes of the triads to create nine different voicings as specified by the **Voicing dial** (directly above the left inlet of **p voicing**).

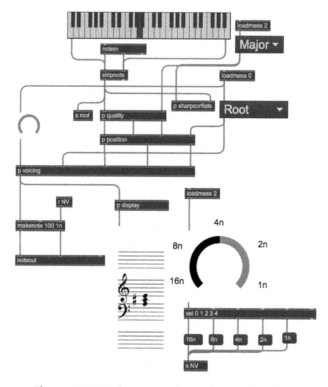

Figure 4.31: Triad Generator **in patcher mode in Max.**

To begin, the root note is received as a MIDI note from the **kslider** or **notein**, and **stripnote** removes the note-ending message (a MIDI note number with 0 velocity). In the **p quality** subpatcher (figure 4.32) the third and fifth above the root are added to form the triad. By adding intervals with different semitone amounts, we can create different qualities of triad, and for these amounts we refer to the intervals between triad notes (see page 70). Thirds are either major (four semitones) or minor (three), and fifths are either diminished (six), perfect (seven), or augmented (eight). To switch between these possibilities, we use a **gate 4** object with four outlets, which sends the root note (entering the object via the right inlet) to either +3 or +4 to add the third, and also sends the root note to either +6, +7, or +8 to add the fifth. The **gate 4** outlets correspond to the different triad qualities. Which gate is used depends on a number supplied by a **umenu** in the main part of the program that **gate 4** receives in the left inlet. The **umenu** names the four qualities and sends out the following values: 0 for diminished, 1 for minor, 2 for major, or 3 for augmented.

The **p quality** subpatcher has two inlets (to receive data) for the root note number and for the quality, and three outlets for each triad tone (root, third, and fifth). These outlets connect to the next subpatcher (**p inversion**), where we create the inversions.

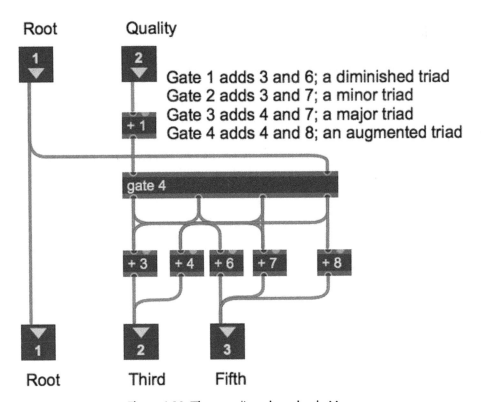

Figure 4.32: The p quality **subpatcher in Max.**

To create the three positions (root, first, and second inversion), we need to transpose certain chord tones by octaves. The root-position triad requires no transpositions. A first-inversion triad requires the root to be transposed up one octave, leaving the third as the lowest note. A second-inversion triad requires that we transpose both the root and third, leaving the fifth as the lowest note. To create these positions, we route the two *transposing* triad tones separately using two **gate 2** objects (figure 4.33). The right **gate 2** outlet is for transposition, and the left outlet leaves the note in place.

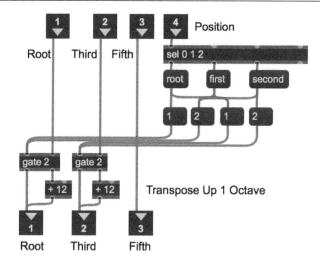

Figure 4.33: The p position **subpatcher in Max.**

The **p position** subpatcher has three inlets and three outlets for the triad tones, and a fourth inlet to choose the position. This fourth inlet receives data from **Position umenu** which lists Root, First Inversion (^{6}), and Second Inversion ($^6_4$) in a drop-down menu.

Triad Generator's next stage is the **p voicing** subpatcher, which spreads the upper two chord tones into higher octaves to create various voicings (figure 4.34). Our use of the term *voicing* refers only to how the two upper chord tones are distributed vertically, but in a general sense voicings can include inversions. In this context, however, we exclude inversions as we have already created a way to make them. Therefore, all the voicings maintain the same bass note while the upper voices are being transposed. The **p voicing** subpatcher needs to accomplish two tasks: (1) isolate the nontransposing bass chord tone based on the inversion; (2) spread the two upper pitches out according to voicing numbers.

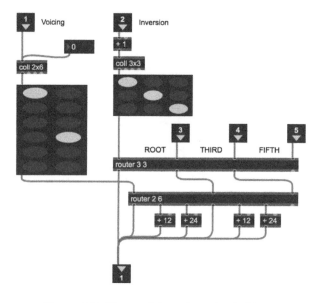

Figure 4.34: The p voicing **subpatcher in Max.**

To isolate which chord tone is in the bass, we first use a **router 3 3** object with three inlets and three outlets. A **router** is like a **gate** and a **switch** combined: it can send any inlet to any outlet. With this object, we send the note which will *not* be transposed—the lowest note—to the left outlet. The middle outlets of the **router 3 3** are sent to another **router 2 6**, which sends chord tones to be transposed to create different voicing.

The **router 3 3** sends data from inlets to different outlets based on the input of a **matrixctrl** (**matrix switch control**, a shaded rectangle with oval shapes inside it) object, which it receives at the left inlet. The **matrixctrl** objects have **cells** (the oval shapes in rows and columns). If a **cell** is lighted, a connection is made between an inlet (numbered by columns) and an outlet (numbered by rows). The **coll 3x3** object has a data collection of three settings for the **matrixctrl**, one for each chord position (root, first inversion, and second inversion). Figure 4.35 shows the data collection with groups of three digits representing the column, row, and on (1) or off (0) settings for the **matrixctrl** object. The "on position" data groups are circled. In the first line, we see column 0/row 0 cell is on, as well as the cells at column 1/row1 and column 2/row 2. The next two lines turn cells on and off to produce the three routings required to isolate the bass notes.

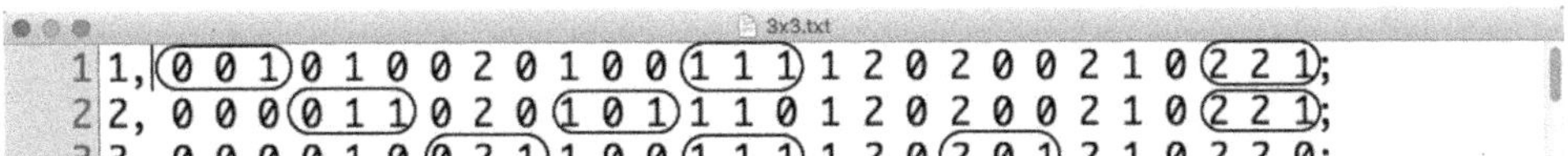

```
1, 0 0 1 0 1 0 0 2 0 1 0 0 1 1 1 1 2 0 2 0 0 2 1 0 2 2 1;
2, 0 0 0 0 1 1 0 2 0 1 0 1 1 1 0 1 2 0 2 0 0 2 1 0 2 2 1;
3, 0 0 0 0 1 0 0 2 1 1 0 0 1 1 1 1 2 0 2 0 1 2 1 0 2 2 0;
```

Figure 4.35: The coll **data for** matrixctrl **of** router 3 3 **in Max.**

With a root-position setting, the **coll 3x3 matrixctrl** sends the root chord tone out of **router 3 3**'s left outlet so that it won't be transposed. For a first-inversion triad, the objects send the *third* out the left outlet, and for a second-inversion chord the *fifth* is sent out the left outlet. The two transposing chord tones are sent out the middle outlets to create different voicings by transposition to **router 2 6**.

The **router 2 6** object has two inlets and six outlets. The **router 2 6** is controlled by a second **matrixctrl** with two columns and six rows—corresponding to the inputs and outputs. This **matrixctrl** receives messages by a **coll 2x6** object with data settings for nine possible combinations of transpositions (the data collection is shown in figure 4.36), based on a voicing number received from the **umenu** in the main patcher. By sending the chord tones that can be transposed to the **router 2 6** object, we can create voicings by transposing the chord tones up either one or two octaves, or by keeping them at their original pitch level.

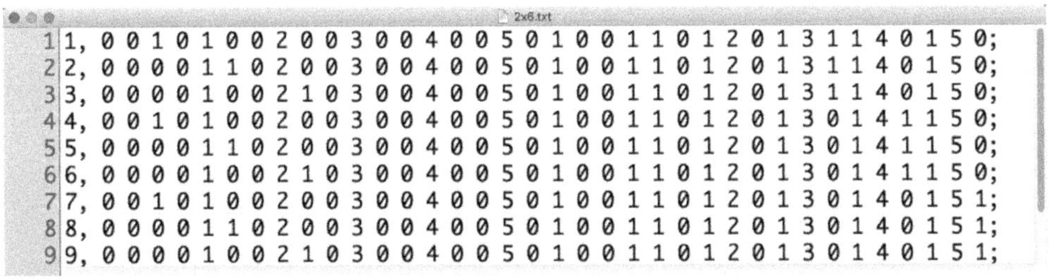

```
1, 0 0 1 0 1 0 0 2 0 0 3 0 0 4 0 0 5 0 1 0 0 1 1 0 1 2 0 1 3 1 1 4 0 1 5 0;
2, 0 0 0 0 1 1 0 2 0 0 3 0 0 4 0 0 5 0 1 0 0 1 1 0 1 2 0 1 3 1 1 4 0 1 5 0;
3, 0 0 0 0 1 0 0 2 1 0 3 0 0 4 0 0 5 0 1 0 0 1 1 0 1 2 0 1 3 1 1 4 0 1 5 0;
4, 0 0 1 0 1 0 0 2 0 0 3 0 0 4 0 0 5 0 1 0 0 1 1 0 1 2 0 1 3 0 1 4 1 1 5 0;
5, 0 0 0 0 1 1 0 2 0 0 3 0 0 4 0 0 5 0 1 0 0 1 1 0 1 2 0 1 3 0 1 4 1 1 5 0;
6, 0 0 0 0 1 0 0 2 1 0 3 0 0 4 0 0 5 0 1 0 0 1 1 0 1 2 0 1 3 0 1 4 1 1 5 0;
7, 0 0 1 0 1 0 0 2 0 0 3 0 0 4 0 0 5 0 1 0 0 1 1 0 1 2 0 1 3 0 1 4 0 1 5 1;
8, 0 0 0 0 1 1 0 2 0 0 3 0 0 4 0 0 5 0 1 0 0 1 1 0 1 2 0 1 3 0 1 4 0 1 5 1;
9, 0 0 0 0 1 0 0 2 1 0 3 0 0 4 0 0 5 0 1 0 0 1 1 0 1 2 0 1 3 0 1 4 0 1 5 1;
```

Figure 4.36: The coll **data for** matrixctrl **for** router 2 6 **in Max.**

To view the triads in the grand staff, **Triad Generator** includes a **nslider** object. We prepare the **nslider** by setting the **Display Mode** to *Polyphonic* (capable of displaying more than one note) in its **inspector**. The color scheme is also changed to make the notation easier to read.

When it receives MIDI notes or chords, the **nslider** object displays only sharps by default. A B♭ major chord thus incorrectly becomes A#, D, and F. If we want it to display flats, the MIDI note numbers must be made negative, which we can do by multiplying them by −1. If we multiply all MIDI notes numbers by −1, however, all accidentals become flats. What we really want is to separate chords which will use sharps from those which will use flats. Table 4.7 shows which accidental (sharp or flat) to use to create triads with the most usual spellings.

Table 4.7: Sharps or flats for triad.

FLATS or SHARPS	Use Sharps	Use Flats
Major	C, D, E, G, A, B Pitch classes: 0, 2, 4, 7, 9, 11	D♭, E♭, F, A♭, B♭, G♭ Pitch classes: 1, 3, 5, 8, 10
Minor	C#, D, E, F#, G#, A, B Pitch classes: 1, 2, 4, 6, 8, 9, 11	C, E♭, F, G, B♭ Pitch classes: 0, 3, 5, 7, 10
Diminished	C#, D#, F#, G#, A#, B Pitch classes: 1, 3, 6, 8, 10, 11	C, D, E, F, G, A Pitch classes: 0, 2, 4, 5, 7, 9
Augmented	C, D, E, F, G, A, B Pitch classes: 0, 2, 4, 5, 7, 9, 11	D♭, E♭, G♭, A♭, B♭ Pitch classes: 1, 3, 6, 8, 10

We use both the triad's root-note number and its quality to sort the triads into which use flats or sharps. To simplify the sorting process, we will consider all major triads built on the same pitch name to be the same triad, regardless of octave, be it middle C (MIDI note 60) or the octave above or below (MIDI notes 72 or 48). In practical terms, this means that we have to determine the **pitch class** for each triad root. Pitch classes are numerical representations of pitch names that don't indicate octave positions. In naming pitch classes, all pitches (regardless of enharmonic spelling or octave position) of the same letter name are represented by the same number. Pitch class numbers are: C=0; C#/D♭=1; D=2; D#/E♭=3; E=4; F=5; F#/G♭=6; G=7; G#/A♭=8; A=9; A#/B♭=10; B=11. Conveniently, when we divide each triad's root-note number by twelve, the remainder will be the pitch class, and the **modulo** object (**% 12**) object outputs the remainder of a division by twelve.

When we have this root-tone pitch-class (the output from **% 12**), choosing sharps or flats can be done with four **select** (**sel**) objects in the **p sharpsorflats** subpatcher (figure 4.37). Each **sel** object is linked to a quality: diminished, minor, major, or augmented. When a quality is selected, the **gate 4** sends the root-note number to one of the **sel** objects, which compares the incoming number with each argument, banging out the corresponding outlet if there is a match. These matches are for triads that use flats. If no match occurs, a bang is sent out the far right outlet so that sharps are used.

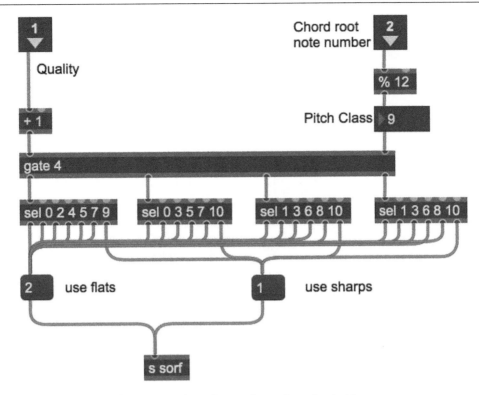

Figure 4.37: The p sharpsorflats subpatcher in Max.

With a pair of **send** and **receive** objects (**s sorf**, **r sorf**—for sharps or flats—located in the **p sharpsorflats** and **p display** subpatchers, respectively), we send either a 1 (for sharps) or a 2 (for flats) to the **p display** subpatcher (fig 4.38).

Three other requirements for **nslider** to display chords correctly from input lists are: (1) chord-tone note numbers should be in ascending order; (2) the word "chord" is added before the values; (3) chord tones are represented by lists containing note and velocity numbers. The **nslider** can also accept MIDI note numbers and MIDI velocity values into the left and right inlets, but with a **message** we can list several pairs of MIDI notes and velocities to create chords.

To create these chord messages for **nslider**, we'll group the chord tones with the **zl.group 3** object, and sort them in ascending order with the **zl.sort** object. Next, if the triad requires that we use flats, we'll send the chord-tone note numbers to a **multiply two numbers** object (*** -1**) via the right outlet of **gate 2** to make the note numbers negative. The triad's note numbers are then joined with a list of velocities (100) with the **zl.lace** object, which interlaces lists of the same length. Velocity values are usually used to change the volume of MIDI notes, but these "dummy" velocities are included only to supply the **nslider** with required data to display the triads. We use a **prepend chord message** to add the word "chord" to the beginning of the message, and finally bang the **message** out to the **nslider** via a **button** to the **message** where all the elements are gathered. This **button** is banged by the output of **zl.sort**, and as it is on the lower left side of the subpatcher, it sends the **message** after all other tasks.

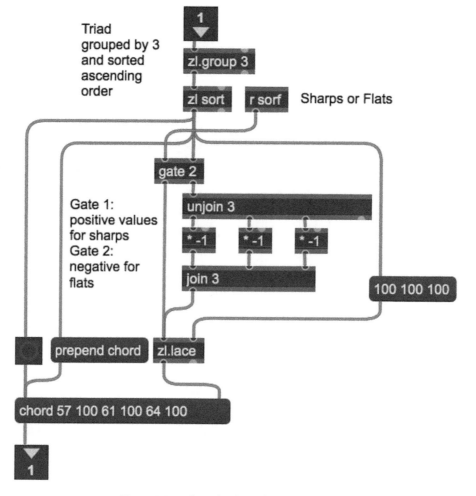

Figure 4.38: The p display **subpatcher in Max.**

The main patcher has three **loadmess** objects which send messages (values) when the patcher is opened. These **loadmess** objects send the value 2 to the quality **umenu**, the voicing **dial**, and the note-value **dial**, and the value 0 to the voicings **dial**. These values ensure that when the patcher is opened the **dials** are always at the same setting. The **Note Values** patching is included to enable us to change chord durations. The note value itself is sent to the **makenote** object via the **s NV** and **r NV** object pair.

4.10 Chord Identification in Logic

To help us identify triads we can use various tools, such as Logic's **LCD Key Signature/ Chord**, Finale's **Chord Analysis**, or **Triad Identifier**, a Max patcher. In Logic, when a chord is played on an attached keyboard, we can see the word **Key** change to **Chord** in the **LCD Key Signature/Chord**. The chord is identified by name, as shown by the example in figure 4.39, where a G augmented triad is being played.

Figure 4.39: LCD display: Chord **showing a G augmented triad is being played in Logic.**

Logic's **LCD Key Signature/Chord** will identify many types of chords as they're being played, although it doesn't differentiate positions, such as root, first, or second inversions. In other words, no matter in which position or voicing you play a chord, just the triad name (root and quality) is displayed. Alternate interpretations can occur. The chord C4, F#4, A4 is a second inversion F# diminished triad, but Logic's **LCD Key Signature/Chord** displays it as an Am⁶ chord. This alternate chord designation is for the minor triad with an added major sixth, not for a first-inversion diminished triad.

Logic's **LCD Key Signature/Chord** displays an identification for every received chord, even when the chord is hard to recognize in terms of standard harmonic practice. The pitches C4, C#4, and D4, for instance, form neither a triad nor a recognizable standard harmonic chord but are identified as **D no 3 ⁷/maj⁷**, a very unusual chord.

If the **Control Bar**'s **LCD** does not have the **Key** display, change the display settings by control-clicking in the **Display Mode Pop-up Menu** and choose **Beats & Project** display mode (figure 4.40).

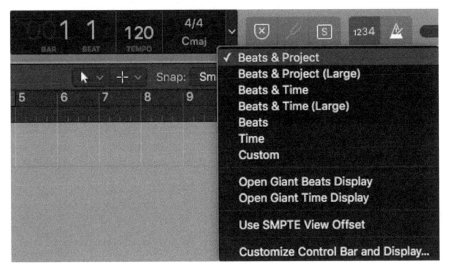

Figure 4.40: Selecting Beats & Project **for the** LCD display **in Logic.**

Logic will also identify chords in the **Piano Roll Editor**. To see this identification, select the notes of the chord, then look at the top section of the **Piano Roll Editor Inspector**. The selected chord's root and quality (a D minor triad) are displayed in parentheses as part of the text "3 Notes selected (D m)" (figure 4.41).

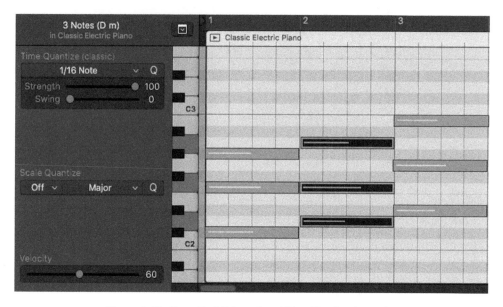

Figure 4.41: Piano Roll Editor **chord identification in Logic.**

4.11 Chord Identification in Finale

Finale's **Chord Analysis** tool identifies notated chords, and adds the chord symbols above the staff. This can be helpful in the process of adding chord symbols to a lead sheet. To use this function, select a section of music and then select **Plug-ins → Scoring and Arranging → Chord Analysis**. The **Chord Analysis** dialog window allows the user to specify certain aspects of the analysis (figure 4.42); the default setting produces an analysis for the chords is also shown in figure 4.42.

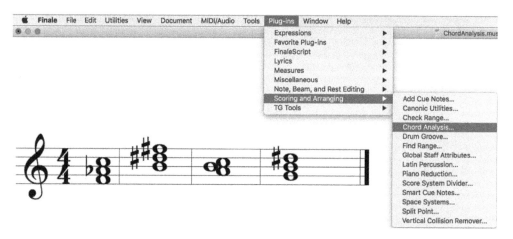

Figure 4.42: Chord Analysis **in Finale.**

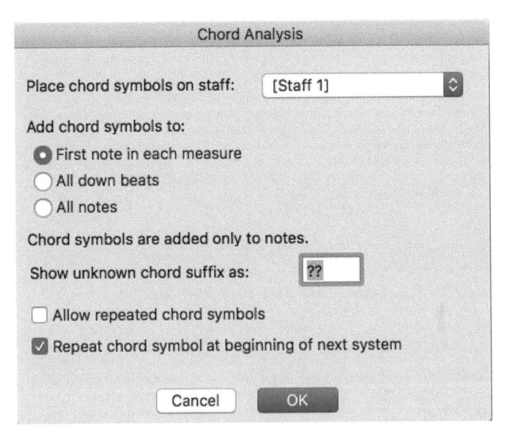

Figure 4.42: Continued

Figure 4.43: Finale's Chord Analysis **results.**

Finale's **Chord Analysis** doesn't analyze all combinations of pitches. Although mm. 1, 2, and 4 are analyzed correctly in figure 4.43, the chord analysis for the third measure displays A**??** to indicate an unknown chord with an A as the lowest note. In the **Chord Analysis Dialog** window, we see this "??" as the response to "unknown chord" suffixes.

Finale's **Chord Analysis** shows inversions in the format of a chord symbol with a slash; the first symbol is a root with a chord type, and the pitch after the slash is the bass tone, which varies depending on the inversion. The **Chord Analysis** output in figure 4.44 shows a C minor triad in root position, and in first and second inversions. The pitches E♭ and G are shown after the slash for the first and second inversions respectively. The B major triad's inversions, however, are notated as having an E♭ and G♭ even though the pitches are (correctly for B major) spelled as D# and F# (figure 4.44).

Figure 4.44: Chord Analysis **identifying triads in inversion in Finale.**

4.12 *Triad Identifier*

Triad Identifier identifies the root and interval structure between the chord tones to then name a triad's root, quality, and inversion when a triad is played on an attached keyboard (figure 4.45). If you play something other than a triad, or if the patcher doesn't get the identification with the initial input, then the **Quality and Inversion message** will read "Maybe not a triad." Playing an actual triad a second time will produce an identification.

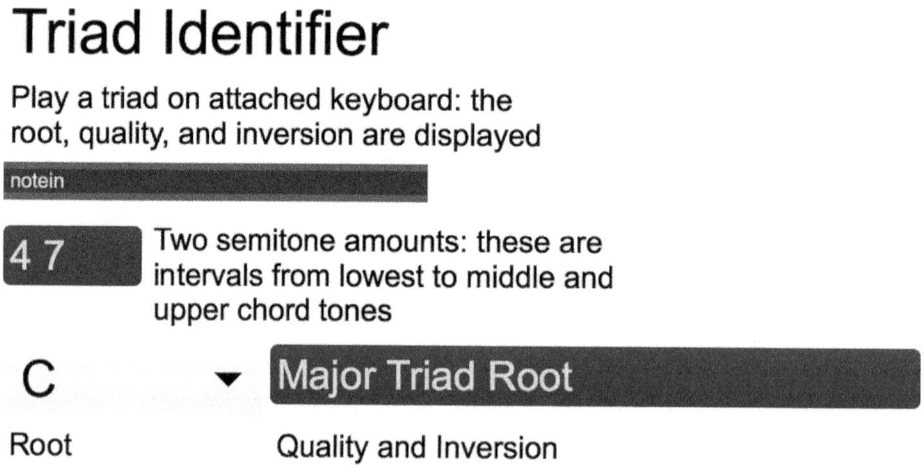

Triad Identifier

Play a triad on attached keyboard: the
root, quality, and inversion are displayed

notein

4 7   Two semitone amounts: these are
intervals from lowest to middle and
upper chord tones

C   ▼   Major Triad Root

Root   Quality and Inversion

Figure 4.45: Triad Identifier **in Max.**

4.13 Max Patcher 8: *Triad Identifier*

Triad Identifier has three subpatchers which perform different tasks: **p detectintervals**; **p matchtriads**; and **p selectinversion**. These subpatchers are shown in **Triad Identifier's** patcher mode (figure 4.46).

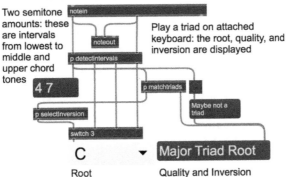

Figure 4.46: Triad Identifier **(patcher) in Max.**

The **p detectintervals** subpatcher (figure 4.47) determines chord tones and the intervals between them. Its first task is to group three pitches with the **quickthresh** and **zl.stream 3** objects. The **quickthresh** object takes a "snapshot" of incoming MIDI data. Its three arguments (in milliseconds) control aspects of how **quickthresh** opens and closes, analogously to a camera's shutter speed. The **zl.stream 3** object then makes the numbers into a list of three items, and the **zl.sort** object arranges them in ascending order. When you play a chord on the piano with the notes sounding together, they arrive as MIDI data one after the other, since MIDI notes are transmitted individually (or serially). Which note will arrive first in the MIDI stream is unknown, so sorting them in ascending order is critical.

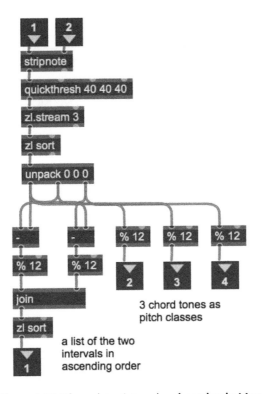

Figure 4.47: The p detectintervals **subpatcher in Max.**

Once we have the MIDI note numbers in ascending order, we can determine the intervals between the chord tones as the number of semitones between the lowest note and the next highest, and the lowest and highest note. For a closed root position triad these correspond to two intervals: (1) between the root and the third, and (2) between the root and the fifth. For closed first inversions, the two intervals formed are (1) between third and fifth and (2) between the third and root, and for closed second-inversion triads, they are (1) between the fifth and root and (2) between the fifth and third. We can determine the triad quality and inversion based on these intervals because each type of triad in each inversion has unique pairs of intervals. By matching the pair of intervals identified with pairs of intervals in a preset list, we can identify the quality and position.

Before this matching happens, however, we must ensure that all the intervals are represented by the smallest possible values. In other words, if the triad is spread over several octaves (or in open voicing), we need to determine the intervals as if the triad were in closed voicing. Otherwise our list of intervals for triad types would have to be impossibly large.

Just as we use pitch classes to represent all the octave positions of a given pitch, we can use **interval class** to represent all intervals with the same order of pitches, regardless of octave. We use the **modulo** object (**% 12**) in **p detectinterval** to determine this **interval class** of the intervals—reducing any compound interval to a simple one. As an example of why we need this, the major third and major tenth (a major third plus an octave) are different intervals, but they have the same interval class, and the E in either octave position can be the third in a C major triad (figure 4.48).

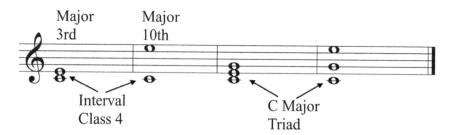

Figure 4.48: Interval class as opposed to interval.

The first output of **p detectinterval** is a list of two interval classes between the triad's chord tones, that is between the lowest and middle and between the lowest and highest. We match it with a list of possible interval classes for our triads. There are ten discreet interval-class pairs, as shown in the **p matchtriads** subpatcher (figure 4.49). Each pair of interval classes makes up the arguments for each of the ten **match** objects. When a **match** object receives these values that match its arguments, it sends out a bang to a **message** with the triad name.

The augmented triad is not differentiated by inversion, because the interval classes are four and eight in every position (root position or in first or second inversion). Although the notation can indicate inversions, the sound of closed augmented triads is always the same, and the intervals formed are always four semitones (equivalent to major thirds). Any augmented triad will be thus identified as being in root position.

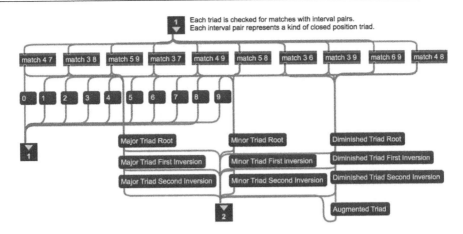

Figure 4.49: The p matchtriads subpatcher.

The triad name **messages** indicating quality and position are sent out outlet 2. Once we know the triad type and have the triad in closed position, we can use this information to determine the root. For root-position triads, the lowest note is the root. For closed-position first-inversion triads the highest note is the root, and for closed-position second-inversion triads the middle note is the root.

The numbers generated in **p matchtriads** that reflect a triad's quality and position are sent to **p selectinversion** from outlet 1. Major triads are represented by 0, 1, and 2 for root, first, and second inversion, respectively. Minors and diminished chords are represented by 3, 4, 5 and 6, 7, 8—with the same pattern for positions, and finally, augmented chords are represented by 9. In the **p selectinversions** subpatcher 0, 3, 6, and 9 will bang a one to the outlet for root position; 1, 4, and 7 bang a two for first inversion; and 2, 5, and 8 bang a three for second inversion (figure 4.50). This inversion number (one for root, two for second inversion, and three for first inversion) then controls a **switch 3** which has coming into it the three chord tones as pitch classes (from the **p detectintervals subpatcher**). Whichever one of these is the root of the chord is sent by **switch 3** to a **umenu,** which then displays the name of the root.

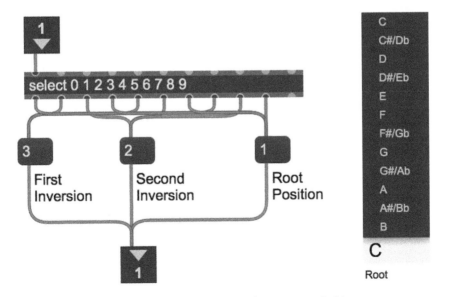

Figures 4.50: p selectinversion **and root** umenu **in Max.**

4.14 Exercises

4.14.1 Exercise 1: Triad Quiz

Triad Generator helps us learn triads by playing and showing them in musical notation—providing us with an interactive reference for triads. We can also modify the patcher, adding objects and instructions, to make it a testing device, as shown with **Triad Quiz** (figure 4.51).

To use **Triad Quiz**, we click on the **? New Chord** button to hear an unidentified triad with a randomly selected root, quality, and position. The **nslider** (notation display) becomes blank, but we see the root tone—in the example, it's F3. Next, we can select what we think the triad's quality and position are with the **Triad Selection umenu** (figure 4.51). In the following example, a F major triad in first inversion was heard and was correctly identified. To check the answer, we click on the **! Check answer** button.

We can hear the chord repeatedly by pressing the space bar, and we can hear only the bass note (lowest tone) by clicking the **Bass only** button. To limit the triads to just one specific inversion or to root position, we uncheck the **Change Position** toggle. Root position is often the easiest to identify. If our selection is correct, the **message That's correct** appears below the **Triad Select umenu**. If it's not correct, the **message** reads **Try again!** We can click on the grayed-out note in the **kslider**, the root of the triad, to see the notation in the **nslider**. Identifying triads can be very challenging, and individualized (nonpressured) practice is a good way to learn and build confidence.

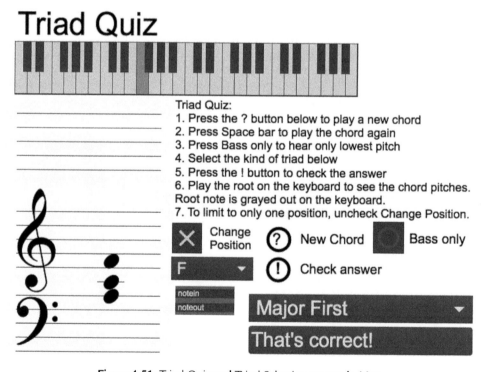

Figure 4.51: Triad Quiz **and** Triad Selection umenu **in Max.**

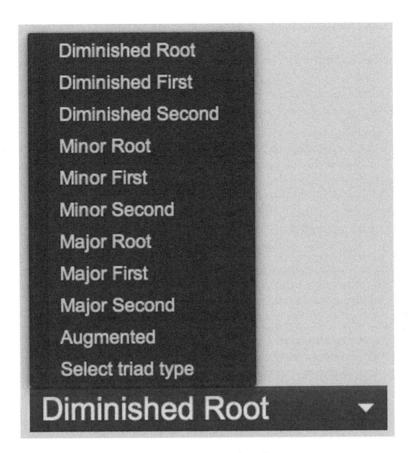

Figure 4.51: Continued

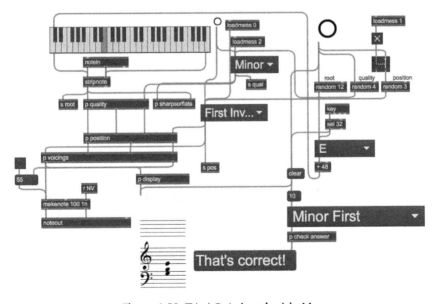

Figure 4.52: Triad Quiz (patcher) in Max.

Triad Quiz works by sending random values to the root, quality, and position **umenus** (figure 4.52), creating an unidentified triad. Each of the four qualities in the **Quality umenu** can be selected by a numerical value (0 for diminished, 1 for minor, 2 for major, and 3 for augmented), while each of the three positions in the **Position umenu** can be selected by numerical values 0, 1, or 2. The root **umenu** has twelve names for each of the pitches, and these can be retrieved by values 0–11.

To randomly send out values in these ranges we set each of three **random** object's argument to a value one greater than the largest number in each parameter range mentioned previously. The **random 12** object creates values between zero and eleven for the root tone. The **random 4** object creates values between 0 and 3 for the quality, and **random 3** creates values between 0 and 2 for the position. The root **umenu**'s values are augmented by forty-eight to place the triads in the middle register (relatively close to middle C), then sent to the **kslider** to show the root and play the new triad. The **nslider** is cleared by receiving a **clear** message.

When we press the space bar, the **key** object sends out the ASCII (American Standard Code for Information Interchange) value 32, which causes **sel 32** to bang both the root **umenu** (which plays the chord) and the **clear message** for the **kslider**.

When we select what kind of triad is played with the **Triad Selection umenu**, it sends out a number between zero and nine to the **p check answer** subpatcher's right inlet (figure 4.53). Each of these numbers corresponds to a triad type, both indicating quality and position. Triad 0 (the first item in the **umenu**), for instance, is a root-position diminished chord. Each number is then used to select a unique value to identify the triad (10, 11, 12, 20, 22, 24, 30, 33, 36, 40) with a **sel** object, and this value is then sent to the right inlet of a == object (two equal signs). The (==) **compare numbers for equal-to condition** object does just what its name indicates. If the numbers entering the left and right inlets are equal, then the == object sends out a 1. If they are not equal, it sends out a 0. The numbers entering left inlet of the == object are generated by the two **umenus** specifying triad quality and position, and these enter the **p check answer** subpatcher via **send** and **receive** objects pairs. To create the unique values for each triad, that is for each combination of quality and position (the list 10, 11, 12, 20, 22, 24, 33, 36, 40), we (1) add 1 to the quality **umenu** values, (2) add 10 to the position **umenu** values, and (3) multiply them.

For any augmented triad (these will send out a 4), we send the number 40 to the == object via a **sel 4** object connected to the **quality umenu**. This operation is on the left side of the multiplication, so it happens last. If the identification is correct and the numbers match, the **sel 0 1** object bangs the "That's correct" to a **message** viewable in presentation mode. If the numbers don't match, then the "Try again!" is sent to the **message**.

To be able to play the bass note alone, we use the **p voicing** subpatcher function of isolating the bass note. Although the main function of **p voicing** is not included in **Triad Quiz**—all the triads are in closed position—the isolation of the bass note that **p voicing** does is helpful because hearing the bass note can help us to identify triad positions. We route the bass-note number to a **message** box on the left side of the patcher. To hear this bass note alone, a **button** will bang the number into the left inlet of the **makenote 100 1n** object, then on to the **noteout** object.

Finally, to provide us with the triad's notation, the **! Check answer button** bangs all three **umenus** (root pitch, quality, and position), sending the triad to the **nslider** without the **clear message.**

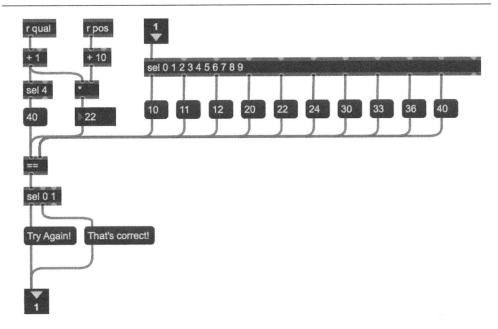

Figure 4.53: p check answer **subpatcher.**

4.14.2 Exercise 2: Practice Writing Triads with Finale

Write a list of some possible triads, including root, quality, and position, and mixing up the parameters, as, for example: (1) F minor root, (2) E♭ major root, (3) B major first inversion, (4) G minor second inversion, (5) C# minor first inversion. Using Finale's **Simple Entry** tool, insert whole notes into a treble clef staff to create the triads in your list, applying accidentals when needed by clicking on the sharp or flat before inserting the note.

Select all the triads and choose **Plug-ins → Scoring and Arranging → Chord Analysis** to check your work (figure 4.54). Remember that Finale represents inversions as slash chords with the bass note (either the third or the fifth) as a pitch name after the slash. Also keep in mind that some **Chord Analysis** examples will have enharmonic spellings. In the following examples, the F# of the B major chord (the fifth of the chord in the bass for a second-inversion triad) is written as "Gb." Additionally, the C# minor chord in first inversion is given as a D♭ minor chord with an E in the bass. As C# minor and D♭ minor are enharmonically equivalent, the triads sound the same even though the notated chord is C# minor/E.

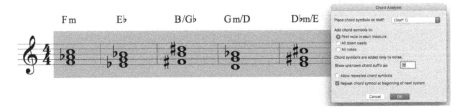

Figure 4.54: Chord Analysis **for triads in Finale.**

4.14.4 Exercise 3: Accompany Songs with Chord Trigger

In Logic, set **Chord Trigger** to **Multi** → **Parallel Chords** →**Triads**, as described on pages 78–79. As we've learned, it will play root-position diatonic chords. We can use this setting to play accompaniments for songs such as **Bingo** or **Shenandoah** (figure 4.55), and also to accompany many similar songs that use only diatonic chords.

Using the music in figure 4.55, play the notes in bass clef on an attached MIDI keyboard. The accompaniment for each song will be with root-position triads. Once the accompaniment feels comfortable and can be played in time (we can add an **Apple Loop Beats** to provide a beat), sing the melody along with it. For some, the sung melody notes might be too high, but we can use the **Chord Trigger's** **Chord Transpose** function to transpose the output down to a more comfortable key for lower voices.

Using **Chord Trigger's** **Multi** set you can create an infinite number of accompaniments or harmonic progressions. As you learn more chords, such as the seventh chords in Chapter 5, it will be possible to accompany more songs! To create your own chords, **Clear** the two chords in **Factory Default**, then input chords with the **Learn** button.

Figure 4.55: Two traditional songs with Chord Trigger **accompaniment. Sing the song while playing the trigger notes in bass clef.**

Seventh Chords and Extensions, Chord Patterns

5.1 Constructing Seventh Chords

Seventh Chords are constructed by adding a note a third above a root-position triad. There are five standard seventh chords built on the major, minor, and diminished triads: **Major Seventh**, **Dominant Seventh** (also known as **Major/minor Seventh**), **Minor Seventh**, **Half-Diminished Seventh** (also known as **Minor Seventh ♭5**), and **Diminished Seventh** (figure 5.1). Table 5.1 shows the triad basis for the seventh chords, the interval qualities between the fifth and the seventh and between the root and seventh, and possible Roman numerals with figures for these chords.

Figure 5.1: The five standard seventh chords.

Major 7th   Dominant 7th   Minor 7th   1/2 Diminished 7th   Diminished 7th

Table 5.1: Seventh chords: triads plus a seventh.

7th chord name	Major 7th	Dominant 7th	Minor 7th	½ Diminished 7th	Diminished 7th
From root to 7th	Major 7th	Minor 7th	Minor 7th	Minor 7th	Diminished 7th
From 5th to 7th	Major 3rd	Minor 3rd	Minor 3rd	Major 3rd	Minor 3rd
Triad Basis	Major	Major	Minor	Diminished	Diminished
Symbols	I^{M7} (in C)	V^7 (in F)	ii^7 (in B♭)	$vii^{\varnothing 7}$ (in D♭)	vii^{o7} (in D♭)

Only major or minor thirds are used between the adjacent chord tones of seventh chords in closed position. The Roman numeral symbols shown here are possible descriptions for the seventh chords in the keys indicated in the parentheses—we'll discuss these more in later parts of this chapter and in subsequent chapters.

5.2 Chord Trigger's Seventh Chords

Other seventh chords are possible, but are less common than the standard five. Logic's **Chord Trigger Extended Harmonies** includes some less common seventh chords and some **extended chords** as well as the standard ones (figure 5.2). From this list we can see two different names for the same chord: **Half-Diminished 7th** and **Minor 7 Flat 5**. The nonstandard seventh chords in the **Extended Harmonies** list are the **Augmented Dominant**

7th, **Augmented Major 7th**, and **Minor Major 7th**. These chords are occasionally heard in jazz, but are less common in classical or rock music. In the music in figure 5.3 that was created from the **Chord Trigger Extended Harmonies** drop-down menu, the first nine chords are seventh chords, and the last four are extended chords. We call these **extended** because they add notes (in thirds) above the seventh chords. We'll discuss extended chords further in *Section 5.11, Extended Chords* in this chapter.

Figure 5.2: Chord Trigger: Extended Harmonies **in Logic.**

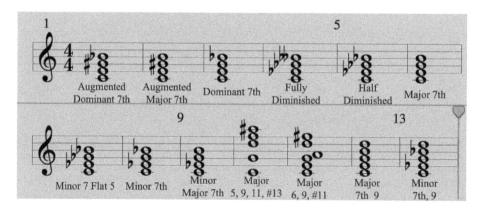

Figure 5.3: Some of the Extended Harmonies **chords viewed in** Score Editor **in Logic.**

5.3 Creating Seventh Chords with Finale

Just as we did for triads, we can use Finale's **Chord** tool to create seventh chords. The **Chord** tool allows us to type in a chord name (the root and the quality) in a blank measure in a Finale file. By exporting the file as a MIDI file, then importing it back into Finale, we will see the chord's musical notation. The example in figure 5.4 shows the names of the five standard seventh chords and their musical notation. Setting the Finale → **Enharmonic Spellings** to **Favor Flats** ensures that all but the diminished seventh chord is spelled correctly. The C diminished seventh will include an A as the seventh; respelling this note enharmonically to B♭♭ maintains the thirds between chord tones.

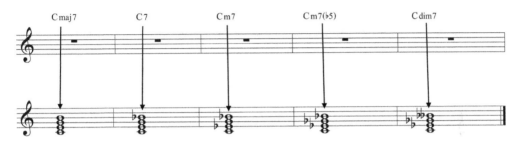

Figure 5.4: Chord **tool seventh chord notation in Finale.**

5.4 Inverting Seventh Chords with Finale and Logic

As seventh chords have four pitches, they can be inverted three times. The figures that accompany Roman numerals to indicate inversions or root position can include three numbers, but they are usually abbreviated to just one or two numbers to make them easier to read, as shown in table 5.2. These seventh chord figures form a sequence of numbers counting backwards from seven to two, as in ^{7}, $^6_5$, $^4_3$, and ^{2}, although the third-inversion seventh chord figure can also be written as $^4_2$. Each figure represents interval distances from the lowest chord tone, although the quality of the intervals varies for different chords.

Table 5.2: Seventh chord inversion figures.

Root		First Inversion		Second Inversion		Third Inversion	
Complete	Abbr.	Complete	Abbr.	Complete	Abbr.	Complete	Abbr.
7	7	6	6	6	4	6	2
5		5	5	4	3	4	
3		3		3		2	

For root-position chords the lowest chord tone is the root. The lowest note of a first-inversion seventh chord is the third, while the lowest note of a second-inversion seventh chord is the fifth, and for a third-inversion seventh chord it's the seventh.

We can use the same tools in Finale and Logic to invert seventh chords as we did to invert triads (in Chapter 4). The following images show Finale's **Canonic Utilities Chord Inversion**

Up inverting a C major seventh chord three times, and Logic **MIDI Transform** doing the same inversions (figs 5.5 and 5.6).

Figure 5.5: Canonic Utilities **seventh chord inversions in Finale.**

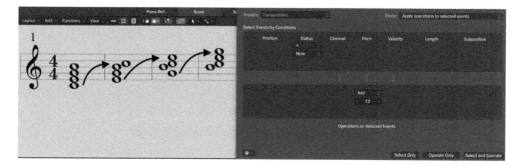

Figure 5.6: MIDI Transform/Transposition **seventh chord inversions in Logic.**

We can use these tools to invert the seventh chords in the opposite direction as well. If we apply the **Canonic Utilities Chord Inversion Down** on the C major seventh chord, we'll get a third-inversion chord, with a B3 as the bass (or lowest) note. Similarly, we could use **MIDI Transform** to change this chord from root position to third inversion by setting the **Pitch** to **Sub 12** in the **Transposition** preset and apply **Operate Only** to the top note of the chord, B4.

5.5 Seventh Chords from Major Scales

The seventh chords that can be created from the pitches of the major scale include major seventh, minor seventh, dominant seventh, and half-diminished seventh. Fully diminished chords can be created from the pitches of the harmonic minor scale.

The following example shows the different seventh chords that can be built on successive scale degrees in C major (figure 5.7). The top line shows the chords in root position, and the three lower staves show the first, second, and third inversions for these chords. The symbols and figures after the Roman numerals indicate the qualities and inversions of the seventh chords. Capital Roman numerals with a **Maj** represent major seventh chords. Dominant seventh chords have only the figures with uppercase Roman numerals. Lowercase Roman numerals with just the figures represent minor seventh chords. The half-diminished chords have a ∅ symbol before the figures. To indicate a fully diminished chord, a ° symbol is used between the Roman numeral and the figures. Seventh chords always have a figure in Roman numeral notation. Root-position triads, on the other hand, have no figures, but for all qualities a root-position seventh chord figure is [7].

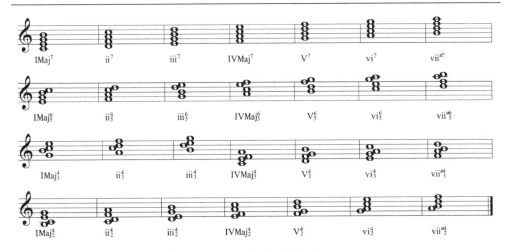

Figure 5.7: Seventh chords in C major.

These chords can be created in Logic with **Chord Trigger** and **MIDI Transform**. The **Text** tool can create the Roman numerals in Logic, whereas in Finale we can use the **Lyrics** tool to create Roman numerals. To create the chords seen in figure 5.7, set **Chord Trigger** to **Multi** → **Parallel** → **Sevenths**, and play a C major scale. Then follow the procedure just outlined for creating inversions with the **MIDI Transform**.

5.6 Seventh Chords from Minor Scales

More seventh chords can be derived from the minor scales than from the major scales because the sixth and seventh scale degrees can be raised or lowered. We see these alternate scale degrees in the three scale forms—natural, harmonic, and melodic minor. The example in figure 5.8 shows all sixteen possible seventh chords in the diatonic collections in A minor. The less common ones are enclosed. The minor dominant chord (the E minor seventh chord in the first measure of the second line), for instance, is only occasionally heard. Also included are some nonstandard seventh chords, such as the minor major seventh (iM⁷), and the augmented major seventh (III⁺⁷). The minor major seventh chord can be heard in different contexts, such as in the second measure of the accompaniment of *My Funny Valentine* by Richard Rodgers and Lorenz Hart, or in a spine-tingling setting on the downbeat of m. 39 of Wolfgang Amadeus Mozart's *Piano Sonata No. 10* (K. 330) ii. *Andante Cantabile*.

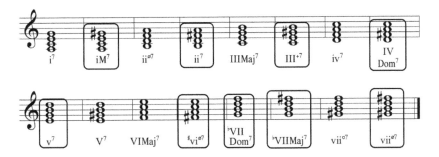

Figure 5.8: All seventh chords from the A minor scale—less-commonly heard chords are enclosed.

In figure 5.9 we have all the standard seventh chords derived from the A minor scale in root position and in the three inversions. Although these versions of the minor-scale seventh chords are heard more often than the nonstandard ones, both the Rodgers and Hart and Mozart examples demonstrate how effective the occasional inclusion of a nonstandard chord can be.

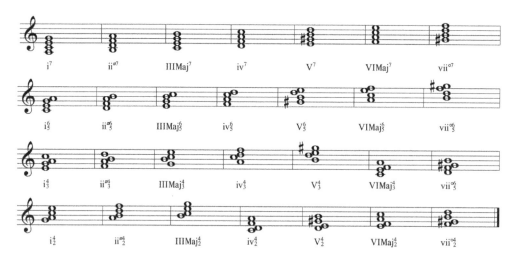

Figure 5.9: Seventh chords in A minor.

To create all the seventh chords in the minor keys in Logic, we first need to create a custom **Multi** set of A minor chords with **Chord Trigger**. For the session shown in figure 5.10, we include all the inversions in the **Multi** set as well, so that we can forego all the **MIDI Transform** operations. This **Multi** set has twenty-eight chords in A minor (seven scale degrees in four positions). We can automate the **Chord Transpose** amounts in **Chord Trigger** to change keys throughout the circle of fifths (as we did for major and minor triads). In figure 5.10 we see the beginning of a Logic session with the musical notation of all the seventh chords in all the minor keys—all 336 of them (12 x 28) in a **Score Editor**. We can also see the **Chord Trigger** notes and automation.

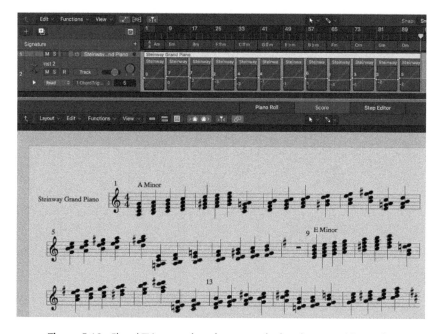

Figure 5.10: Chord Trigger: **minor-key seventh chords created in Logic.**

5.7 Seventh Chord Generator

To create any seventh chord, we can use the Max patcher **Seventh Chord Generator** (figure 5.11), which, like **Triad Generator**, produces chords based on selections from user input via **umenus**. With the **Seventh Chord Generator**, any of the five possible standard seventh chords, in any of the four positions (root position and three inversions), and with a selection from among twenty-seven voicings, can be heard and the musical notation viewed.

Some spelling issues occur—such as diminished seventh chords which have both a sharp and a flat. One example is a F# diminished seventh, which contains both a F# and an Eb. While the **nslider** object can display sharps and flats simultaneously, for the two instances of these chords (F# and C# diminished sevenths) we'll forego the extra programming needed to make this happen. Additionally, there are two diminished chords that require double-flats (C diminished has a Bbb and F diminished has an Ebb), but the **nslider** is limited to single sharps or flats.

In figure 5.11, we see a G minor seventh chord in root position with voicing 11. This voicing has both the seventh and the third raised one octave from the closed-position chord with a root on G3. The chord will sound for the duration of a quarter note at the **Transport**'s tempo setting, and the MIDI output can be sent to Logic or Finale by setting **noteout** to **from MIDI 1**.

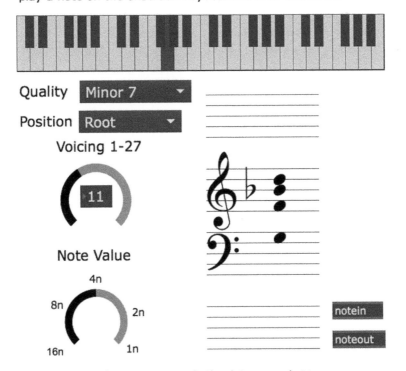

Seventh Chord Generator

Select Quality, Position, Voicing, and Note Value, then play a note on the onscreen keyboard to hear the chord

Quality Minor 7

Position Root

Voicing 1-27

11

Note Value

4n

8n   2n

16n   1n

notein

noteout

Figure 5.11: Seventh Chord Generator **in Max.**

5.8 Max Patcher 9: *Seventh Chord Generator*

The **Seventh Chord Generator** is similar in design to the **Triad Generator**—the significant difference being that it outputs four-note chords as opposed to three-note chords (figure 5.12)

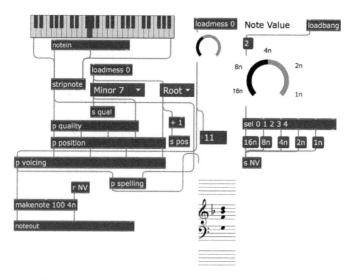

Figure 5.12: Seventh Chord Generator **(patcher) in Max.**

Seventh Chord Generator's first task is to make the chords with different qualities, which it does by adding intervals (produced by adding semitones) to the root tone. In figure 5.13 we see how **Seventh Chord Generator** creates the five qualities of seventh chords in the **p quality** subpatcher. Outlet 2 produces either a major or a minor third. Outlet 3 produces either a diminished or a perfect fifth, and outlet 4 produces either a diminished, a minor, or a major seventh.

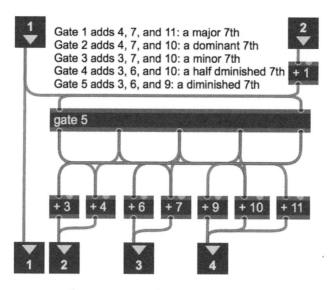

Figure 5.13: p quality **subpatcher in Max.**

The next stage is to transpose chord tones up one octave to create inversions with the **p position** subpatcher (figure 5.14). For root position, no chord tones are transposed. The first inversion requires us to transpose the root up one octave. The second inversion transposes the root and third up one octave, and the third inversion transposes the root, third, and fifth up one octave. A **umenu** with a list of the positions (root and inversions) in the main patcher sends a value to inlet 5 of **p inversion**. The values indicate position or inversion, with 0 for root, and 1, 2, and 3 for first, second, and third inversion, respectively. This value is received by the **sel 0 1 2 3** object, which bangs one of the **messages** based on the value received.

Each of the four **messages** sends either a 1 or 2 to each of the three **gate 2** objects to select either transposition of twelve semitones up (one octave up) or no transposition. The combined transpositions create the inversions required.

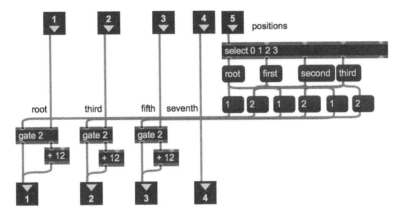

Figure 5.14: p position **subpatcher in Max.**

After creating the inversion where needed, we need to voice the chords such that the upper three tones can be spread out from the bass by various octave amounts. Figure 5.15 shows the **p voicing** subpatcher. Two tasks are required: (1) isolate the nontransposing bass chord tone, and (2) transpose the upper three chord tones. These tasks are done with the **router 4 4** (4 x 4) and the **router 3 9** (3 x 9) objects, respectively. We isolate the nontransposing chord tone with the **router 4 4**, then transpose the remaining three chord tones in twenty-seven possible voicings with **router 3 9**. As we are using these objects in the same way as we did in the **Triad Generator**, the **p voicing** subpatcher's **routers** are controlled by **matrixctrl** and **coll** objects which connect inputs to outputs.

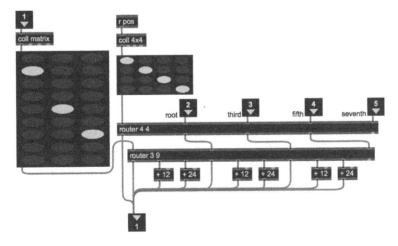

Figure 5.15: p voicing **subpatcher in Max.**

Next, to ensure that chords are spelled as accurately as possible, we determine which seventh chords will use sharps and which will use flats. For seventh chords that mix accidentals (F# and C# diminished), **Seventh Chord Generator** chooses just one type and spells certain pitches enharmonically. Which accidentals will be used for the seventh chord qualities is shown in table 5.3. The pitch-class numbers (pc) are used to identify the roots of the chords (tab. 5.3).

Table 5.3: Sorting chords for flats or sharps.

Flats or Sharps	Use Flats	Use Sharps
Major Seventh	Db, Eb, F, Ab, Bb pc: 1, 3, 5, 8, 10	C, D, E, F#, G, A, B pc: 0, 2, 4, 6, 7, 9, 11
Dominant Seventh	C, Db, Eb, F, Ab, Bb pc: 0, 1, 3, 5, 8, 10	D, E, F#, G, A, B pc: 2, 4, 6, 7, 9, 11
Minor Seventh	C, D, F, G, Bb pc: 0, 2, 5, 7, 10	C#, E, F#, G#, A, B pc: 1, 4, 6, 8, 9, 11
Half-diminished Seventh	C, D, Eb, E, F, G, A, Bb pc: 0, 3, 4, 5, 7, 9, 10	C#, F#, G#, B pc: 1, 6, 8, 11
Diminished Seventh	C, D, Eb, E, F, G, A, Bb pc: 0, 2, 3, 4, 5, 7, 9, 10	C#, F#, G# pc: 1, 6, 8

The task of separating seventh chords notated with flats from those using sharps happens in **p spelling** (figure 5.16). The **nslider** object displays negative MIDI note numbers with a flat, and positive MIDI note numbers with a sharp. Making the MIDI note numbers negative must be separate from playback, as negative numbers aren't recognized as MIDI note numbers. The root pitch enters the subpatcher through inlet 2, and the seventh chord quality (as a value between 0 and 4) enters through the **r qual** object. With the **gate 5** and five **sel** objects (one **sel** object for each quality), the selection of whether to use flats or sharps is made. Based on this selection, the actual chord (note numbers and velocities) is sent through one of the two outlets of the **gate 2** object. The first gate sends the MIDI note numbers of the chord through without alteration for sharps, whereas the second gate multiplies all the values times −1 so that flats will be used in the **nslider**.

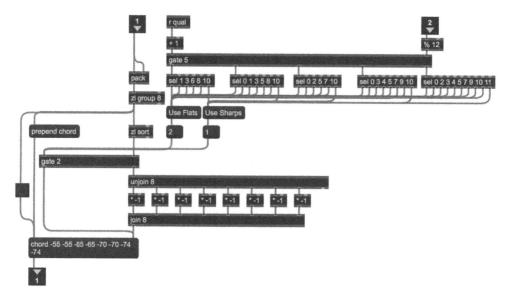

Figure 5.16: p spelling **subpatcher in Max.**

In the Exercises section of the chapter, we'll discuss how **Seventh Chord Generator** can be modified to practice chord recognition. Additionally, the process of creating chords with manipulatable parameters (root, quality, position, and voicing) is an integral part of programming chord progressions, which we will discuss in Chapters 7 and 8 with the **Diatonic** and **Chromatic Progression Generators**.

5.9 Chord Patterns, Logic's Arpeggiator

Chords with notes sounding simultaneously and close together are **block chords**. Block chords are frequently used in music, but a chord's notes can be arranged in many ways. Our two chord generators (triad and seventh chord) demonstrate how to expand chords vertically with different voicings, but chords can also be expanded horizontally, so that they become more like melodies. Consider the first two measures of Frederic Chopin's *Etude Op. 10, no. 1* in C major (fig 5.17). Listening to the music, we're dazzled at the speed and range of the notes. Looking closer, however, we can see that it's not really complicated; all the notes are from a C major triad played as a four-octave **arpeggio** or **broken chord** (notes sounding separately) pattern.

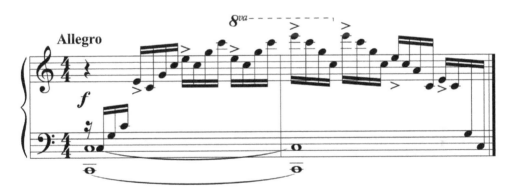

Figure 5.17: The first two measures of Chopin's *Etude Op. 10, no. 1* in C major.

Recognizing chords in complex broken-chord passages can be a challenging aspect of music theory, but with practice and by using one's ear, the task becomes easier. Expanding harmonies in broken-chord patterns is likewise a useful process in creating music with varied textures.

Logic's **MIDI FX Arpeggiator** creates patterns for individual chords, and we can use it to become familiar with the task of creating broken-chord patterns of all kinds. We could, for instance, recreate the right-hand sixteenth-notes part of the Chopin *Etude Op. 10, no. 1*. First, we see how the first four notes (C3–G3–C4–E4)—a C major triad with an added C—form a repeated pattern that is transposed up an octave four times, then transposed down by an octave four times.

The **Arpeggiator** setting to create this pattern must have four stages in **Grid** mode, corresponding to the four notes in the pattern. The **Rate** is **1/16** (sixteenth notes), and we use the (1) up/down pattern; (2) **Variation** mode two; and (3) **Oct. Range** of 4 (fig 5.18).

Figure 5.18: Arpeggiator **creates Chopin** *Etude Op. 10, no. 1,* **mm. 1–2 right hand, in Logic.**

With these settings in place, we input the first two chords in measures 1–4 on track 2 with the **Arpeggiator**. If we route and record its output to track 1, we'll see the music as per figure 5.19.

Figure 5.19: **Chopin's** *Etude Op. 10, no. 1* **as created with the** Arpeggiator **in Logic.**

In the original musical score, the highest part of the pattern (the last beat of the first measure and the first beat of the second measure) has an **ottava alto (8va . . .)**, indicating the notes sound one octave higher than notated. In the Logic **Score Editor** (figure 5.19), these notes are shown at the actual pitches. Chopin's *Etude Op. 10, no. 1* has broken chords throughout the piece, but as these chords do not always use the pattern we created, we would need many different **Arpeggiator** settings to create all the chord patterns to recreate the entire piece.

We can also use the **Arpeggiator** in **Live**, as opposed to **Grid** mode, so that it responds to notes played on a connected MIDI controller. In **Live** mode, if we choose the **Latch Transpose Mode**, the Arpeggiator will "learn" an arpeggio pattern played on the keyboard. If we then play a single note on our MIDI keyboard, the arpeggiator will play the same arpeggio pattern based on that note. Next, we go to the **Keyboard** section in **Arpeggiator** and choose both a key and a scale form from among the seventeen possibilities (the major and the three minor scale forms are included). The **Arpeggiator** will then constrain any chord pattern to that scale. If we choose the key of C and the major scale, for instance, then play a C major seventh chord (C–E–G–B), anytime we then play a single note in the C major scale, **Arpeggiator** will play the seventh chord that corresponds to that scale degree.

Earlier in this chapter, we learned that the seventh chords based on the scale degrees of the major scale are : I^{maj7}—major seventh, ii^7—minor seventh, iii^7—minor seventh, IV^{maj7}—major seventh, V^7—dominant seventh (or major/minor seventh), vi^7—minor seventh, vii^{o7}—half-diminished seventh. We can use the **Arpeggiator** in **Latch Mode** to play all these chords.

Figure 5.20: Arpeggiator **constrained to C major and set to a major seventh chord in Logic.**

In figure 5.20, we see the **Arpeggiator** set to **Play**, **Latch**, and **Transpose Mode** so that it will play arpeggios continuously based on input, and will also transpose them. The **Keyboard** setting also shows that the **Arpeggiator** will be constrained to C major (that is, it will only play notes from the C major scale) and that the current pattern is a C major seventh chord. In this setting, playing any single note in the C major scale will produce the seventh chord with the correct quality for that scale degree. This **Arpeggiator** setting will also work for diatonic triads in C major with this setting.

Arpeggiator is a good tool for learning about how chords can be arranged in different patterns, and there are countless other ways to arrange chords besides the examples outlined here that we could create by manipulating parameters. **Arpeggiator** has over fifty presets which are available via a drop-down menu **Factory Default → Factory**. Many individual patterns are available by navigating to **Pattern → Grid → Custom →** drop-down menu.

5.10 Chord Patterns in Finale

Finale has its own tools for creating and manipulating chord patterns. A C major triad is in the first measure (figure 5.21). To create the second measure, where each chord tone is repeated, copy m. 1 into m. 2, then navigate to **Plug-ins → Note, Beam, and Rest Editing → Rhythmic Subdivisions**, and choose **Subdivide Entries into Rhythmic Duration** (eighth note). This is one possible pattern from the **Rhythmic Subdivisions** plug-in, as shown in figure 5.22.

Figure 5.21: Chord patterns in Finale.

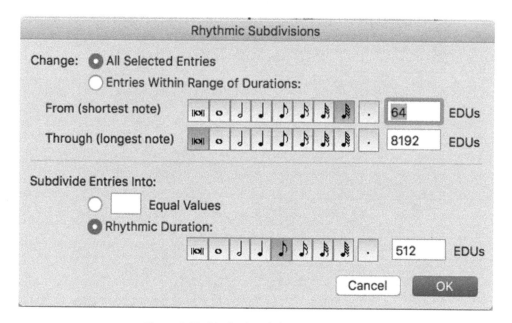

Figure 5.22: Rhythmic Subdivisions **in Finale.**

Next, we can drag m. 2 forward to paste it in m. 3. In m.3, we'll rearrange some of the pitches by hand, using either **Simple** or **Speedy Entry**. Select a note-head and drag it to a nearby chord tone. The pattern in figure 5.21 is to move every other note up by two chord tones (C → G; E → C; G → E; etc.). We then copy and move m.3 to m. 4, 5, and 6. M. 4 is transposed up one octave with the **Transposition** tool. M. 5 is transposed up one octave, then retrograded with the **Canonic Utilities** tool, and m. 6 is retrograded (no transposition) with the **Canonic Utilities** tool (see page 136) (figure 5.23).

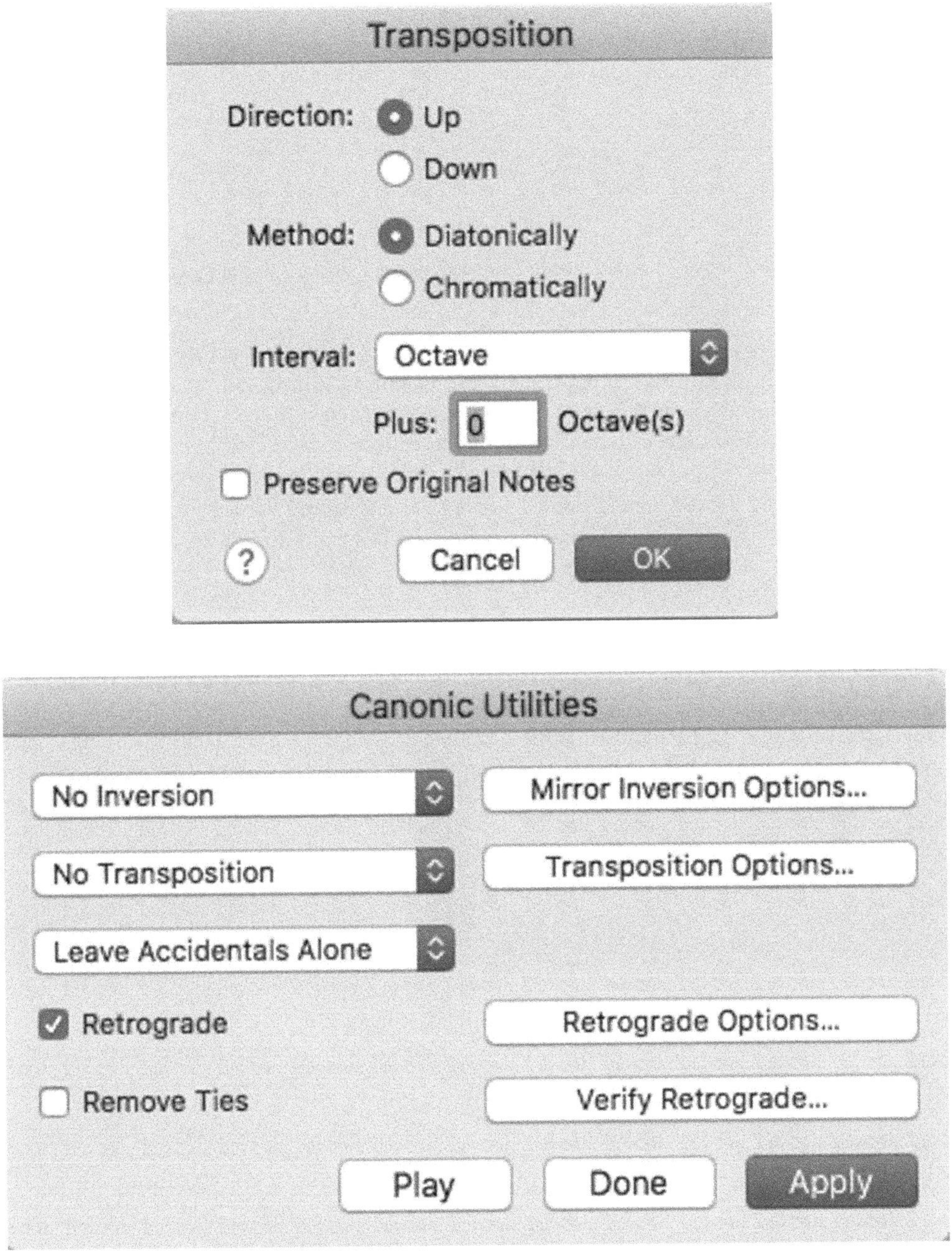

Figure 5.23: Transposition **and** Canonic Utilities **in Finale.**

5.11 *Extended Chords*

Both Finale's **Chord** tool and Logic's **Chord Trigger** provide examples of five- and six-note extended chords. The chord labels of these extensions help us to understand how they are related to seventh chords or triads. In figure 5.24 are some examples of five- and six-note chords from

Logic's **Chord Trigger Extended Harmonies** set. Some of the pitches are rearranged to help show how the chords are built in thirds. The first two are five-note chords which are created by adding ninths to a major seventh chord and to a minor seventh chord. The third example (also a five-note chord) starts with an altered triad (the *sus* chord, a triad with the third replaced with a perfect fourth) and adds a minor seventh and major ninth. The fourth chord has six notes and adds a major sixth, ninth, and raised eleventh to a major triad (figure 5.24).

Figure 5.24: Chord Trigger: Extended Harmonies **examples in Logic.**

Although these chords are more complex, they can sometimes substitute for triads or seventh chords. The **Maj$^{7\,9}$** chord can be used in place of a major triad or major seventh chord, and the **Min^{79}** in place of a minor triad or minor seventh chord. The **Sus$^{7,\,9}$** chord will potentially work as a substitute for a minor seventh chord or a dominant seventh chord. The **Maj$^{6,\,7,\,\#11}$** chord, on the other hand, is tonally ambiguous, and it might be difficult to substitute it for a triad or seventh chord. This chord is a **bitonal** chord, containing both a C and D major triads. Perhaps it's a C major triad with A, D, and F# pitch extensions, but we can also hear it as a D dominant seventh in third inversion with G, and E extensions added below, or a sort of D$^{7,\,9,\,11}$.

Finale's **Chord** tool provides access to over 100 different chord types, including many extended chords. Many of these extended chords are used in contemporary jazz, but are not as common in classical music. To see the entire set of extended chords in Finale: with the **Chord** tool selected, double-click on a measure to bring up the **Chord Definition** window, then click on the **Chord Suffix Selection** button (figure 5.25). By following the procedure outlined on pages 75–77, we can see the musical notation for any chord available in the **Chord** tool.

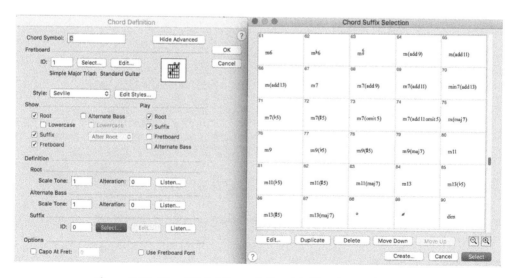

Figure 5.25: Chord Definition **and** Chord Suffix Selection **in Finale.**

5.12 Exercises

5.12.1 Exercise 1: Seventh Chord Quiz

Just as **Triad Quiz** can help us learn how to identify triads aurally, the **Seventh Chord Quiz** allows us to develop aural identification of seventh chords (figure 5.26). Clicking the **(?) New Chord** button plays a randomly generated new seventh chord and erases the previous chord from the **nslider**. **Seventh Chord Quiz** plays a random seventh chord by root, quality, and position. We then identify the seventh chord on the **umenu** list of seventh chord types and press the **(!) Check answer button** to see if our selection is correct.

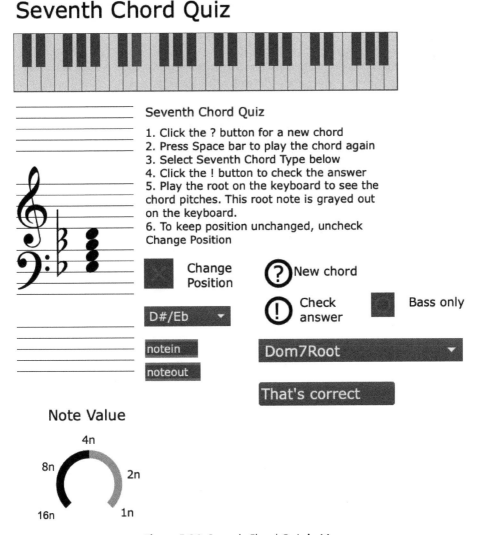

Figure 5.26: Seventh Chord Quiz **in Max.**

To limit to only one position (root position is the easiest to identify), uncheck the **Change Position** toggle. To hear the chord again, press the space bar, or to hear the bass tone alone, press the **Bass only** button. Clicking on the grayed-out note in the **kslider** will play the chord again and display the notation in the **nslider**.

The modifications of **Seventh Chord Generator** to create **Seventh Chord Quiz** are essentially the same as those that changed **Triad Generator** into **Triad Quiz**, except that larger values are required in several places because there are *five* qualities and *four* positions for seventh chords, as opposed to the four qualities and three positions of triads (figure 5.27). The **random 12** object sends out values from 0–11 to select one of the twelve pitches as a root. The **random 5** and **random 4** objects randomly select qualities and positions, respectively, and the **random 4** object can be deselected by a toggle to limit the position to whichever was last selected.

The **Seventh Chord Type Selector umenu** has seventeen possible selections, numbered 0–16. There are four for the major seventh chord in the four positions (root, first, second, and third inversions), and four also for each of the dominant seventh, minor seventh, and half-diminished seventh chords, as each chord can be heard in four positions. There is only one selection for the diminished seventh, because this chord (like the augmented triad) sounds the same in any inversion in closed position. As the interval structure for a closed diminished seventh chord is always three minor thirds, we can't select an inversion just by listening—inversions of diminished seventh chords are only a question of notation.

Once the user has selected which chord is being played from the **Seventh Chord Type Selector umenu**, then the **p check answer** subpatcher can determine if the selection is correct (figure 5.28). The **p check answer** subpatcher in **Seventh Chord Quiz** works in the same way as Triad Quiz's **p check answer** subpatcher.

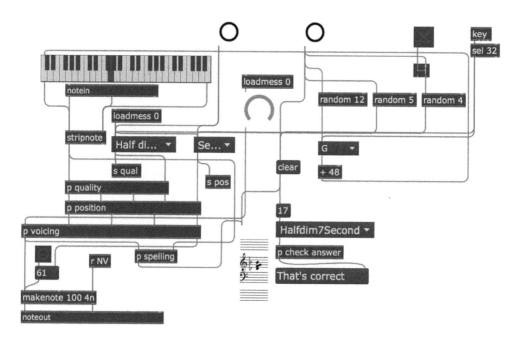

Figure 5.27: Seventh Chord Quiz **(patcher).**

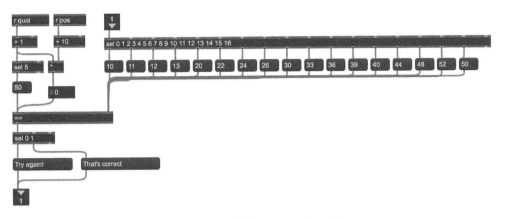

Figure 5.28: p check answer **subpatcher.**

5.12.2 Exercise 2: 12-Bar Shuffle Blues *Accompaniment with Logic Chord Trigger*

A basic form of the *12-Bar Shuffle Blues* consists only of dominant seventh chords (figure 5.29). The tonic, subdominant, and dominant chords all have this quality. To create the chords using Logic's **Chord Trigger**, we can select **Single** → **Extended Harmonies** → **Dominant 7th**. (Or, for a slightly different set of chords, select **Multi** → **Keyboard Voicing** → **Blues Left Hand**.) Input the trigger notes as follows into a **Software Instrument** track with this **Chord Trigger** setting to play the progression. In the top staff of the music (figure 5.29) are the notes of the C blues scale on which we can base a blues improvisation. Use a **Software Instrument** track for this, adding the **Transposer MIDI FX** set to the **C Minor Blues** to constrain this instrument to the six notes shown in figure 5.29. Add an **Apple Loop Beats** for the twelve measures (such as **Chicago Blues Drumset**) for a rhythmic foundation, and start improvising! To add different chords, create a **Multi** set. Conversely, turn off the **Transposer** for melodic freedom!

Figure 5.29: *12-Bar Shuffle Blues.*

5.12.3 Exercise 3: Create a Finale Song Accompaniment

Creating a song accompaniment in Finale can help us learn about seventh chords, as many popular songs use seventh chords throughout, such as the standard *How High the Moon* by Nancy Hamilton and Morgan Lewis. Our first task is to locate the lead-sheet format of the song so that we can see the chord symbols. As Finale's **Chord** tool has such a large number of chord types, we should be able to find almost any chord in the **Chord Suffix Selection**.

With the **Chord** tool, we can type the chords directly into the score, or type in the root and then find the suffix. The five standard chords can be input as shown in the second line of table 5.4—each based on C, and with no spaces between the characters. The third line has some common alternate symbols for these same chords (tab. 5.4).

Table 5.4: Lead sheet chord symbols for the five standard seventh chords.

	Major Seventh	Dominant Seventh	Minor Seventh	Half-diminished Seventh	Diminished Seventh
Chord tool symbol	CMaj^7	C^7	Cm^7	Cm^7 (b5)	Cdim^7
Alternate			C-^{7}	C-7 b5 or Cø^7	C°^{7}

Typing into the score with a common time signature allows us to place chords on every quarter-note beat, and in the following example the chords are placed at every downbeat unless there is more than one chord per measure (figure 5.30). To make the song accompaniment more lively, we can add a drum pattern from **Plug-Ins →Scoring and Arranging → Drum Groove**, such as **12 Bar Bop Blues** (figure 5.31).

To see the notation for these chords, we can export the file as a SMF (standard MIDI file) and import it back into Finale. To play or sing the tune along with the accompaniment, it can be helpful to have a count-off (several beats heard before the downbeat). Finale's **Click and Countoff** window (available from the **Playback Controls** window) allows you to specify certain parameters for the count-off. With MIDI notes as the source, Channel 10, and notes 42 and 51 selected, the count-off will use some of the same sounds we hear in the drum pattern itself (figure 5.32).

Figure 5.30: Accompaniment to Hamilton and Lewis's *How High the Moon* in Finale.

Figure 5.31: Drum Groove **in Finale.**

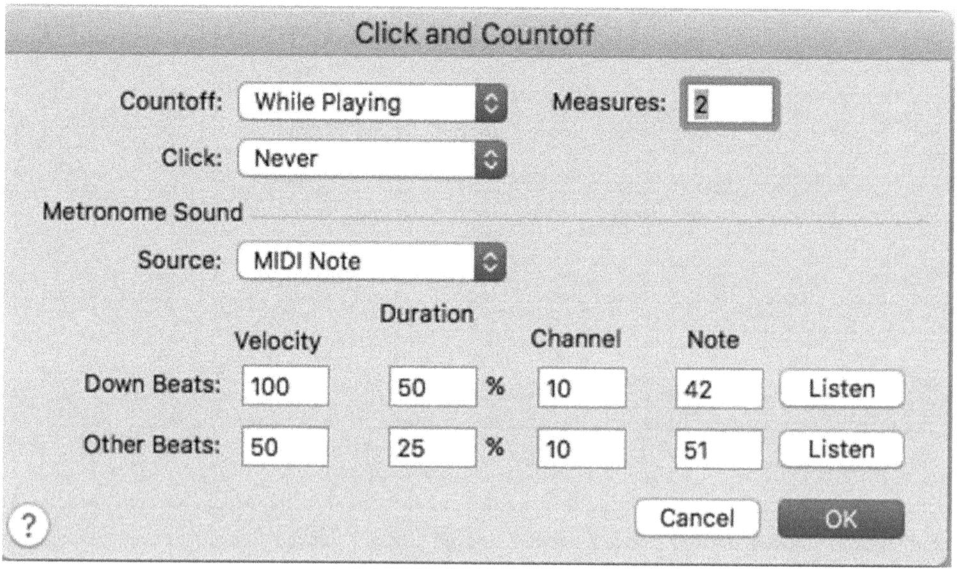

Figure 5.32: Click and Countoff **in Finale.**

CHAPTER 6

Melody

6.1 Melody and Motives

A **melody** is a distinct and recognizable sequence of pitches and durations, but that knowledge doesn't tell us much about what makes a good melody. How to compose a good melody is not easily prescribed, but we can learn how melodies can be constructed from component parts. Melodies combine all the musical concepts we have discussed so far. The pitch materials of melody can include intervals, scales, arpeggiated triads, and seventh chords. The rhythmic materials can include any kinds of durations arranged in any kinds of meter and tempo, from simple durations to advanced rhythmic concepts. In this sense, while tonal chords (triads and seventh chords) are of known quantity, melodies are open-ended.

As examples of scales and chords being used in melodies, we hear a descending major scale in the opening melody of *Joy to the World* by George Frederic Handel and an arpeggiated major triad in *The Blue Danube Waltz* by Johann Strauss (figure 6.1). While the rhythms of both melodies help make these melodies distinct and recognizable, the pitches are clearly derived from the basic building blocks of music—the scale and the triad.

Figure 6.1: Handel's *Joy to the World* (C major scale), and Strauss's
The Blue Danube Waltz (C major triad).

Many melodies contain portions of scales and chords, but some melodies' pitches might be better described as a series of intervals, rather than in terms of scales or triads. In the opening melody of *A Fine Romance* by Jerome Kern and Dorothy Fields (figure 6.2), we recognize that all the notes are from the C major scale. We can also hear the notes of an A minor triad in the first three pitches and a C major triad in the last three measures, but the effect overall is of a series of melodic intervals changing directions (M3 down, M6 up, M2 down, M2 up, m7 down, P8 up, etc.).

Figure 6.2: Kern and Fields, *A Fine Romance* (excerpt). A rhythmic motive is in brackets.

Although it might be hard to discern a pattern in these intervals, the melody of *A Fine Romance* is not random. In addition to all of its pitches being in the C major scale, the melody repeats the same short rhythmic pattern (quarter, half, quarter, whole) in successive pairs of measures: 2–3, 4–5, and 6–7. In figure 6.2, each instance of the rhythmic pattern is marked with a bracket above the notes. This recurring pattern is a **motive**, a small but recognizable and recurring unit of rhythms, pitches, or combinations of both. In *A Fine Romance*, we can also hear that each motive starts with a descending major second interval, and the last note of each instance is lower than the first pitch, specifically by the intervals of a minor seventh for the first instance, and by a perfect fifth for the last two. While aspects of the motive are changing in this short segment of music, its repeating rhythm and shape provides continuity.

Motives occur throughout all kinds of music. Possibly the most famous motive is heard in the opening measures of Ludwig van Beethoven's Fifth Symphony in C minor. These first four notes have become universally recognizable (figure 6.3):

Figure 6.3: Beethoven's Fifth Symphony. Opening motive transposed and modified.

In this symphony, we hear the motive (three repeated short notes followed by a long lower note) repeated five times in the first nine measures, but transposed several times and with different starting pitches for each transposition (G, F, G, Ab, Eb). At the same time, the interval from the third to fourth note changes throughout (M3, m3, M3, m2, m3), but the motive's rhythm and shape keep it recognizable. The opening motive of Beethoven's Fifth Symphony is repeated hundreds of times, and in various forms, throughout the entire symphony. Throughout history, composers have used motives in their music, but this symphony is groundbreaking in how pervasive the opening motive is.

Motives are often part of melodies, and melodies are often the most memorable part of a piece of music. Motives are sometimes quite recognizable, but at other times can be somewhat disguised or blended into the musical texture. In popular music, a memorable melody might be considered a **hook**—the part of a song that grabs people's attention and makes them remember the song—but hooks can also be rhythmic or melodic motives that are shorter than a full melody and possibly combinable into larger units. Additionally, we can expand the idea of melody to include musical lines of different kinds. Bass lines, the lowest parts of a musical texture, provide support for the harmony, but if they are melodic in their own right, so much the better. Similarly, interior musical lines, be they accompaniment patterns or countermelodies (melodies that are heard along with the main melody and that can play a secondary role), often work best if they have a melodic quality. In all cases, main melodies, bass lines, and interior musical lines often incorporate motives.

We'll use motives to develop an understanding of melody in this chapter, but we will always want to keep in mind that creating melodies involves more than generating material from motives—creating a good melody being one of music's more elusive goals.

6.2 Motives and Transposition

To help us understand the process of creating melodies through repeating and varying motives, we can create a melodic phrase from a randomly generated motive in Logic. In the following example, we'll repeat the motive three times in all, and transpose the second and third instances. By generating the motive randomly, however, we can repeat this semi-automated process many times and compare results without having to think up new motives.

1. In a new Logic session, create four quarter notes on middle C in a MIDI region (figure 6.4a).

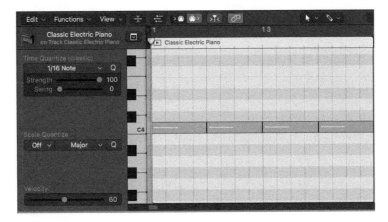

Figure 6.4a: Piano Roll Editor **in Logic.**

2. Open **MIDI Transform**, choose **Random Pitch**, **Velocity**, and **Length** preset with these settings: Pitch → C4–C5; Velocity → 127–40; and Length → 020 0–001 0. Choose **Select and Operate** (figure 6.4b).

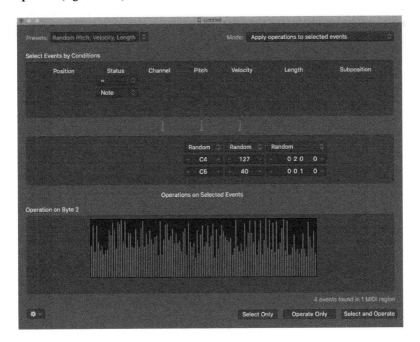

Figure 6.4b: MIDI Transform: Random Pitch, Velocity, Length **in Logic.**

3. Edit the notes in the **Piano Roll Editor** to eliminate overlaps or gaps, limiting the notes to a single measure. Keep the differences in durations to create identifiable rhythms (figs 6.4c and d).

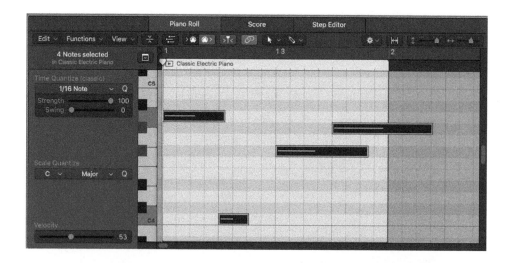

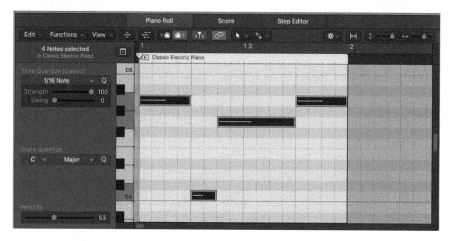

Figures 6.4c and d: Piano Roll Editor **in Logic.**

4. Select the measure, and option/drag it forward so there are two additional copies in mm. 2–3
5. Open **MIDI Transform** and the **Transposition** preset and select **Add 2**, then **Select and Operate** to transpose the m. 2 up two semitones. Repeat the process with m. 3, with **Add 4** to the **Transposition** preset so that the motive is transposed up four semitones. (Or choose to transpose down with **Sub** and/or different transposition amounts.)
6. In **Piano Roll Editor**, **Scale Quantize** all the notes of the three instances of the motive to C major. Join the regions together to view a single melody.

Figure 6.4e: A C major melody with repeating motives.

The melodic phrase in the **Score Editor** (figure 6.4e) consists of a motive repeated three times in **sequence**. A melodic sequence occurs when a motive repeats at different pitch levels, or, to put it another way, when the motive is transposed. We could vary this melody by making the motive descend sequentially instead of ascend, or by changing the transposition intervals, or by combinations of both processes. We can listen to how the motive is changed during each of the steps and use our ears to guide in selecting the transposition amounts and the number of repetitions.

We made sure that the sequence of motives always stays in C major by **Scale Quantizing**, which results in a **tonal sequence**. In a tonal sequence, the motive remains in the same key, and intervals will be adjusted to match the scale pitches accordingly. A **real** sequence, on the other hand, keeps the actual intervals the same. The pattern of intervals is replicated exactly, and certain notes will no longer be in the original scale or key. In our previous example, we could have **Scale Quantized** just the motive, then transposed it—resulting in a real sequence. With a real sequence, it might sound as if the motive is using different scales, or that some notes sound out of key. The difference between real and tonal sequences is shown in the following example (figure 6.5), which transposes the first four notes as a motive twice in both sequences. In the real sequence, the motive's final minor second (F–E) is transposed to G → F# in the second measure—so that it sounds as if the D major scale is used. In the third measure, the added F# and G# make it sound as though the E major scale is used.

Figure 6.5: Tonal sequence vs. real sequence.

Finale's **Transposition** tool, on the other hand, has settings for both tonal and real transposition, effectively joining the transposition and scale-quantize functions with its **Method Diatonically** setting. In this case, *diatonic* means the same as *tonal*, and *chromatic* means the same as *real*. In figure 6.6, we see a motive transposed first diatonically and then chromatically with Finale's **Transposition**.

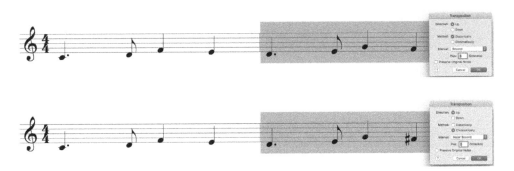

Figure 6.6: Transposition Diatonically **and** Chromatically **in Finale.**

6.3 Inversion and Retrograde

A motive can also be played as a mirror image, or in **melodic inversion**, in which ascending melodic intervals are replaced by descending melodic intervals, and vice versa. Melodic inversion has a connection with harmonic inversion (chord and interval inversion), but it's easier to think of them as separate operations. In melodic inversion, we invert the pitches of a melody or motive around a central pitch, the **axis of inversion** (which might be the first pitch). In Logic's **MIDI Transform** this pitch is called the **flip**, and in Finale's **Canonic Utilities** it's called the **pivot**.

In the following Logic example, the first-measure motive is chromatically inverted around G4 in m. 2, and diatonically inverted around G4 in m.3 (figure 6.7). A **chromatic inversion** is where the exact intervals are used in the inversion, just as in a *real* transposed sequence. A **diatonic inversion**, on the other hand, stays in the same key and adjusts the intervals so that the pitches always stay in the key.

To invert a motive chromatically and diatonically:

1. Copy/drag the motive to be inverted to two locations.
2. With **MIDI Transform → Reverse Pitch** preset set the **Flip** to the MIDI note number of the motive's first pitch (G4=67), then **Select & Operate**.
3. **Scale Quantize** the inverted motives to create the diatonic form, or leave as is to create the chromatic form.

Figure 6.7: A motive inverted around G4 chromatically (m. 2) and diatonically in G major (m. 3).

In Logic, **Reverse Pitch** is synonymous with "invert pitch," and **Flip** is used to define the axis of inversion. We set **Flip** to G4, the first pitch of our motive, so that the motive is inverted around that first pitch. If we set Flip to F#4, on the other hand, the inverted motive will start on F4—the same semitone distance as between G4 and F#4, but in the opposite direction, that is, a semitone below F#4. In other words, if we set the **Flip** to a note other than the motive's starting pitch, we create a *transposed* inversion.

Another means for varying a motive is to play it backwards, or in **retrograde.** To play a motive backwards in Logic, (1) open **MIDI Transform** and set the preset to **Reverse Position**, (2) specify the start and end of the motive by its MIDI-based location, and (3) **Select and Operate** (figure 6.8).

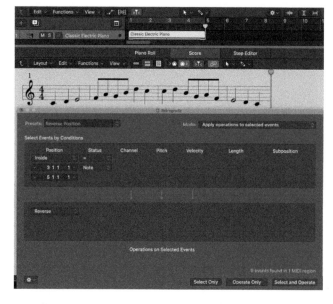

Figure 6.8: MIDI Transform: Reverse Position **in Logic.**

Alternatively, we can retrograde a phrase in Logic with the **Time Handles** in the **Piano Roll Editor**. In the **Piano Roll Editor**, (1) we enable **Time Handles** and select the material to retrograde so that the **Time Handles** appear at the left and right boundaries of the selected materials. (2) We drag the right **Time Handle** towards the left side of the selection—but not all the way past where the left **Time Handle** is, then (3) drag the left **Time Handle** past the right **Time Handle**. At this point, we (4) position the **Time Handles** so their positions are reversed, resulting in a retrograde of the MIDI notes (figure 6.9).

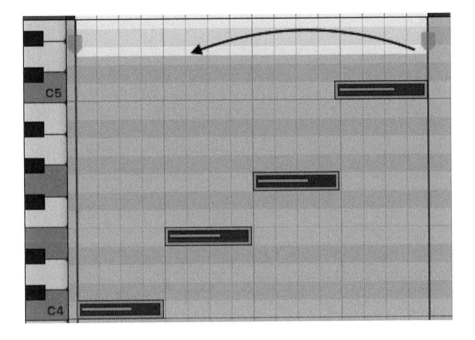

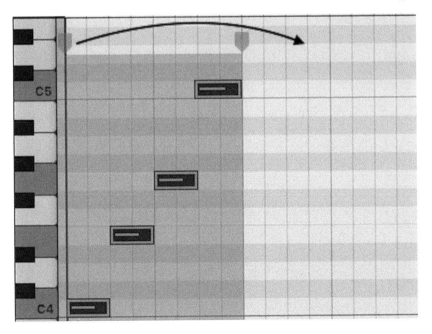

Figure 6.9: Adjusting Time Handles to create retrograde in Logic.

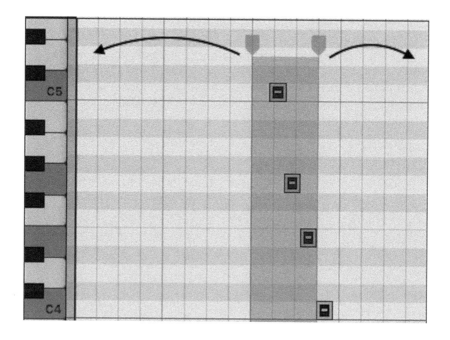

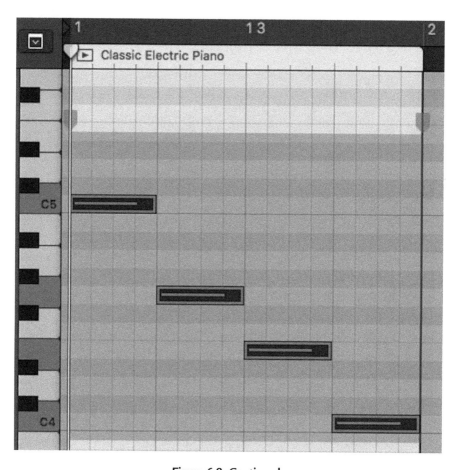

Figure 6.9: Continued

6.4 *Rhythmic Augmentation and Diminution*

We can transform motives rhythmically as well. Rhythmic **augmentation** multiplies durations by a constant value to lengthen them, whereas rhythmic **diminution** divides durations to shorten them. In both cases the resulting rhythm patterns remain proportional to the original. The Logic's **MIDI Transform Preset Half Speed** augments durations by multiplying by 2, and **Double Speed** will create diminution by dividing the durations by 2. Both **Presets** also ensure that the relative positions for durations are maintained, and these **Half Speed** and **Double Speed** presets can also multiply or divide by values other than 2. The following example has an initial motive in the first measure and the **Half Speed** and **Double Speed** versions directly after (figure 6.10). If we wanted to augment selected rhythmic values by 3, we could use the **Half Speed** preset, and change settings for **Position** and **Length** to **Mul 3**. The result would be two dotted quarters, a dotted half, and a dotted whole note (and it would expand the motive to three measures in common time).

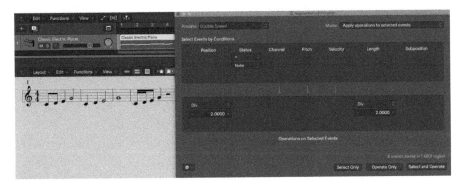

Figure 6.10: MIDI Transform: Half **(augmentation)** and Double Speed **(diminution) in Logic.**

We can apply rhythmic augmentation and diminution to motives in Finale by selecting them and navigating from **Utilities** → **Change** → **Note Durations**. From this **Change Note Durations** window, we can choose **Change All Note Durations By** and select a percentage from the drop-down menu. The 50% and 25% settings will divide all the note values in half or in quarters, respectively (diminution), whereas 200% or 400% will double or quadruple the note value durations (augmentation) (figure 6.11).

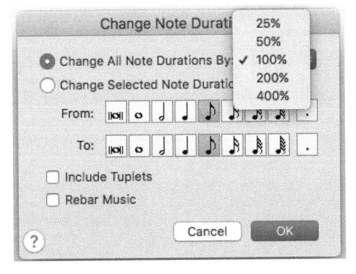

Figure 6.11: Change Note Durations **in Finale.**

6.5 *Canonic Utilities in Finale*

Finale's **Canonic Utilities** can perform transposition, inversion, retrograde, and the combination of any of these functions, either chromatically or diatonically. In the following example we see the same motive inverted around C5 (the axis of inversion or **pivot note**) both diatonically and chromatically. The diatonic inversion keeps the motive in the same key, while the chromatic inversion keeps all the intervals the same (figure 6.12).

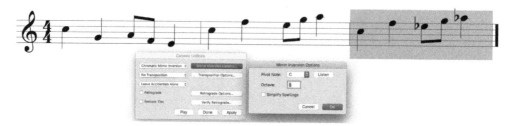

Figure 6.12: Canonic Utilities: Diatonic **and** Chromatic Mirror Inversion **in Finale.**

The **Retrograde** setting of **Canonic Utilities** reverses the motive, similarly to Logic's **MIDI Transform Reverse Position** (figure 6.13).

Figure 6.13: Canonic Utilities: Retrograde **in Finale.**

6.6 *Finale Motivic Analysis*

We can use Finale's **Canonic Utilities** and **Transposition** to show how composers have transformed motives in their music—known as **motivic analysis**. As we listen to motives in different forms in music, we can even discern which operations were used.

J. S. Bach's Two-part Inventions were written for keyboard students, but, as Bach wrote in a handwritten score he gave to one of his own students, the pieces were also designed so that students could "acquire a strong foretaste of composition." In the first invention, Bach shows how a single motive can be transposed and inverted in many ways to create a coherent and lively piece. The music (figure 6.14) shows how the opening motive is transformed in the first four measures. As described in the preceding sections, these transformations can all be done in Logic or in Finale using **Transposition** and **Canonic Utilities** tools: diatonic transpositions in mm. 1–2, and diatonic transpositions with inversion in mm. 3–4. When operating on a motive diatonically, the quality of interval of operation is not typically given because we're always within the scale, or operating diatonically.

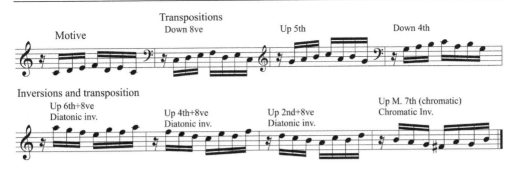

Figure 6.14: Bach's *Invention No. 1*. The opening motive transposed and inverted.

The following music shows the first six measures of *Invention No. 1* (figure 6.15). The transposition of the motive on the first two beats of m. 5 is down a minor seventh chromatically, not diatonically. Because Bach transposes the motive chromatically, we hear F#s, not from the original key of C major, but instead from G major.

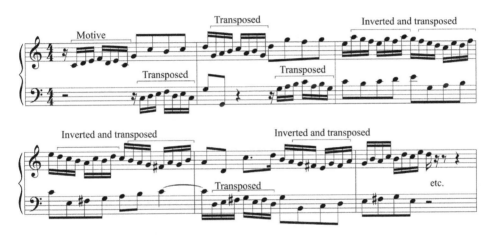

Figure 6.15: Bach's *Invention No. 1*. Measures 1–6.

Motives are heard in many kinds of music, and are often transposed both tonally and chromatically. In the traditional song *The Oak and the Ash*, the simple three-note motive marked A in the music (fig 6.16) is transposed up a second (diatonically) in m. 2, then transposed up a second and inverted in m. 7. The inversion appears to be real because the intervals formed match the initial motive (M2, m2), and are not part of the F natural minor scale. The E♮, however, is in the harmonic-minor form of F minor, and so this motivic transposition is actually tonal with respect to the E harmonic minor scale. The song also contains a rhythmic variant of motive A (the variant is marked as motive B in figure 6.16).

Figure 6.16: Motives in *The Oak and the Ash*.

6.7 Diatonic Melody Generator

The **Diatonic Melody Generator** (figure 6.17) generates diatonic melodies of up to thirty-five notes by combining repetitions of three-, four-, five-, or six-note motives which can be transposed, inverted, or retrograded. The number of notes in the motive is chosen in the top left portion of the screen (**Motive Length**), and the motive notes are input via the onscreen keyboard (**Motive Pitches**, a **kslider** object). The rhythmic values of the motive are selected on the top right side of the patcher (**Motive Rhythms**), and include values between sixteenth and whole notes. Melodies are constructed by adding pitch and rhythmic motives together. The length of the melody is set by the **Melody Length** dial and is optimally a multiple of the motive length.

The melodies always stay within the key and use one of the four main scale forms (major, natural, harmonic, or melodic minor) indicated by the **Key** and **Scale umenus**. With **Diatonic Melody Generator** we can explore the process of combining motives into larger musical phrases. In the lower right corner, we've also added some buttons to create motives and melodies with random processes—we'll discuss these in this chapter's Exercises.

As shown in figure 6.17, we've input a four-note motive that outlines a C major triad (C–E–C–G). This motive in C major is shown in the **message** marked **P** (for prime) as 0 2 0 4. We base these numbers on a kind of modified C major scale degrees system with 0 as the tonic pitch C. Starting on middle C as 0, the ascending numbers 0, 1, 2, 3, 4, 5, 6, 7 move up the C major scale from C4 to C5. The descending numbers go down the scale from C4 to C3 as 0, −1, −2, −3, −4, −5, −6, −7. The numbers continue in either direction (above 7 and below −7) to extend the melodic possibilities into the entire treble and bass clef registers. The 2 in our motive is a note *two scale steps* above C4 (that is, E4), and the 4 is *four scale steps* above C4 (or G4).

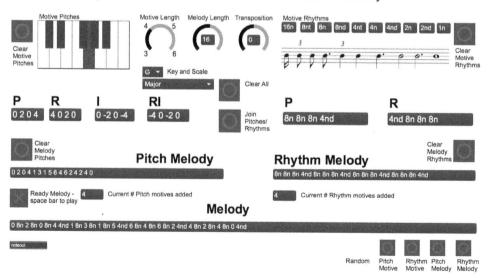

Figure 6.17: Diatonic Melody Generator **in Max.**

Three **messages** to the right of the prime show operations on the motive: **R**—the motive in retrograde; **I**—the motive inverted; and **RI**—the inverted motive in retrograde. To add one of these forms to the **Pitch Melody** (a list of the pitches to be included in the melody), click on the **message**. When we change the key with the **Key** and **Scale** drop-down menus, all the forms are transposed. If we change the key to D major or F minor, for instance, the forms are all transposed to the new key as shown in figure 6.18.

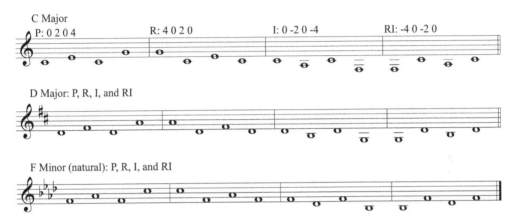

Figure 6.18: P, R, I, and RI forms of 0 2 0 4 in three keys.

The rhythmic motive can be played forwards (**P** for prime) or backwards (**R** for retrograde). For rhythmic motives that are the same backwards or forwards, like a musical palindrome, **P** and **R** will be identical. We click on a rhythm form to add it to the **Rhythm Melody** (a list of only the rhythms to be included in the melody).

Once we have the pitch and rhythm motives, we combine them. First, to hear just the motive, we set the **Melody Length** to be the same as **Motive Length** (in this case 4), then we click **Join Pitches/Rhythm**. Next, we toggle on the **Ready Melody** and press the space bar to hear the melody. We can also step through the notes by toggling off **Ready Melody** and pressing the space bar to play individual notes.

In the **Diatonic Melody Generator** shown in figure 6.17, we have it set to a sixteen-note melody (**Melody Length** = 16). The pitch motive is four notes, and we have added four forms to the melody: **P** at **0** transposition; **P** at **1** (transposed up one scale degree); **I** at **6** (the inversion transposed up six scale degrees); and **I** at **4** (inverted at the fourth scale degree). The rhythmic motive consists of three eighth notes and a dotted quarter note (8n–8n–8n–4nd)—equal to one measure in $^6_8$ time. Two prime forms of the rhythmic motives are in mm. 1–2, and two retrograde forms are in mm. 3–4. The following music shows the resulting melody (figure 6.19).

Figure 6.19: The melody produced by Diatonic Melody Generator in figure 6.17.

The repeated motive, transposed and inverted, creates a rising and falling melody and also outlines a chord sequence in C major: C major, D minor, E minor, and C major. We could also analyze the chord progression in Roman numerals: I–ii–iii–I.

For a second example, a six-note motive is repeated four times using the four forms of the melodic motive at different transpositions (**P** at **0**; **R** at **1**; **RI** at **3**; **I** at **4**) to create a twenty-four-note melody (figure 6.20). The rhythmic motive is repeated as **P, R, P, R**. The motive in prime form is C–E–G–F–E–G (0 2 4 3 2 4), and the rhythmic motive is a dotted quarter, eighth, dotted eighth, sixteenth, dotted eighth, and a sixteenth (4nd–8n–8nd–16n–8nd–16n). The rhythmic pattern fits into one measure of common time, and we can record the melody with this time signature. Chords were added to accompany the melody: C major, F major $^6_4$, G dominant $^4_3$, and C major. The melody shows how using recurring motives provides consistency and coherence.

Figure 6.20: Diatonic Melody Generator **playing P, R, RI, and I forms with accompaniment.**

6.8 Max Patcher 10: *Diatonic Melody Generator*

The patcher image of **Diatonic Melody Generator** (figure 6.21) identifies six parts, each with its own function: (1) create pitch motives; (2) create rhythm motives; (3) select pitch motives at various transpositions and forms (**P, R, I, RI**) to create the **Pitch Melody**; (4) select rhythm motives (**P** or **R**) to create the **Rhythm Melody**; (5) join the pitch and rhythm motives together to make the melody; (6) choose the key and modality (major scale or one of the minor scale forms), and play the melody. Each of these six parts of the patcher is demarcated by dotted lines (figure 6.21).

In the first area, pitches of the motives are selected. The settings in **kslider**'s **Inspector** have been modified so that the **kslider** outputs numbers from 0 to 12, with the low C key outputting 0. The **kslider** sends these numbers to the **p SortAndTranspose** subpatcher (figure 6.22), whose purpose is threefold: (1) change the pitches into scale degrees; (2) collect pitches according to the motive length; (3) transpose the scale degrees. The pitch-to-scale-degree operation is done by the **coll pitch2SD**. In the **coll pitch2SD**, all the numbers are mapped to a modified scale degree-system which starts with 0 as the first scale degree. (0 and 1 are mapped to scale degree 0—the tonic or first scale degree, 2 and 3 are mapped to scale degree 1, 4 is mapped to scale degree 2, etc.). Any note played on the keyboard automatically becomes a scale degree—much as Logic's **Transposer's Can't Go Wrong** setting will constrain all inputted notes to a given scale.

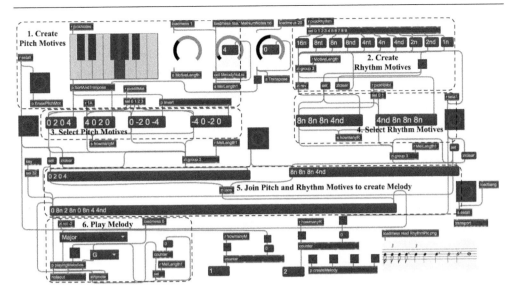

Figure 6.21: Diatonic Melody Generator **(patcher) in Max.**

The **zl.group 3** object then groups together scale degree numbers according to **Motive Length** number, which is received by **r MotiveLength**. The motive is now sorted by length through the **gate 4** object: three-note motives out gate 1; four-note motives out gate 2; five-note motives out gate 3; and six-note motives out gate 4. Each outlet from **gate 4** is connected to an **unjoin** object with the corresponding number of outlets for that length motive, and each **unjoin** object sends the pitches to **addition** objects (+) for transposition.

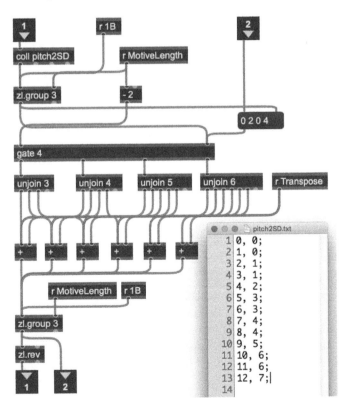

Figure 6.22. p SortAndTranspose **in Max.**

The transposition amount comes from the **Transposition Dial** via **r Transpose/s Transpose** pair. The transposition can either be ascending (positive numbers) or descending (negative numbers). It's worth reminding ourselves that we are transposing tonally by *scale degree* amounts, not semitones. After the transposition, the pitches are grouped again by length.

At this stage, the motives are in retrograde, because **zl.group** groups received elements from right to left, or in reverse order. To produce the prime form, we reverse the retrograde form with a **zl.rev** object. This prime form is sent to the **p invert** subpatcher to create inversions of the motive (figure 6.23), and both the prime and retrograde forms are sent to their respective **messages**, marked **P** and **R** in the patcher.

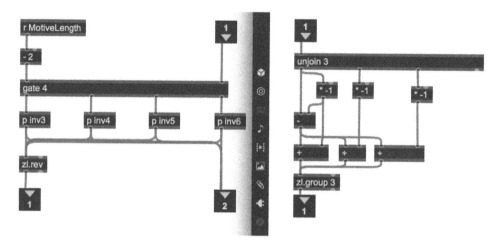

Figure 6.23: The p invert **(left) and** p inv3 **(right) subpatchers (**p inv 3 **is a subpatcher within a subpatcher) in Max.**

In the **p invert** subpatcher, the motives are again sorted by length and sent to one of the four subpatchers (**p inv3, p inv3, p inv5, p inv6**), each of which inverts the motive around the first note. To create the inversion, the following operations are performed on the scale degree numbers: (1) multiplication by −1, (2) subtraction of this product from the axis number, then (3) summing the product and subtraction. The inverted motives are sent out to a **zl.rev** object and then out outlet 1 for the **I** form, and out outlet 2 for the **RI** form.

We now have the four forms of the pitch motive which can be added to the melody in any order and at any scale degree transposition. As we click on the pitch motives in the **Select Pitch Motives** part of the patcher (4), they are added to the **Pitch Melody**. The number of items in the **Pitch Melody** box is controlled by the **Melody Length** dial, which sends a message to a **zl.group** object to group incoming pitch motives. The melody is complete when the correct amount of scale degree numbers are collected, and then these scale degree numbers appear in the **Pitch Melody** box.

To create the rhythmic motives, we select note values to be grouped together in the part of the patcher labeled (2). The motive length is again set in **zl.group 3**, and we use **zl.rev** to reverse the prime form. The rhythmic motives are sent to two messages for the prime and retrograde forms. Just as we added pitch motives to the **Pitch Melody**, we click on **P** or **R** rhythmic motives to add them to the **Rhythm Melody** in the **Select Rhythm Motives** part of the patcher (4). The number of items is again controlled by the **Melody Length dial** via a **zl.group** object.

The pitch and rhythm melodies are held in the two message boxes labeled **Melody Pitches** and **Melody Rhythms** (5). Clicking the **Join Pitches/Rhythms button** connected to these messages causes the **zl.lace** object to interleave both lists—alternately taking elements from the two lists to create a single list with both elements. The interleaved list sent from **zl.lace** is sent to the **Melody message**, and we have our melody!

The next stage is to play the melody, which happens in part (6). The output of the **Melody message** (with scale degree numbers and rhythm symbols) is sent to both the **p playingMelodies** subpatcher (figure 6.24) and a **zl.rot -2** object. The **zl.rot -2** object rotates the contents of the list, in this case taking the first two elements and placing them at the end to continuously loop the melody.

The **p playingMelodies** subpatcher first slices off two elements from the list (note number and rhythm) with **zl.slice 2**. These pairs are separated by an **unpack** object. Notice that because the rhythms are alphanumeric symbols, we specify the arguments of **unpack** as **0** (for numbers) and **sym** (for symbols). The rhythmic values are sent to the **makenote** object to control the duration of the notes, and scale degree numbers are sent to the **coll** objects to be converted into pitch numbers (MIDI note numbers).

Because **coll** object index numbers must be positive, the scale degrees numbers are shifted into a positive range by adding twenty-seven with the **addition** object (**+ 27**). The numbers are then sent to one of four **coll** objects (one **coll** object for each scale form) via a **gate 4** object. Each **coll** stores a scale-degree-to-MIDI-note-number mapping with different scale forms (major and three minor scale forms). Which **gate 4** outlet sends out the incoming pitch numbers is controlled by the **Scale umenu**.

Next to the **p playingMelodies** subpatcher, we see a portion of the **coll majorscale** contents on the right side (figure 6.24). The lowest MIDI note is a 14 (D0), three octaves below middle C, and the highest note is 108 (C8). Before getting to the **makenote 60 4n** object, we can add or subtract values to or from the MIDI note numbers to create key transpositions. We get the values for these key transpositions from the **Key umenu**. Our **Key umenu** goes from G to F# as 0 to 11. As C is the fifth element of the **umenu**, we subtract five from the **umenu** output before sending it on. For the key of C, we are thus adding zero to keep the MIDI notes as they are. But for other keys, we add or subtract semitone amounts to every note, from −5 for G to +6 for F#. After this, the MIDI note numbers are sent to **makenote**'s left inlet as the alphanumeric rhythmic values are sent to the right inlet to create durations.

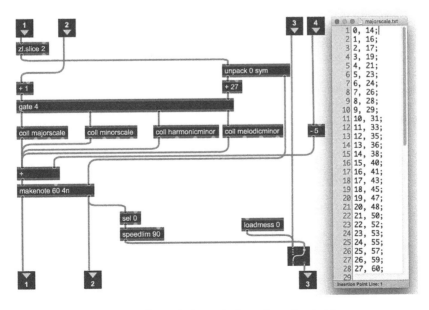

Figure 6.24: The p playingMelodies subpatcher in Max.

In order to have the melody play in rhythm, we use MIDI's note-on endings to trigger new notes. When a note ends, **makenote** sends out the note number and a velocity of 0 (this MIDI message—a note number with 0 velocity—is used to turn notes off). This 0 note velocity is sent to a **sel 0** object which then sends out a bang (with an added **speedlim** object to ensure that the bangs don't transmit too quickly). This bang is sent out outlet 3 to the **Melody message** to trigger another note.

The **counter** object in the **Play Melody** (6) part of the patcher counts the notes that have been played in the melody. When the melody note count reaches the **Melody Length** number, the **sel** object bangs (it is set at this **Melody Length** number), and this toggles off **Ready Melody**, which in turn disconnects the retriggering of notes described previously.

The patcher also has a number of **set messages** which clear the motives or melody in their respective **messages**. When clearing these **messages**, we also initialize the **zl.group** objects with **zl.clear messages** so that all stored elements are erased and their lengths are reset. The five **Clear** buttons (figure 6.17) can be applied to any specific pitch or rhythm motives, pitch or rhythm melodies, or all of these. In that way, one can redo various elements while leaving other elements as they are.

The patcher has an image (using a **fpic** object) showing the notation for possible rhythmic values. There are also two **counter** objects which report how many pitch or rhythm motives have been added to the **Pitch Melody** and **Rhythm Melody** so that we can keep track as we add motives. These two **counter** objects send their values to **Current # Pitch motives added** and **Current # Rhythm motives added**.

6.9 Exercises

As a music theory exercise, creating melodies from motives provides insight into how music is constructed. We can hear motivic development in many melodies, but we also know that composing melodies involves other aspects besides motivic development. In fact, composing melodies is so elusive that many music theory texts hardly mention it at all, and focus instead on harmony and form. Nevertheless, melody construction based on motives provides good opportunities to develop our understanding of many music theory topics, including scales, arpeggiated chords, transposition, and melodic transformations.

6.9.1 Exercise 1: Create a 4-Measure Melody using Finale or Logic

Pick any major or minor key and consider the scale associated with that key. First, compose a one-measure motive in that key. Copy and paste the measure three times so that you have four measures. Using the tools mentioned in this chapter, vary the motive by transposition, inversion, and/or retrograde, or combinations of those. To keep the motive in the key, **Scale Quantize** measures after certain operations as needed in Logic, or use the diatonic settings for operations in Finale. Consider the shape of the melody and whether it has forward momentum.

In the following example (figure 6.25), the first measure was diatonically transposed up a fourth to create the second measure. The first measure was diatonically transposed up a third and retrograded to create the third measure, and the first measure retrograded to create the fourth and final measure.

Figure 6.25: A four-measure melody based on a one-measure motive.

In Logic, use **MIDI Transform**:

1. To transpose measures, use **Transposition** (then quantize afterwards).
2. To retrograde measures, use **Reverse Position** (set **Position** to the measure itself).
3. To invert measures, use **Reverse Pitch** and set **Flip** to first pitch (then scale quantize).

In Finale, use **Transposition** and **Canonic Utilities**:

1. To transpose measures, use **Transposition** (from **Utilities**); choose **Diatonically**.
2. To retrograde measures, use **Canonic Utilities** (from **Plug-ins**) and choose **Retrograde**.
3. To invert measures, use **Canonic Utilities** (from **Plug-ins**) and choose **Diatonic Mirror Inversion**. Open **Mirror Inversion Options** and select the starting pitch of measure as **Pivot Note** to invert around that note.
4. **Canonic Utilities** also has a transposition function, but separating this task by using the **Transposition** tool may be helpful.

The possibilities to expand this exercise include: (1) create larger melodies with larger motives; (2) use multiple motives, and/or by connecting motives with other material; (3) include rhythm augmentation and diminution; (4) use partial motives in various ways, or add partial motives together.

6.9.2 Exercise 2: Create Melodies with Diatonic Melody Generator

We can use **Diatonic Melody Generator** to create melodies and send the output to Logic or Finale (with the **from Max 1** setting of **noteout**) to see the notation. In creating melodies with motives we will use different forms and their transpositions. If we repeat a motive multiple times and transpose each one up a step, for instance, we can create a melodic sequence. If we start with a rhythmic motive such as eighth–eighth–quarter–quarter, then switch to sixteenth–sixteenth–eighth–eighth, we have created rhythmic diminution. We can experiment with these creative processes, and we can also recreate known melodies.

Following are the steps to create two motivic melodies from (1) Ludwig van Beethoven, and (2) Stevie Wonder.

(1) Beethoven melody:

1. Press **Clear All** to start.
2. Set **Motive Length** to 3 and **Melody Length** to 24.
3. Enter C–D–C to create a 0 1 0 pitch motive, and select these motive forms in order to create the **Pitch Melody**: P +2, P +4, P 0, P +2, P −2, P 0, P +1, P +2, P +3.
4. Enter 8n–16n–16n for a rhythm motive; add 8 of them to the **Rhythm Melody**.
5. Press **Join Pitches/Rhythms**, set **Key and Scale** to G major.
6. Toggle **Ready Melody** on, and press space bar to hear the melody.
7. Compare to the opening of Beethoven's Sonatine, Op 79, iii. Vivace, for piano.

(2) Wonder melody:

1. Press **Clear All** to start.
2. Set **Motive Length** to 5 and **Melody Length** to 15.
3. Enter C–D–E–D–C to create a 0 1 2 1 0 pitch motive, and these motive forms to create the **Pitch Melody**: P +4, P +2, P 0.
4. Enter 8n–8n–8n–4n–4nd as the rhythmic motive, add 3 of them to the **Rhythm Melody**.
5. Press **Join Pitches/Rhythms**, set **Key and Scale** to E major.
6. Toggle **Ready Melody** on, and press space bar to hear the melody.
7. Compare to the opening of Stevie Wonder's *Joy Inside My Tears*.

6.9.3 Exercise 3: Create Melodies Algorithmically with Diatonic Melody Generator

As we saw with **Rhythm Generator**, we can apply algorithmic techniques in studying aspects of music theory. Along the same lines, the **Diatonic Melody Generator** has a set of **Random** buttons that automatically generate motives and melodies. In figure 6.26, the four **buttons** added to the patcher's lower right corner for algorithmically creating pitch motives, rhythm motives, pitch melodies, or rhythm melodies are circled. To add a new randomly generated component, click on one or more of the buttons and follow the steps outlined in the chapter to create melodies.

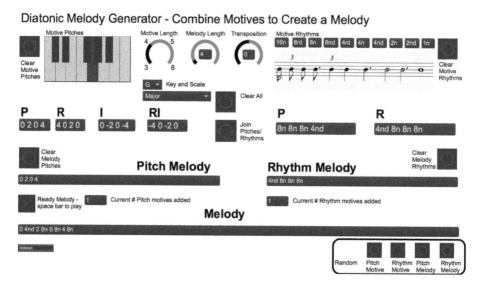

Figure 6.26: Diatonic Melody Generator: Random Pitch Motive, Rhythm Motive, Pitch Melody **and** Rhythm Melody **in Max.**

The randomness of the material will usually be obvious and lead to unconvincing results. In listening to these melodies, we have further proof that creating good melodies from motives requires inspiration and internal logic—something missing from random processes. On the other hand, it's easy to keep generating material until we hear something that sounds as if it might work, and every so often we will come across an interesting motive or melody. We can use critical listening skills to decide what might make the algorithmic output sound better, and (for those who want to explore algorithmic concepts farther) we could program more specific decision-making, rather than relying on the **random** object alone.

To create this algorithmic expansion, we created **p createMelody** (viewable in patcher mode) with four **buttons** (viewable in presentation mode) (figure 6.27).

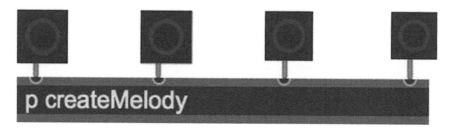

Figure 6.27: p createMelody **and** buttons **in Max.**

The **p createMelody** subpatcher connects to four areas of the main patcher via **send** and **receive** objects, and we see the four **send** objects at the bottom of the **p createMelody** subpatcher (figure 6.28). These four **send** objects are: (1) **s pickNotes**—to pick notes for the motive; (2) **s pickRhythm**—to pick rhythms for the motive, (3) **s pickMMot**—to pick pitch-motive forms for the melody, and (4) **s pickRMot**—to pick rhythm forms for the melody.

When the **Random – Pitch Motives button** is pressed, the **uzi** object rapidly bangs out a number of bangs determined by its argument, as set by **r MotiveLength.** These bangs trigger a **random 13** object to send out values between 0 and 12, and these values are collected by a **zl.group 3** object whose argument is also set by **r MotiveLength.**

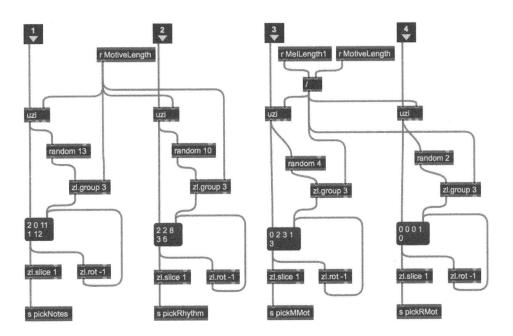

Figure 6.28: p createMelody **subpatcher in Max.**

The resultant list is sliced and rotated by **zl.slice 1** and **zl.rot -1**, and list items are sent out one at a time. The same process is replicated for the other algorithmically determined parameters. For the melody components, the number of motives to be created (the values used by the **uzi** and **zl.group** objects) is determined by the melody length divided by the motive length. This is the number of motive forms that make up the melody.

The **send** objects are sent to four **receive** objects in the main patcher (viewable in patcher mode), as shown in figure 6.29, to select pitches, rhythms, melodic forms, or rhythmic forms.

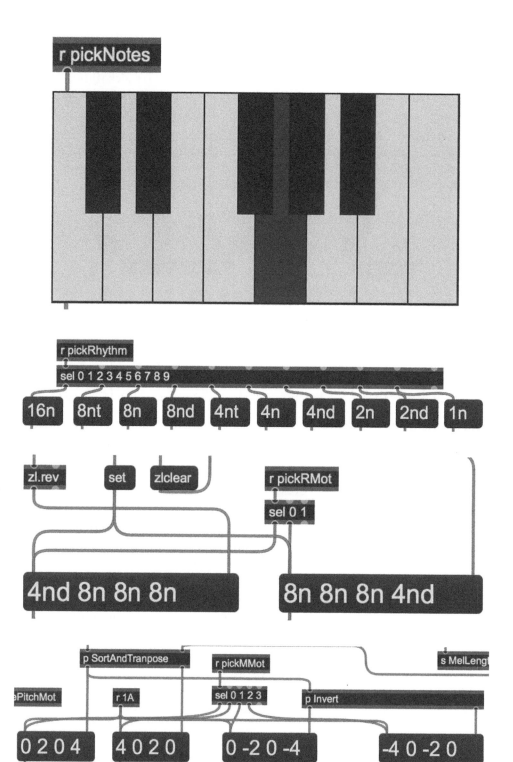

Figure 6.29: Four receive **objects** (r pickNotes, r pickRhythm, r pickRMot, r pickMMot) **from** p createMelodies **subpatcher in Max.**

CHAPTER 7

Harmonic Progressions

7.1 Chord Trigger *and Progressions*

When we play song accompaniments using **Chord Trigger** (see Chapter 4's Exercise 3), we should hear that the succession of chords makes sense—chord progressions actually do *progress* from one chord to the next. We've probably been hearing progressions like these for our whole lives, and we've learned their logic intuitively by ear. But what makes a good chord progression? And what creates this progression—this sense of motion—from one chord to the next? We'll approach this question by considering how to build chord progressions one chord at a time—starting with single-chord harmonies. Our starting point, however, is how melody fits together with harmony.

7.2 Single-Chord Harmony, Non-Chord Tones

A single-chord harmonic accompaniment heard throughout a piece of music is a harmonic **drone**. Drone accompaniments have existed throughout music history and are found in many musical cultures, although they aren't the usual harmonic practice in western classical and modern forms. Examples of single-chord accompaniments (harmonic drones) include Aretha Franklin's *Chain of Fools* (based on a C minor chord throughout, and composed by Don Covay) and Bob Dylan's *Ballad of Hollis Brown* (based on an E minor chord throughout). As an example in classical music, the piano part of Franz Schubert's song *The Hurdy-Gurdy Man* consists of a B minor drone as it imitates the droning hurdy-gurdy instrument.

When we listen to a sustained D minor triad played with an ascending chromatic scale or D melodic minor scale, as shown in figure 7.1, we hear that the notes that are in both the triad and the scales (the chord tones) sound more consonant. The notes that are not part of the chord are **non-chord tones**, and these are dissonant (see page 46) to varying degrees. In the following music, the non-chord tones from chromatic and D melodic minor scales are shown in parentheses. In the top line, we see that some notes (those with the arrows pointing forward) are **resolving** to chord tones. These notes are **tendency tones**. The effect of these tendency tones resolving can be described as a release of tension, or resolving dissonance.

Figure 7.1: Non-chord tones in chromatic and melodic minor scales with D minor triad.

Figure 7.1: Continued

Listening to each of the two scales separately along with the D minor triad, we hear how the varying degrees of dissonance (clashing quality) of the non-chord tones and the resolutions of the **tendency tones** create a melodic quality.

When a melody has a non-chord tone between two chord tones, the note is called a **passing tone**.

Other named non-chord tones include **neighbor tones**, which move by step above or below a chord tone, then return to the same chord tone, and **incomplete neighbor tones**, which move by step to or from a chord tone (figure 7.2). **Chromatic non-chord tones** (such as the E♭ **chromatic neighbor tone** in the following music) are non-chord tones which are also outside of the key.

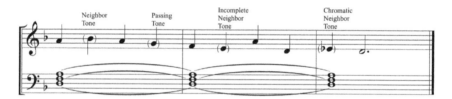

Figure 7.2: Non-chord tone names.

Non-chord tones are heard in all kinds of music, but how they are used depends on the musical style. In some kinds of music, specific rules govern their use. Music with a drone harmony demonstrates how non-chord tones themselves can create tension and interest. In the Aretha Franklin and Bob Dylan songs mentioned previously, the non-chord tones create a kind of tension when heard against the drone harmony, a tension which is released as the non-chord tones move to chord tones.

We can hear these non-chord tones, the passing and neighbor tones, in the familiar round *Frère Jacques*. These are noted in the following example with **P** (passing) and **N** (neighbor) above the notes (figure 7.3). The climactic fifth and sixth measures have more non-chord tones than other measures, creating melodic tension before the peaceful chord tones in the last two measures. While the song doesn't need or usually have an accompaniment such as guitar or piano, it is another example of a drone harmony, because when it is sung as a round we hear only an F major triad.

The F major chord is the **tonic** chord, and the non-chord tones resolve to the tonic's chord tones. We can also say that the F major chord has a **tonic function**—its root (F) is the basis for the scale, and the final tonic chord and note provide a sense of closure at the end.

Figure 7.3: Non-chord tones in *Frère Jacques*.

7.3 Two-Chord Harmonic Progressions, Chord Functions

Harmonic progressions become possible when we have more than one chord, and we'll start with the most fundamental two-chord harmonic progression, that using (I) tonic and (V) dominant chords. The interval between the roots of the chords can be either a perfect fifth (I → V ascending) or perfect fourth (I → V descending), the **root motion** of a I–V progression. The I–V progression sounds familiar and works well as the harmonic accompaniment for some traditional songs, such as *Oats, Peas, Beans, and Barley Grow* (figure 7.4). The tonic (I) is C and the dominant (V) is G. The chords' root tones are in the bass line.

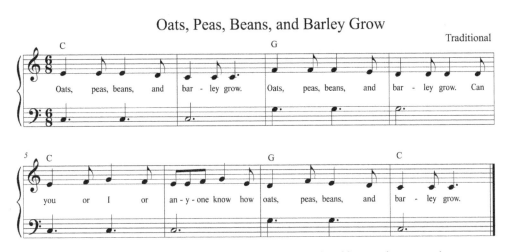

Figure 7.4: *Oats, Peas, Beans, and Barley Grow*: two-chord harmonic progression.

Playing the bass line with a Logic **Chord Trigger** (in the **Multi/Parallel Chords/Triads** setting) creates C and G major triads as accompaniment. We hear the sense of home key in the tonic C, and the sense of tension with the dominant chord G. If, as an experiment, we keep playing the G dominant chord in the last measure, we'll notice something interesting. The C in the last measure of the melody will be an unresolved non-chord tone, and it will be a strange way to end the song. If we replace the last C in the melody with a G major chord tone, such as B3, it will be a chord tone, but it will still sound a bit strange—as if something is left hanging and still in need of resolution. Our musical intuition tells us that the G chord needs to resolve back to C based on the **function** of these two chords. The G dominant chord's function is to lead us back to the tonic chord C.

The three diatonic functions are: **tonic**, **dominant preparation** or **subdominant**, and **dominant**. These functions help us explain how chords work together in progressions. The tonic-function chord is the resting chord or tonal home. At a song's beginning the tonic is established, and when we hear it at the end, we are satisfied that the song is complete. The dominant function chord works well after the tonic chord, but when we hear the dominant chord our expectation is that more chords will follow, including an eventual return to the tonic. The dominant-preparation function chord leads us away from the tonic and to the dominant.

The following chart shows the harmonic functions of each chord in the diatonic collection (figure 7.5), and what the usual movements between the chords are in much of tonal music. For some forms of modern music, we could also include an arrow leading from the dominant function back to the dominant preparation. The last three chords in a standard twelve-bar blues form, for instance, proceed from V–IV–I. The tonic chord is usually the final chord in any harmonic progression. The mediant and submediant chords are in the dominant-preparation column, but they can also have other functions as well.

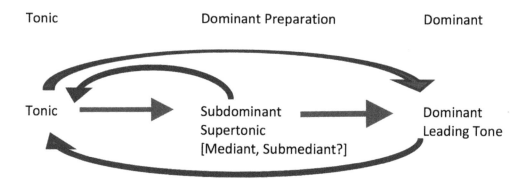

Figure 7.5: Harmonic function in major keys.

In *Oats, Peas, Beans, and Barley Grow*, C major has a tonic function and G major has a dominant function. We could, however, replace the G major triad—the dominant—with the B diminished triad—the vii° leading tone chord. This **chord substitution** doesn't necessarily work in every context, but it does work here, as the diminished triad can have a dominant function. Chord substitutions can be used to create variation in harmonic progressions. Exchanging the leading-tone chord for the dominant chord is one example, but we can also exchange the submediant chord for the tonic in some cases, or the subdominant for the dominant in others.

7.4 Cadences

The final two chords in *Oats, Peas, Beans, and Barley Grow* together with the melody's ending note create the sense of finality. The move from dominant to tonic function is a **cadence**—the end of the musical **phrase** (a completed musical thought). Cadences can be purely melodic, but they often include harmonic progressions. A final cadence sometimes also includes a slowing down of the tempo—a ritardando. The final cadence in this song is a **perfect authentic cadence**—authentic because it ends on the tonic, and perfect because (1) the melody ends on the tonic tone and (2) the final two chords are in root position. Examples of five common cadence types (perfect authentic, imperfect authentic, half, plagal, and deceptive) are shown in figure 7.6.

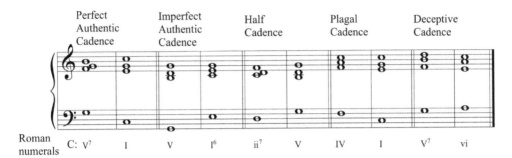

Figure 7.6: Cadence types.

We can create versions of these five cadence types with **Chord Trigger's Multi Parallel Songwriter Right Hand** setting. The following example shows the trigger notes in the first track. This track has the **Chord Trigger MIDI FX**, and its output is being sent to track 2 (figure 7.7). In the next example, we changed track 2 to a piano track in the **Score Region Inspector**, and we took notes out of the treble clef and added notes in the bass clef. These changes were done to create a balanced four-part texture with connections between the chords (figure 7.8).

Figure 7.7: Chord Trigger **cadences in Logic.**

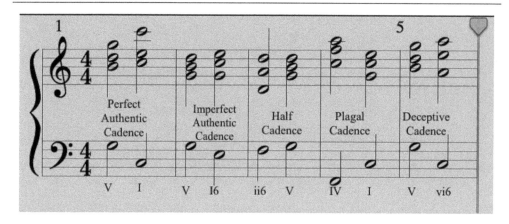

Figure 7.8: Modified Chord Trigger cadences.

The accompaniment for *Oats, Peas, Beans, and Barley Grow* uses the tonic and dominant chords and ends with a perfect authentic cadence. If we experiment again with the harmony and play an A in the accompaniment in the last measure, **Chord Trigger** with **Multi/Parallel Chords/Triads** will play an A minor triad at the end, creating a **deceptive cadence** of V → vi. But once again, the sense of completion will be lacking. We'll discuss the other cadence types (**Imperfect Authentic Cadence, Plagal Cadence,** and **Half Cadence**) in the pages ahead.

7.5 Creating a Three-Part Progression in Finale

With Finale's **Transposition** tool, we can create a standard C major diatonic progression with all seven chords of the diatonic collection. The progression's bass line alternates descending fifths and ascending fourths—known as a **descending fifths diatonic progression**. First, we create eight measures in C major with a $^2_4$ time signature in the grand staff and place a C major triad in the first measure. Selecting the measure, we copy and paste this into the next measure.

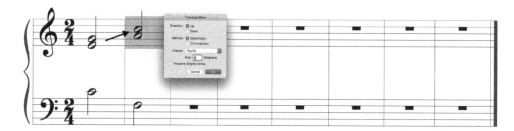

Figure 7.9: First steps for progression with all the diatonic triads in Finale.

Next, select the bass note of m. 2 only, and from **Utilities**, select **Transposition** and **Down/Diatonically/Fifth**, and press **OK**. Select the treble clef notes in m. 2 and this time select **Up/Diatonically/Fourth**, and press **OK**. The results are in the first two measures in figure 7.9. We then copy both staves of mm. 1–2 into mm. 3–4, and transpose mm. 3–4 down diatonically by a second in figure 7.10. Next we take all of mm. 1–4, copy and paste them into mm. 5–8, and transpose them down diatonically by a third. In m. 8, we come back to C major, and we have a progression that includes all seven diatonic triads in C major (figure 7.11).

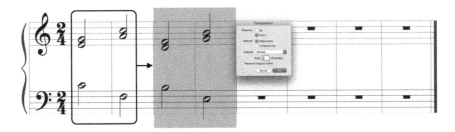

Figure 7.10: Using the Transposition **tool to create a diatonic progression in Finale.**

C: I   IV   vii°   iii   vi   ii   V   I

Figure 7.11: Descending fifths progression in C major.

In this progression, we'll hear a familiar-sounding descending fifth/ascending fourth bass line. By keeping the **Transposition** tool set to **Diatonically**, we made sure that all the triads were diatonic (in C major). The **Key Signature** tool will change the key signature *and* transpose the progression to any of the twelve major and minor keys (using natural minor scale). As an example, figure 7.12 is the progression transposed down to B♭ major.

Bb: I   IV   vii   iii   vi   ii   V   I

Figure 7.12: Transposing the progression with the Key Signature **tool in Finale.**

Within this progression we can find two common examples of a tonic → dominant preparation → dominant → tonic progression. If we omit mm. 3–6 of figure 7.11, we'll hear the I–IV–V–I pattern, as in the first four measures in figure 7.13, and if we omit mm. 2–5, we'll hear the I–ii–V–I pattern (figure 7.13). Many examples of I–IV–V–I exist, including Joni Mitchell's *The Circle Game* and Norman Meade's *Time is on My Side* (made famous by the Rolling Stones). The I–ii–V–I is also common and can be heard in many popular songs, including Irving Berlin's *Anything You Can Do.*

Figure 7.13: Two four-chord progressions.

This chapter's exercises include more Logic **Chord Trigger** examples, as well as exercises based on the circle-of-fifths progression mentioned previously. To explore how to arrange the chords in a progression by alternating positions and voicings, we can also use the **Diatonic Progression Generator**, explained in the next section.

7.6 Diatonic Progression Generator

The **Diatonic Progression Generator** (figure 7.14) is an eight-step chord sequencer for creating harmonic progressions using chords derived from major or minor scales. With the **Diatonic Progression Generator**, we can control the following chord parameters: octave, Roman numeral, position (root, first, second, or third inversion), voicing, and rhythmic value. We can change the key or mode (major or minor) and store two progressions.

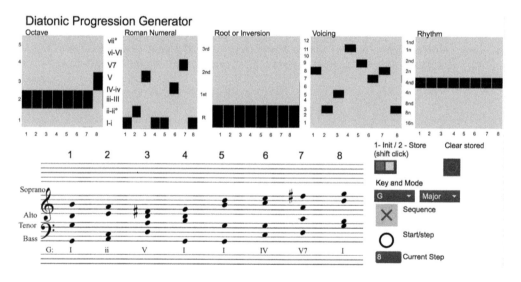

Figure 7.14: Diatonic Progression Generator **playing two common patterns in Max.**

The five tables across the top of the screen display the parameters for each chord at each of the eight steps. These parameters can be changed by clicking in the table to shift the points (the black box shapes that represent values), or by dragging a point up or down. The leftmost **Octave** table allows the user to select an octave position for each chord. With two selected, for instance, the root of a G chord will be G2, in the chords 1, 4, and 5 in the **Diatonic Progression Generator** as shown in figure 7.14. From the **Roman Numeral** table we choose which of the seven chords in the diatonic collection we wish to hear (V and V⁷ are both dominant chords). The Roman numerals in major keys are: I–ii–iii–IV–V or V⁷–vi–vii°, and in minor keys are: i–ii°–III–iv–V or V⁷–VI–vii°. The minor-key chords are based on the harmonic minor scale, with the exception of the mediant (III) chord which has the lowered seventh scale degree. For C minor, the lowered seventh scale degree is B♭, heard in the mediant chord (E♭ major). The **Root or Inversion** table allows the user to select between root (R), first and second inversions (1st and 2nd), and the third inversion (3rd) for the V⁷ chord. The **Voicing** table allows the user to select from among twelve voicings for each chord—that is, the octave positions of the three upper notes. The bass note may be any of the chord tones, depending on the setting of the **Position** table. The **Rhythm** table controls the rhythms of the chords, and we can choose between nine rhythmic values (16n, 8n, 8nd, etc.) listed at the table's left side. With the **Rhythm** table we can try out how the progressions sound with different rhythms.

The notation area displays the chords. The display's limitations are that: (1) rhythm values and key signatures are not shown; (2) each progression has either sharps or flats but not both; and (3) chord tones are not always exactly aligned. We can avoid these limitations by sending the progression to Logic or Finale with the **noteout** object set to **from Max 1** and displaying the notation in either of those programs with the key selected.

The **Key and Mode** drop-down menu is where we select the key in its major or minor form. The transport controls are on the lower right side (**Sequence, Start/step, Current Step**). When the **Sequence** is toggled on, the **Start/step** button will play the sequence with the selected rhythms. If **Sequence** is toggled off, **Start/step** will step through the progression (without the rhythm). Clicking on **Current Step** plays the currently selected chord.

To help us understand harmonic progression principles, we add Roman numerals and the key to all the examples of **Diatonic Progression Generator**, including figure 7.14.

7.7 Voice Leading

Progressions are often written in the standard **four parts**, but three, five, or even two part progressions are also possible. As triads have only three pitches, triads in four-part progressions **double** a chord tone. The most common doubled note is the root of the triad, but other chord tones can be doubled. The **Diatonic Progression Generator** doubles the root of triads except for the leading tone chord, where the third is doubled. Doubling the root works well in many situations, but we should be aware that other triad tones besides the root can (and sometimes should) be doubled. The V⁷ chord is the only seventh chord available and always has the four chord tones.

Part of our focus with the **Diatonic Progression Generator** will be **voice leading**—writing the four parts to create a balanced and classical sound. We can think of voice leading as how the separate tones in chords follow one another through a progression to create four independent musical lines. We might want sometimes to tweak the progressions in Logic and Finale, but **Diatonic Progression Generator** is a good place to start as it allows us to hear different versions of progressions easily.

Traditional four-part writing with good voice leading is designed to create music with consistent harmonic richness, where each chord sounds connected to the next. Good voice leading avoids chords jumping around by large intervals, sounding clunky, or having a thin texture. To create good voice leading, we think of the music being comprised not only of chords (vertically constructed) but also of four simultaneous melodic lines (horizontally constructed). In other words, we listen to how the musical lines work together. In four-part harmonic progressions, the four lines (or **voices**) are **soprano**, **alto**, **tenor**, and **bass**, in that order from highest to lowest. These voice names (which are also the singing parts of a mixed chorus) are shown in the previous progression (figure 7.14), and in four-part harmony exercises we use these names for the musical lines even if we're not creating music for a chorus.

To examine the individual linear aspects of a harmonic progression, we identify the **motion** created between any two voices as they move forward from one chord to the next. Motion exists between each possible pair of voices. When one four-part chord moves to another, there are six motions to consider: soprano/alto, soprano/tenor, soprano/bass, alto/tenor, alto/bass, and tenor/bass, as shown in figure 7.15.

Figure 7.15: Four-part progressions (as seen in m. 1) have six motions between voices.

There are five possible motion types: (1) **static**—neither voice moves melodically; (2) **oblique**—one voice moves (up or down) while the other voice remains stationary; (3) **parallel**—both voices move in the same direction with the same intervals; (4) **similar**—both voices move in the same direction but with different intervals; (5) **contrary**—both voices move in opposite directions (figure 7.16). The voice-leading motions in figure 7.15 are contrary except for those between the soprano and bass and between the alto and tenor, both of which are similar. Good voice leading avoids certain types of motion. The first voice-leading rule is: (1) avoid parallel motion of perfect intervals of fifths and octaves.

Types of motion between voices

Figure 7.16: Voice-leading motion types.

We can also demonstrate what the music looks and sounds like when we ignore the rule to avoid parallel motion of perfect intervals by taking the progression shown in figure 7.14 and set all the chords' voicings to seven in the **Voicing itable** (figure 7.17). The alto and the bass voices move in parallel octaves, and the tenor and bass have many parallel fifths. These parallel intervals are shown with the lines connecting the notes of the first four chords. The rule against parallel intervals does not apply to thirds or sixths. In fact parallel thirds or sixths are desirable in many contexts.

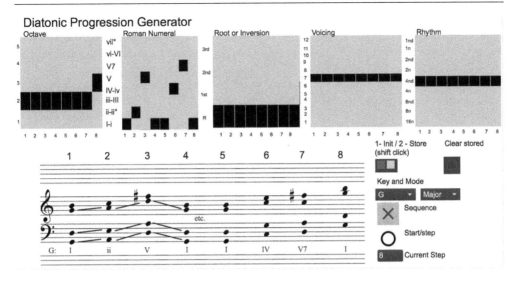

Figure 7.17: Parallel perfect intervals in Max.

A second rule is: (2) keep the voices separated (with minimal overlap), with more space between the lower voices than between the higher voices. A third rule relates to dominant seventh chords: (3) the dominant seventh's tendency tones resolve by step. When the seventh scale degree (or **leading tone**—the third of the dominant seventh) appears in the soprano or bass, it resolves upwards to the tonic. The **seventh** of a dominant seventh always resolves down to the third of the tonic chord in a V⁷–I or i context.

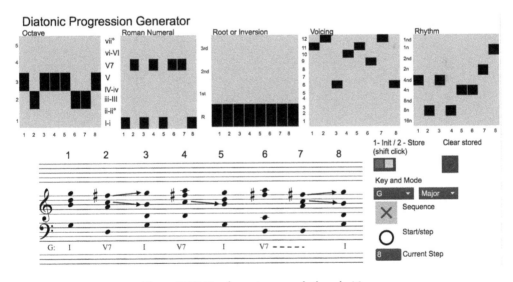

Figure 7.18: Tendency tone resolutions in Max.

The progression in figure 7.18 is based on the I–V⁷ chord progression. To clarify, lines showing how the seventh-chord tendency tones resolve are added. When the leading tone (F#) is in the soprano, it resolves up to the G, and the sevenths (C) of the V⁷ chord always resolve down to the third of the I chord (B). The seventh of chord 6 doesn't have to resolve because the chord is repeated, and chords 7 → 8 resolve correctly. In other words, the resolution of seventh-chord tendency tones can be delayed if the chord is repeated.

How one hears and reacts to voice-leading rules is *subjective*. In many contemporary musical styles, these voice-leading rules are not followed. For instance, metal music's **power chords** (the root and fifth only, without the third) are often played in parallel motion, creating parallel perfect intervals and parallel motion between perfect intervals. In fact, parallel perfect intervals sound fine in many situations. In the context of the kind of voice leading we're describing here, however, the rule against parallel perfect intervals helps ensure that the four-part texture remains consistent, and that one always hears four *independent* voices. In short, it creates a traditional style of harmony.

One reason to study traditional voice leading is that it helps us develop an understanding of harmony's linear aspects. And to be clear, the three voice-leading rules mentioned are only a beginning—we are taking an introductory approach here.

7.8 Inverted Chords

Inverted chords in progressions also follow voice-leading rules. The I–V[7] progression seen in figure 7.19 has all four positions of the dominant seventh chord. Chord 2 is in first inversion (V^6_5); chord 4 is in second inversion (V^4_3); chord 6 is in root position (V^7); and chord 7 is in third inversion (V^4_2).

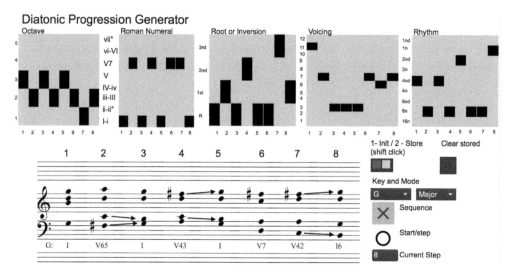

Figure 7.19: I–V[7] progression with inversions in Max.

In each case where the dominant seventh chord resolves to a tonic chord, the tendency tones are resolved by step (as shown with the arrows). The seventh goes down to the third, and the leading tone goes up to the tonic when in an outer voice. A first-inversion dominant seventh (V^6_5) resolves to a root-position tonic chord, so that the leading tone in the bass can resolve up to the tonic. A third-inversion dominant seventh (V^4_2) resolves to a first-inversion tonic chord (an imperfect authentic cadence), so that the seventh can resolve down to the third of the tonic.

7.9 Common Tones

Next, we'll explore progressions using the tonic and other chords that share chord tones with the tonic. If two chords share the same pitch, these pitches are **common tones**.

Keeping common tones at the same pitch level when progressing from one chord to another creates desirable smoothness. The mediant (iii) and submediant (vi) chords share two common tones with the tonic chord in the major keys, and the subdominant (IV) and dominant (V) chords share one chord with the tonic chord. In the previous progression (figure 7.19), the common tone Ds are kept in place between the tonic and dominant in chords 1 → 5 and 7 → 8.

In the following example, in F major, we hear the tonic alternate with the mediant, submediant, and subdominant chords, keeping common tones where possible (figure 7.20). The harmonic motion of IV to I, heard in chords 6 → 8, is an example of a plagal cadence.

The plagal cadence is often referred to as the "Amen" cadence, as it is heard at the end of many traditional religious musical works. Ideally, the following example should align all the chords tones in chords 4 and 7.

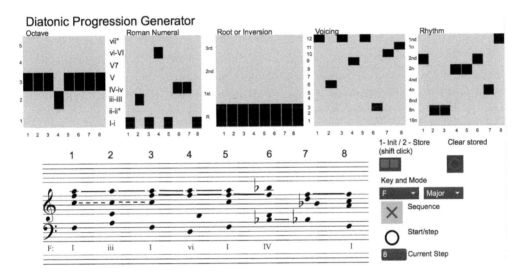

Figure 7.20: Common-tone progression in Max.

Common-tone progressions are heard in many musical contexts. John Lennon and Paul McCartney's *Eleanor Rigby* alternates E minor (tonic) with C major (submediant) throughout, where E and G are common tones. Similarly, both Jimmy Page and Robert Plant's *Ramble On* and Bob Marley's *Running Away* alternate tonic and subdominant chords. *Ramble On*'s chords are E and A major (E is the common tone), and *Running Away*'s chords are G and D minor (D is the common tone).

7.10 Descending-Fifths Progressions

The root motion of a descending fifth, which we can hear with a V–I progression, is a strong harmonic progression. As we learned earlier in this chapter, this falling-fifth root motion can be used to progress through all the diatonic chords in a major key collection: I–IV–vii°–iii–vi–ii–V–I. We hear the falling fifth or ascending fourth throughout the next example (figure 7.21). These are perfect fourths and fifths, except for the ascending *augmented* fourth from the subdominant (IV) to the leading tone chord (vii°).

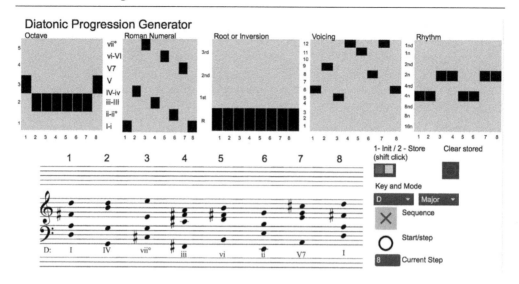

Figure 7.21: Descending-fifths progression in D major in Max.

The falling-fifths progression can also be created in minor keys (figure 7.22). In the following we see the same progression in D minor. By transmitting the output of **Diatonic Progression Generator** to Finale and setting the key as D minor, the accidentals have been corrected. **Diatonic Progression Generator** spells the C#s as Db in D minor, one of its limitations due to the fact that it uses only one type of accidental for any key, based on the key signature.

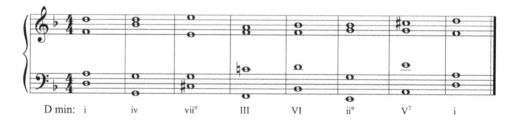

Figure 7.22: Descending-fifths progression in D minor.

7.11 Harmonic Sequences

The root-motion descending-fifth interval used in the previous progression is a **harmonic motive** (analogous to the melodic motives described in Chapter 6). The falling-fifth motive is transposed down by a second three times in the progression, creating a **harmonic sequence**. Other harmonic sequences are possible by transposing different harmonic motives. Johann Pachelbel's *Canon in D* is based on a root-motion sequence of a descending fourth followed by an ascending second, which is repeated three times in the first six chords. At chord 6 the pattern discontinues as it progresses I → IV → V and ends with a half-cadence, which leads back to the first chord (figure 7.23). The eight-measure harmonic sequence is repeated twenty-eight times in the piece.

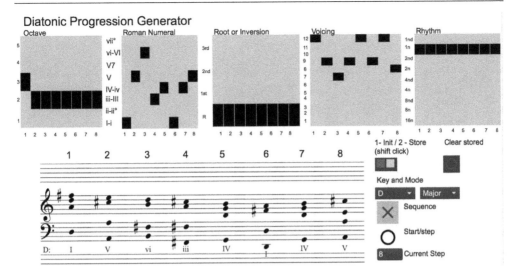

Figure 7.23: Pachelbel's *Canon in D* in Max.

Harmonic sequences can use other intervals as well. The following sequence, in E♭ major, has a descending third followed by an ascending fourth (figure 7.24).

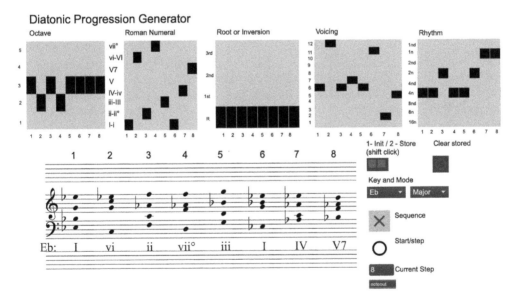

Figure 7.24: Descending-thirds, ascending-fourths progression.

The final example (figure 7.25), in E major, demonstrates a sequence of descending thirds in the bass, alternating between major and minor thirds.

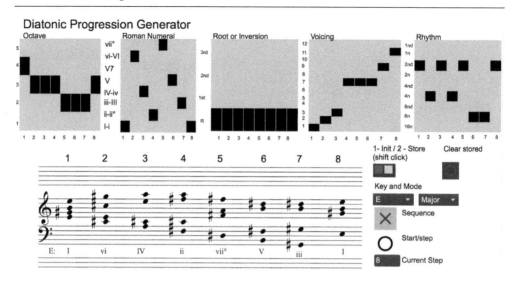

Figure 7.25: Descending-thirds progression.

7.12 Patterns

Harmonic progressions often use patterns based on types of root motion, and we've described some of these previously. Along with these patterns, progressions tend to be organized by functions (tonic, dominant preparation, dominant). But we can't assume that successful harmonic progressions only use known harmonic patterns.

In this chapter's exercises section, we'll explore randomly generating values for the **Diatonic Progression Generator**'s five **itables**. Most of what is generated does indeed sound random (and not very usable). These randomly generated progressions, however, afford us the opportunity to think about how we can make them better by adjusting their parameters. Alternatively, we could constrain the randomness to accord with harmonic function by adding more programming to the patcher to control which kinds of chords could be used in which locations. Along these lines, algorithmic and computer music pioneer David Cope has written extensively on the process of programming the computer to create music that follows traditional harmonic principles. Ultimately we can think of the **Diatonic Progression Generator** as a kind of harmonic-progression sketch pad—providing easy-to-work-with demonstrations of diatonic progressions in many different forms.

7.13 Max Patcher 11: *Diatonic Progression Generator*

In harmonic progressions (both in exercises and in real music) the fifth chord tone of a triad is sometimes omitted and the third and root can both be doubled. The triad can even be represented by three roots and one third in four-part harmony. For the sake of programming simplicity, however, the triads created with **Diatonic Progression Generator** always have all three chord tones, and these special situations of omitted chord tones are avoided.

With the **Key and Mode umenu** objects we select from twelve possible keys in either the major or the minor form. The **Key umenu** has only one setting for each chromatic pitch and avoids enharmonic spellings of keys. The **Mode umenu** sets the key as major or minor. Certain pitches with accidentals, such as C#/Db, G#/Ab, show both the sharp and the flat spellings because the major and minor keys at that pitch use different accidentals. We use C# minor and Db major, and we use G# minor and Ab major. Eb, Bb, and F# are used for both major and minor, although Gb is among the possible keys. Both **umenu** objects send out numbers when banged, and we can think of these numbers as pitch classes (C=0, C#/Db=1, D=3, etc.) or modes (major=0, minor=1).

Five **itable** objects are used to control the octave, Roman numeral, position, voicing, and rhythm parameters. An **itable** object is a 128 x 128 data table when first opened (or **instantiated**). That means there are 128 steps of data (size), and the range for each datum is 0–127. With the **itables' inspectors** we reduce the size to 8, corresponding to the number of steps or chords in the sequence. The **itables'** range depends on which parameter is being controlled; the ranges are 5, 7, 4, 12, and 9 because we have *five* octave positions, *seven* Roman numerals, *four* positions, *twelve* voicings, and *nine* rhythms. Below each **itable** are step numbers (1–8), and to the left of each **itable** we see how the parameters are arranged numerically from bottom to top.

The notation display in the lower half consists of eight **nslider** objects. In the **inspector** we (1) set all **nsliders** to **polyphonic mode**, and (2) hide all the clefs after the first **nslider**. The **nsliders** are aligned to appear as one grand staff. The patcher mode is shown in figure 7.26.

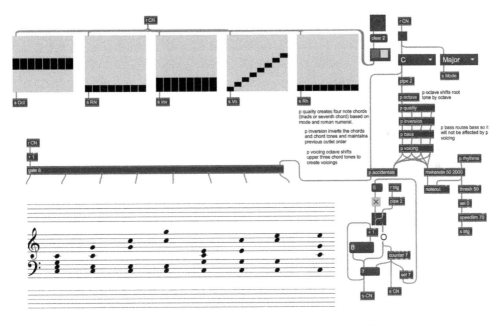

Figure 7.26: Diatonic Progression Generator **(patcher) in Max.**

In figure 7.26 we see seven subpatchers which create and modify the chords below the **Key umenu**: **p octave**, **p quality**, **p inversion**, **p bass**, **p voicing**, **p accidentals**, and **p rhythms**. After **p voicing** the chords are sent out to the **makenote 50 2000** and **noteout** pair which play the chords with the help of **p rhythms**, or alternatively they can be transmitted as MIDI out of the patcher. The output of **p voicing** is also sent to the **p accidentals** subpatcher which determines which accidentals are used for each progression. The output of **p accidentals** is distributed to 8 **nsliders** through the **gate 8** object.

Each chord's duration is sent to **makenote**'s right inlet directly from the **p rhythms** subpatcher (figure 7.27), which receives a value from the **rhythm itable** and translates it into a Max note duration. When the chord ends, **makenote** sends out a velocity value of zero. This zero, as it is connected to a **sel 0** object, creates a bang for the next chord to start. The bang is sent to the transport object via the **s/r chordTrig** objects. The **counter 7** counts from 0 to 7. When it gets to 7 (the eighth chord), the **sel 7** object sends a 0 to the **ggate**, causing it to close and the progression to stop.

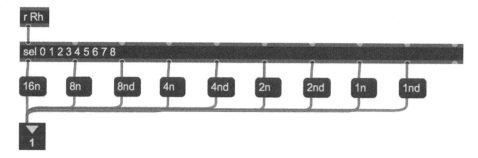

Figure 7.27: The p rhythms **subpatcher in Max.**

When sent to the **itables** via a pair of **send** and **receive** objects (**s/r CN**), the chord numbers advance the index number of all the **itables**, and the **itables** output the value at that index number. These values are sent to the subpatchers via **send** and **receive** objects (**s/r Oct, s/r RN, s/r Inv, s/r Vo,** and **s/r Rh**).

The **Key umenu** (it reads C in figure 7.26) sends a pitch-class number to the **p octaves** subpatcher one inlet. To this number the subpatcher then adds either 24, 36, 48, 60, or 72— depending on the value it received from the **Octaves itable** (**s/r Oct**)—to bring the tonic's pitch-class number to the desired octave (figure 7.28).

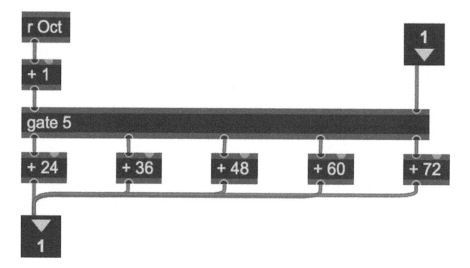

Figure 7.28: The p octaves **subpatcher in Max.**

As an example, if one chooses C major, the pitch-class number is 0; this 0 is added to one of the octave numbers, such as 48—chosen when the **Octaves itable** has a 3 selected. The output of **p octaves** will thus be 48, or the MIDI note number corresponding to C3, an octave below middle C. If we choose G major, which has the pitch-class number 7, and we add 60 with an **Octave itable** value of 4, **p octaves** will output 67, or G4, the G above middle C. These pitches become the root of the tonic chord when they are sent to the **p quality** subpatcher (figure 7.29).

In **p quality**, chords are created based on the selection of the mode and the **Roman Numeral itable**, whose output comes to the subpatcher via **r RN** (receive Roman numeral) object.

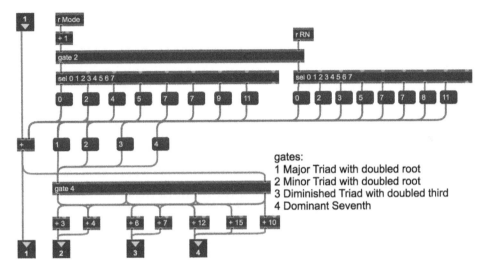

Figure 7.29: The p quality **subpatcher in Max.**

The tonic root note is input through the left inlet (1) from **p octaves**, and the first step is to add an amount to this value to produce the root for the selected Roman-numeral chord. The major and minor keys each have different scale patterns and different chord qualities. The **gate 2** object sends values corresponding to the major-key scale degrees out the left outlet, and minor-key scale degrees out the right outlet.

If the mediant chord in major is selected (the iii chord), 4 is added because in major keys the mediant is built on the third scale degree *four* semitones above the tonic. If the mediant in a minor key is selected (the III chord), 3 is added because the mediant chord is built on the third scale degree *three* semitones above the tonic.

Once the root of the chord is established, values are added to the chord root to create one of four possible chord qualities via the **gate 4** object: (1) a major triad with doubled root; (2) a minor triad with doubled root; (3) a diminished triad with doubled third; or (4) a dominant seventh chord. From left to right, the four outlets at the bottom of the **p quality** subpatcher are the root, third, fifth, and either a minor seventh (+10), octave (+12), or minor tenth (+15). From **p quality** these four note numbers are next sent to **p inversion**, where the chord can be inverted into first, second, or third (for dominant seventh chords only) inversion, or left as a root-position chord.

To invert the chords, **p inversion** (figure 7.30) transposes certain chord tones upwards. The chords used require different kinds of inversions, as described in table 7.1.

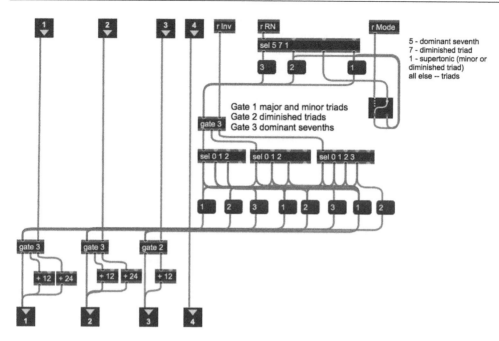

Figure 7.30: The p inversion **subpatcher in Max.**

Table 7.1: Transpositions in p inversion to create inversions.

Chord Type	Position	Root	Third	Fifth
Major/Minor Triad	Root			
	First Inversion	+24		
	Second Inversion	+24	+12	
Diminished Triad	Root			
	First Inversion	+12		
	Second Inversion	+12	+24	
Dominant Seventh	Root			
	First Inversion	+12		
	Second Inversion	+12	+12	
	Third Inversion	+12	+12	+12

The **p inversion** subpatcher receives the Roman-numeral value (0-tonic, 1-supertonic, etc.) via **r RN** and creates routings for the transpositions with the **sel 5 7 1** and **gate 3** objects. The **sel 5 7 1** object: (1) bangs out of the left outlet for dominant sevenths (V7, represented by 5); (2) bangs out of the second from left outlet for diminished triads (vii°, represented by 7); (3) bangs out of the third from left outlet for supertonic (ii, represented by 1); or (4) bangs out the right outlet for all other triads. These bangs then set the **gate 3** object to route the inversion values depending on whether there is a major or minor triad, diminished triad, or seventh chord.

The supertonic chord is minor in the major keys (ii), but diminished in the minor keys (ii°), so **p inversion** receives the mode from **r Mode** to route the ii chords to either 1 (for a minor triad) or 2 (diminished). The **r inv** object sends values to indicate position (root, first, second, and third inversions), and these values are routed by **gate 3** to the three **sel** objects, each of which creates different transposition amounts for the chord tones.

The **p voicing** subpatcher allows us to transpose non-bass chord tones to different octaves to create various voicings, but the bass must remain untransposed to keep the inversion selected. To ensure that the bass chord tone leaves **p voicing** in the same octave position at which it arrived, **p bass** isolates it by means of **router 4 4** controlled by a **matrix switch control** (**matrixctrl**—a rectangle with sixteen oval-shaped cells) (figure 7.31). When **p bass** receives the inversion number from the **Inversion itable** via **r INV**, the number is sent to a **coll fourbyfour** (collection) object. The **coll fourbyfour** object turns the **matrixctrl** cells on or off with a string of values that specify cell by column and row, and the on (1) or off (0) state.

When a cell is on, it is appears illuminated. Each string of values is stored in **coll 4x4control** and is recalled by inputting an index number. Any data entering one of the **router 4 4** inlets can be routed to any of its outlets. The bass note is always routed to **outlet 1**. In figure 7.31c, we see how each inlet (1, 2, 3, 4) is routed to **outlet 1** in turn from left to right by different configurations of the **matrixctrl**, and in figure 7.31b we see the four strings of values in **coll fourbyfour** to create these routings. The top row of cells, visible in the four **matrixctrl** objects, are sent to outlet 1—these are the nontransposed chord tones.

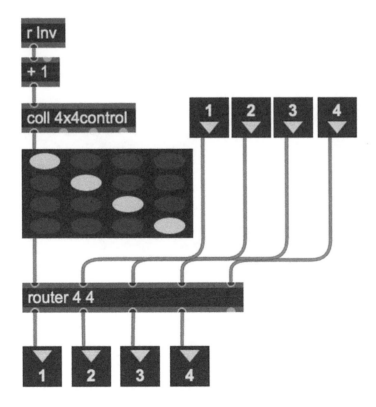

Figure 7.31: From top to bottom: (a) p bass **subpatcher**; (b) coll 4x4control **data**;
(c) matrix control **in four settings in Max.**

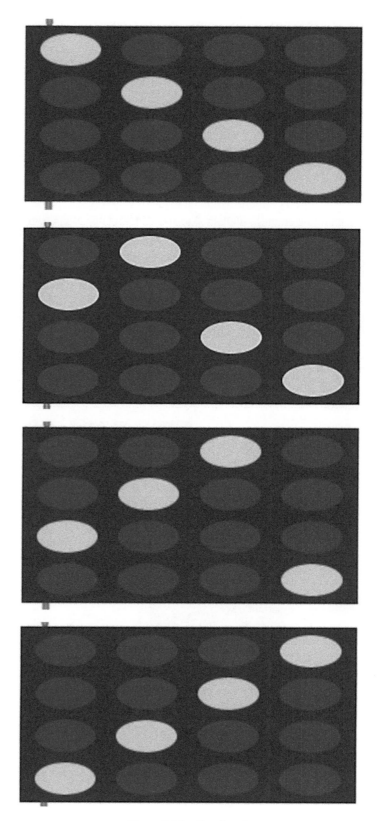

Figure 7.31c: Continued

Once we have isolated the bass note at **outlet 1**, we can move the three upper pitches around to create voicings in **p voicings** (figure 7.32). The three transposable chord tones can be modified by the same objects found in **p bass**: **coll 3x10**, **matrixctrl**, and **router 3 10**. The **router 3 10** has three inlets and ten outlets, and the required **matrixctrl** thus has 3 x 10 cells. Each of the three chord tones can be left untransposed or transposed up one or two octaves, and the middle chord tone can also be transposed up three octaves.

To ensure that we maintain a four-voice texture without doubled chord tones, each of the inversions must be treated separately with regard to voicing. To do this, the **coll 3x10** object has eighty-four matrix control settings. The seven groups of twelve (for the twelve voicings of the **Voicing itable**) are for different categories of chords, as in table 7.2. In this way, voicings can be created for specific inversions, and for the leading-tone chord.

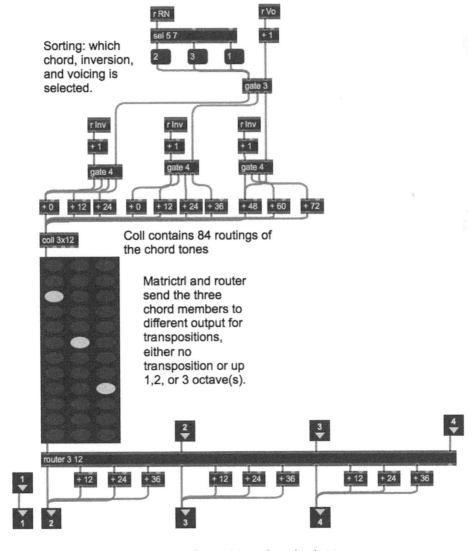

Figure 7.32: The p voicing **subpatcher in Max.**

Table 7.2: The coll numbers for seven categories of chords.

coll #	position	coll #	position
1–12	root	42–54	second
13–25	root leading tone	55–67	second leading tone
26–38	first	68–84	third (V7)
39–41	first leading tone		

The output of **p voicing** subpatcher is sent to the **p accidentals** subpatcher to select sharps or flats (figure 7.33). To display flats, the lists of note numbers entering the **nslider** objects must be negative, but negative note numbers are not played correctly by MIDI devices, so we must have two streams of MIDI: one for playback, and another for display.

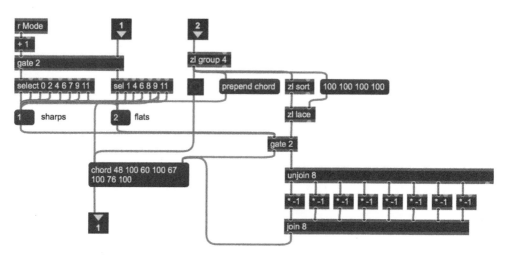

Figure 7.33: The p accidentals **subpatcher in Max.**

As an example, a C minor triad (60, 63, 67) will be displayed as C, D#, G by default in a **nslider**. In order for the triad to have an E♭, it must be (60, −63, 67), but (−60, −63, −67) will also work as −60 and −67 will display as C4 and G4, respectively. To get notes with accidentals to be displayed with flats, we multiply their note numbers by −1 before sending them to **nsliders**, but these negative note numbers are not sent to **noteout** object.

The chord tones are first grouped into a four-element list by **zl.group 4**. The **zl.sort** object sorts them in ascending order, and the **zl.lace** and **100 100 100 100 message** combines the note numbers with dummy velocity values of 100. These velocity values are added because the **nsliders** display chords when they receive a message formatted as: chord, note # 1, velocity 1, note # 2, velocity 2, etc. The word "chord" is prepended (added as the first element) to the message with **prepend chord**. The list of note values and velocities is sent to the **gate 2** object (on the left side of the subpatcher). The **gate**'s left output sends the list as is (positive values), the right outlet sends the list to be made negative by eight **multiply two numbers** (* −1) objects.

The control for this **gate 2** is determined by messages **1** for sharps or **2** for flats. Inlet 1 is for the key (as a pitch-class number), and **r Mode** receives the mode (major or minor). With the **gate 2** and **select** objects in the upper right of the subpatcher, we determine whether sharps or flats will be used. As an example, D major requires sharps. The right-side **gate 2** will route a 2 (D) to its left outlet to the **sel 0 2 4 6 9 11** object which will bang the **1** (sharps). If the key is D minor, which requires flats, then **gate**

2 will route the 2 to its right outlet to **sel 1 4 6 8 11**. The **sel 1 4 6 8 11** object will bang out its right outlet when it receives the 2 (because there's no match), and this bangs the **2** (flats).

Any progression's parameter settings can be stored by a **preset** object in the **Diatonic Progression Generator**. The **preset** object was minimized to just two slots in the **inspector**, but it could be expanded in the **inspector** in order to store more progressions.

7.14 Exercises

7.14.1 Exercise 1: Creating Cadence Progressions with Logic Chord Trigger

Each of the cadence types can be preceded by the tonic chord to create a three-chord progression. Using Logic's **Chord Trigger**'s **Multi - Keyboard Voicings Diatonic Left Hand** set, create these cadence progressions using the trigger notes as indicated in table 7.3 on track 1. Set the **Chord Transpose** number for the key as shown:

Table 7.3: Cadence progressions.

	KEY	Cadence	Roman numerals	Chord Transpose	Trigger notes
1	B major	PAC (Perfect Authentic Cadence)	I–V–I	−1	
2	F major	IAC (Imperfect Authentic Cadence)	I–V–I⁶	+5	
3	C major	Plagal	I–IV–I	0	
4	D major	Half	I–IV–V	+2	
5	B♭ major	Deceptive	I–V–vi	−2	

Set up to record **Chord Trigger**'s output from track 1 onto track 2 by (1) setting the output of track 1 to **External Instrument IAC Driver IAC Bus 1**, (2) creating a polyphonic instrument on track 2, and (3) record-enabling track 2 and disabling recording on track 1. (Remember never to record on a track set to output to an **IAC Bus**.) Change the key signature for each cadence, and set the **Region Style** to **Piano** in track 2's **Inspector**. The output for the first example will look like the first two measures in figure 7.34. Using **MIDI Transform's Transposition**, transpose the notes indicated inside the T-shaped area up one octave to create the perfect authentic cadence (PAC) in B major shown to the right. In addition to being V → I (root-position chords), the PAC melody must end on the tonic note (figure 7.34).

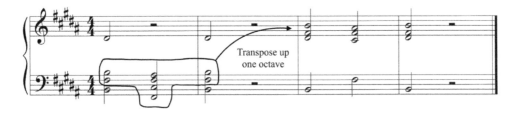

Figure 7.34: PAC in B major.

Use **MIDI Transform Transposition** to arrange notes in the other cadence progressions (2–5). The music in figure 7.35 shows one solution for each cadence type, but others are possible.

Figure 7.35: Four cadential progressions.

We can combine these progressions in various ways to make larger progressions, as follows. We can use any major key with the **Chord Trigger Diatonic Left Hand** to create them.

a. I–IV–V–I–V–I
b. I–IV–I–V–I
c. I–V–vi–IV–V–I
d. I–V–I⁶–V–I

7.14.2 Exercise 2: Chord Progression with Transposition and Canonic Utilities in Finale

1. Create a grand staff with a $^2_4$ time signature in C major.
2. Create a C major triad in the right hand (C4, E4, G4). Copy it nine times to mm. 2–10.
3. Transpose mm. 3–4 up a diatonic second, mm. 5–6 up a diatonic third, mm. 7–8 up a diatonic fourth, and mm. 9–10 up a diatonic fifth. The result will be pairs of these triads: C major, D minor, E minor, F major, and G major.
4. Invert the chords in odd-numbered measures with **Chord Inversion Up** in **Canonic Utilities** (one at a time!).
5. Invert the chords in even-numbered measures with **Diatonic Mirror Inversion Down** in **Canonic Utilities**, setting each **Pivot Note** to the chord's root. Then transpose each chord up one octave. These diatonic inversions will be: C → F; Dm → G; Em → Am; F → Bdim; and G → C.
6. Add bass notes in the left hand. In mm. 2–8 make the bass notes the third chord tone of each chord and transpose them down one octave. For the other three measures, make the bass the triad root and also transpose them down one octave.
7. The repeating root-motion pattern (starting in m. 2) is down a third, up a fourth. The progression includes all the triads in the diatonic collection (figure 7.36).

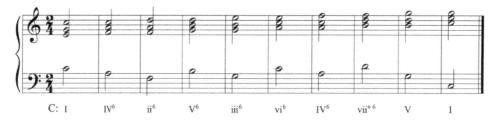

Figure 7.36: **Progression with** Transposition **and** Canonic Utilities.

7.14.3 Exercise 3: Diatonic Progression Generator and Roman Numeral Progressions

First, work out the following exercises in the **Diatonic Progression Generator** by inputting the Roman numerals and positions (table 7.4). Then, modify octaves and voicings to create better voice leading. When you have something that sounds reasonably good, transmit and record it in Logic or Finale to improve any notation or voice-leading issues. Choose different keys for the progressions to explore all the possibilities. Each progression has many realizations and can be completed in any key—and each is based on a real piece of music!

Table 7.4: Diatonic Progression Generator exercises.

Roman Numeral Chord Progressions									
	Mode	1	2	3	4	5	6	7	8
1	Minor	i	i^6	V	i^6	V^6	i	V	i
2	Major	I	V^6	V^7	I	V^4_3	I^6	V^6	I
3	Major	I	V^6	I	V	V^6	I	V	I
4	Minor	I	I^6	V^6	I	IV	ii^6	V^7	I
5	Minor	i	i^6	V^4_3	i	V^4_2	i^6	iv	i
6	Major	I	vii°	I	I^6	IV	ii	V	I
7	Major	I	V^7	vi	I^6	V^4_3	I	V^7	I
8	Major	I	iii	V^4_3	I	iii	ii^6	V^7	I
9	Minor	i	VI	III	I^6	ii°	V	V^7	i

7.14.4 Exercise 4: Modify Diatonic Progression Generator for Random Generation

We can generate random values to create progressions with the **Diatonic Progression Generator**. To do this, we will need to input values in the right and left inlets of the **itables**. The left inlet is for the index numbers to move through the table (X values), and the right inlet sets a value for each column (Y values). In figure 7.37, we see pairs of **receive** objects for both inlets at the top of the **itables** that input values in each table: **r O#** (octave table index); **r Orand** (Octave table values); **r rom#**; **r romrand**; **r pos#**; **r posrand**; **r vo#**; **r vorand**; **r rh#**; **r rhrand**. The **receive** objects get values from a **p randgen** subpatcher (figure 7.37). The five buttons trigger values for each of the **itables** (figure 7.38).

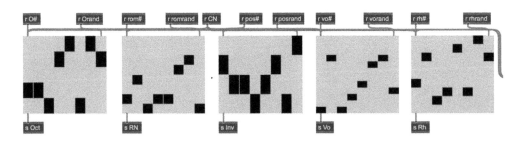

Figure 7.37: Receive **objects inputting values in** Diatonic Progression Generator **in Max.**

Figure 7.38: The p randgen **subpatcher in Max.**

Each **button** is connected (inside the subpatcher) to a series of objects that generate random values for the different ranges of each **itable**. The **metro 50** bangs the **counter 9** from 0 to 9 at a rate of one-twentieth of a second (fifty milliseconds). At 9, the attached **sel 9** object turns off the **metro 50**. The counter also bangs a **random** object that sends out random values within the necessary range for each **itable** (figure 7.39).

The randomness can and usually does generate progressions that don't make sense. Once a progression is created, however, we can alter any parameters to develop it so that it does work better, using our ears and our understanding of harmonic functions.

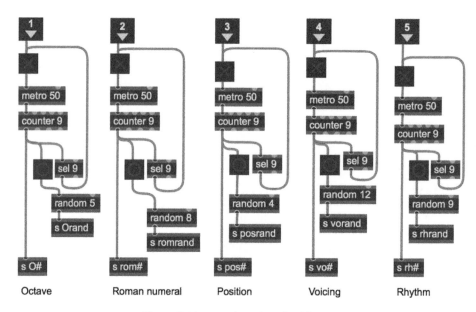

Figure 7.39: p randgen **(patcher) in Max.**

CHAPTER 8

Chromatic Harmony

8.1 Diatonic or Chromatic Harmony, Applied Dominant Chords

All the pitches of **Diatonic Progression Generator**'s chords come from selected key's scale, making the chords and progressions **diatonic** in that key. If we export these progressions to Finale or Logic and set the key signature, then the music shows no accidentals other than the key signature. The one exception is the seventh scale degree in minor progressions, which requires an accidental for the V and vii° chords.

If sharps or flats are added beyond the key, the music is **chromatic** as opposed to diatonic. And **chromatic harmony** results when accidentals occur specifically in chords. If accidentals are added only to the melody, the harmony might remain diatonic while the melody is chromatic. Our focus now is on chromatic harmony.

The most common kind of chromatic harmony is the **applied** (or **secondary**) **dominant**. An applied dominant is a chord that functions as the dominant (V) to a chord in the diatonic collection other than the tonic, such as the supertonic, mediant, subdominant, dominant, or submediant. In almost all cases the applied dominant has an accidental which changes the quality of the chord to major or dominant seventh. The applied dominant of the dominant (V of V) is the most common (figure 8.1). To create that chord, we start with a ii → V progression. If we add a sharp to the third of the ii chord, it becomes major. This D major triad is not part of the C major diatonic collection, but it is the V chord of G. We can add the C5 to the D major triad to create an applied dominant seventh chord. The slash in V/V or V⁷/V indicates the word "of" as in "the five *of* five" or "the five seven *of* five."

Figure 8.1: (1) Supertonic, (2) applied dominant to V, and (3) V⁷/V in a progression.

The V/V chord leads to the V chord and has a subdominant function. In figure 8.1, the V⁷/V in a C major progression hints (very briefly) at G major. As every diatonic collection has only one dominant seventh chord, this D dominant seventh is linked to G major even though we are in C major throughout. This quick linkage to another key is a **tonicization**, and it contrasts with a harmonic **modulation**, a longer stretch of music where the main tonic is supplanted by another key. With a single applied dominant seventh, we are *briefly* importing the V⁷ → I progression from another key, but we don't have an actual change of keys.

8.2 Constructing Applied Dominants

We can create applied dominants for the ii, iii, IV, V, and vi diatonic chords. We can't create applied dominants for I and vii° because the tonic (I) has its regular dominant (V), and the leading-tone chord (vii°) is itself unstable and therefore can't be the resolution for another chord.

Starting with the fifth of each of our target chords, we build either a major triad or a dominant seventh chord on that note to create our applied dominants (figure 8.2). In major keys the applied-dominant triad to the subdominant chord V/IV is also the tonic chord (in this case, a C major triad) so it usually doesn't sound like an applied dominant. In figure 8.2 we've added a question mark to show that this chord doesn't usually work as an applied dominant.

Figure 8.2: Applied dominants in triad and seventh chord form for ii, iii, IV, V, and vi in C major.

8.3 Chord Trigger Applied Dominants

To hear how applied dominants work in chromatic harmony, we can use Logic's **Chord Trigger**, with the **Multi → Keyboard Voicings → Pop Left Hand** setting. If the key is set to C major and we play a C major scale from C2 to A3, we hear diatonic chords: I, ii, iii, IV (add2), V (add 2), vi. The IV (add 2) and V (add 2) triads have an added G and A respectively, making them ninth chords (see Chapter 5, *Section 5.11: Extended Chords*), and instead of being a diminished triad, the vii chord is minor.

If we play a *chromatic* scale from C2 to A3, however, we hear the applied-dominant chords (figure 8.3). These applied dominants are resolving to the ii, iii, V, and vi chords (fig 8.3).

Figure 8.3: Chord Trigger Pop Left Hand—**chords produced with bass notes C2 → A3.**

Except for the V⁷/iii, these applied dominants are first-inversion triads, and the thirds of the chords are in the bass. Following voice-leading rules, the bass notes of each of these applied dominants should resolve up one step to the root of the following chord.

We could use this **Pop Left Hand** setting to create an accompaniment for the traditional *Amazing Grace* that includes two applied dominants, as shown in figure 8.4. To hear the chords, play the notes on the lowest staff in a track with **Chord Trigger Pop Left Hand** enabled. The applied dominant V⁶/V in m. 6 (a D major triad in first inversion) resolves to the V chord (G major add 2), ending this first eight-measure phrase with a half cadence. In the second line the applied-dominant V6/vi resolves to the vi chord. The song then ends with a plagal cadence (IV–I). Other versions of *Amazing Grace* work out the harmony differently; our version with applied dominants is just one possibility.

Our version has parallel perfect fifths and octaves, but adding bass and drums along with our **Chord Trigger** applied dominants and ninth chords creates a nice texture overall.

Figure 8.4: Chord Trigger Pop Left Hand **V⁶/V and V6/vi applied dominants** in *Amazing Grace*.

8.4 *Chord Tool Applied Dominants*

We can create a series of applied dominants with Finale's **Chord** tool by (1) typing the chord roots and chord suffixes above empty measures, (2) exporting the file as a SMF, then (3) opening that same SMF in Finale. Instead of typing all the chords, however, we can use the **Chord Definition** window to create the applied-dominant chords. We can type in the other chords with the **Chord** tool, and the resulting progression is shown in figure 8.5.

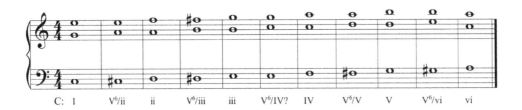

Figure 8.5: Chord Tool **applied-dominants progression.**

Using the **Chord** tool, we type in the chord names for the odd-numbered measures. These measures have the diatonic chords of C major: C, Dm, Em, F, G, Am. Next, with the **Chord** tool still enabled, we double-click in the second-measure staff to bring up the

Chord Definition window (figure 8.6). We adjust the settings in the lower half of the window to create a A/C# chord symbol for this second measure—a chord symbol that indicates an A major triad with a C# in the bass, or a first-inversion A major triad. In this context (preceding the D minor chord), the chord is also a first-inversion applied-dominant triad to the ii chord in C major.

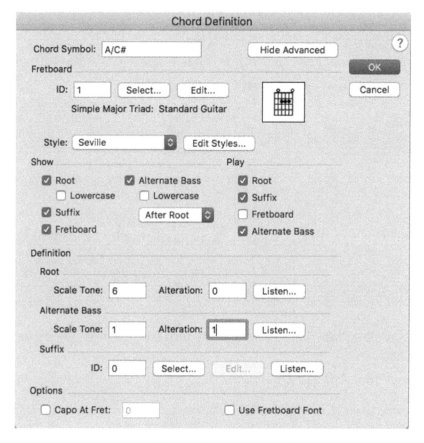

Figure 8.6: Chord Definition **in Finale.**

First, in the **Definition** section, we set the **Root Scale Tone** to **6**, as A is the sixth scale degree in C major, and we set the **Alternate Bass Scale Tone** as **1** with a **1** alteration, which creates a C# (the first scale degree with one semitone-up alteration). Next, in both the **Show** and **Play** sections we check the **Alternate Bass** boxes. The **Chord Symbol** now reads A/C#. The **Definitions** settings for all the applied-dominant chords are shown in table 8.1, and we type these into the even-numbered measures. In each case we consider the scale tones of the roots and alternate bass in relation to the tonic C major (tab. 8.1).

Table 8.1: Settings for applied dominants in Chord Tool Chord Definition.

Measure	2	4	6	8	10
Chord	V⁶/ii or A/C#	V⁶/iii or B/D#	V⁶/IV or C/E	V⁶/V or D/F#	V⁶/vi or E/G#
Root	6	7	1	2	3
Alt. bass	1	2	3	4	5
Alteration	1	1	0	1	1

The chord symbols will appear as in the top line of figure 8.7, and we export these eleven measures as a SMF. Before opening that SMF file with Finale, from the menu item we choose **Finale → Enharmonic Spelling → Favor Sharps**. This will ensure that all the applied-dominant chords are spelled correctly with sharps. Once opened in Finale, the music will appear as per figure 8.7 in the grand staff. To create the version shown earlier in figure 8.5, several editing steps were required. Triads in odd-numbered measures were **Chord Inverted** with **Canonic Utilities**, and each root was then transposed down three octaves. For even-numbered measures, the third of each triad was removed, resulting in a three-part texture. The transposition of diatonic collections of triads and seventh chords to all the keys shown in Chapters 4 and 5 demonstrates how a chord has different functions in different keys. C major, for instance, is the tonic in C major, the subdominant in G major, and the Dominant in F major. Transposing figure 8.7 to all the other keys besides C major will likewise demonstrate how applied dominants function differently in different keys. A major, for instance, is V/ii in C major, V/iii in B♭ major, and V/vi in F major.

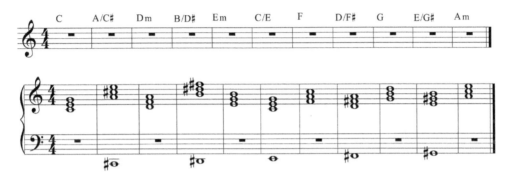

Figure 8.7: Applied-dominant progression with chord symbols (above) and chords (below).

8.5 Copy, Paste, and Transpose Applied Dominants

Another approach to working with applied dominants with Finale relies on copying, pasting, and transposing (diatonically or chromatically). We start with the dominant seventh in first inversion (V^6_5) followed by the tonic chord in root position. By copying the tonic chord to *every other* measure (mm. 4, 6, 8, and 10) and diatonically transposing each chord in turn up by a second, we get the diatonic collection (I, ii, iii, IV, V, vi). Setting the **Method** as **Diatonically** restrains all the pitches to the key. Then, we transpose the dominant seventh in first inversion up by major or minor seconds by turns (M2, M2, m2, M2, M2) with the setting **Method** as **Chromatically**. The result resembles that which we obtained with the **Chord** tool (figure 8.8).

Notice that our bass lines are chromatic scales, and that the accidentals generated for each applied dominant are in the key of the following chord. In D (major or minor), the V chord has a C#, for instance, whereas in E, the V chord has both the D# and F#.

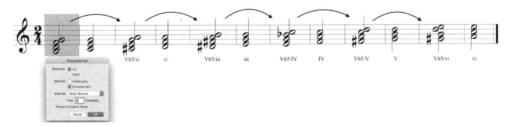

Figure 8.8: Diatonic collection chords preceded by applied dominants in Finale.

Numerous examples of applied dominants can be found in many styles of music, including classical, jazz, and popular. Traditional music theory texts often provide examples of applied dominants from classical music, but examples of applied dominants in popular music are common too. In Leonard Cohen's *Hallelujah*, the chords for the first-verse lyrics "The baffled king composing Hallelujah" include a V⁷/vi → vi progression, and in John Lennon and Paul McCartney's *I Will*, the chord accompaniment for the lyrics "Will I wait a lonely lifetime?" starts with V⁷/IV → IV.

8.6 Applied Leading-Tone Chords

The leading-tone chord can also be used as an applied chord in any of its three forms: a diminished triad, a diminished seventh chord, and a half-diminished seventh chord. We can create a complete set of applied diminished seventh leading-tone chords for triads in C major in Finale (figure 8.9) by using the same copy, paste, and transpose techniques that we used for the applied-dominant sevenths.

Figure 8.9: Applied leading-tone chords for the set of diatonic chords (I, ii, iii, IV, V, and vi).

The other leading-tone chord forms, the diminished triad and the half-diminished seventh chord, can be substituted for the applied-diminished seventh in many musical contexts, and these forms can be also generated by our copy/paste/transpose method.

In the **Chord Trigger, Multi → Keyboard Voicings → Jazz Ballad Right Hand** we hear an applied leading-tone diminished seventh chord (vii°⁷/ii) as well as an applied leading-tone half-diminished seventh chord (viiø⁷/V) (figure 8.10). The resolutions include added chord tones (extensions) above the seventh. The ii⁷ chord has an added major ninth (D, F, A, C, E). The V⁷ chord also has an added major ninth (G, B, D, F, A). Finally, the leading-tone chord in the key (viiø⁴³) is a B half-diminished chord in second inversion with an added ninth as well (C). These added ninths are common chord extensions in jazz, providing a rich harmonic palette.

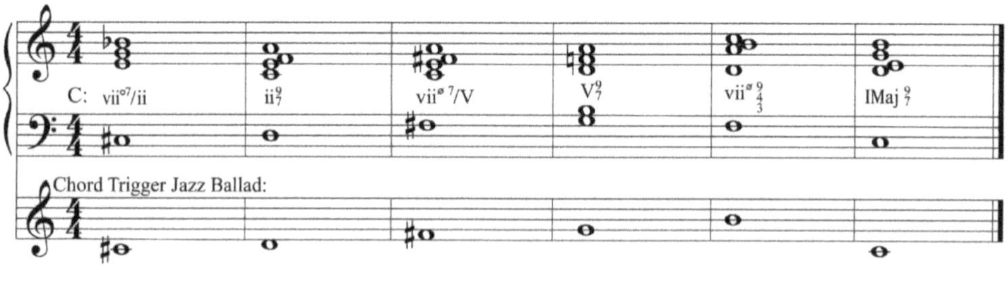

Figure 8.10: Chord Trigger: Jazz Ballad Right Hand.

We can use this **Chord Trigger Jazz Ballad Right Hand** to play the chords for the first eight-measure section of *Have You Met Miss Jones?* by Richard Rodgers and Lorenz Hart (figure 8.11). The **Chord Trigger** notes are in the bottom staff, and the harmonies are in the grand staff. The second measure has an applied leading-tone chord (C# dim[7]) which resolves to a D minor seventh chord. To follow the original harmonic progression, the A[7] chord in m. 6 should be replaced with an A min[7] chord. We can make this change with the **Learn** and **Clear** button in **Chord Trigger**. The added ninths aren't in the original, but work well as added sonorities.

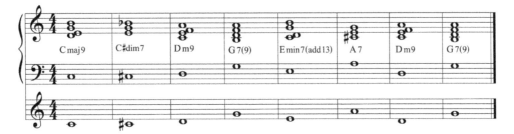

Figure 8.11: Rodgers and Hart's *Have You Met Miss Jones?* **(excerpt) with** Chord Trigger: Jazz Ballad Right Hand.

8.7 Modulation

Applied dominants and leading-tone chords temporarily invoke a different key than the original home-key tonic. Additionally, chromatic harmony can create situations where a new key is established, or where the music moves from one key to another, which is called a **modulation**. Modulations can happen between any two keys, although certain kinds are more common, such as modulations between **close** keys. Close keys either have key signatures that differ by only one accidental, or are relative major/minor pairs that have the same key signature (C major and A minor, for example). The keys Bb and Eb are close, for instance, because their key signatures differ by only one flat. A common example of a modulation between close keys is from tonic to dominant—always a shift of only one accidental. If we start in C major, for instance, we can modulate easily to G major as a close key. Modulation between C and F#, on the other hand, is rare, because C and F# are **distant** from one another; their key signatures differ by six accidentals.

8.8 Chromatic Progression Generator

To explore the concepts related to chromatic harmony, such as applied dominants and modulation, we can use the **Chromatic Progression Generator**. The difference between this patcher and Chapter 7's **Diatonic Progression Generator** is that the **Chromatic Progression Generator** plays chords from any key—a feature we'll need for chromatic harmony. With the **Chromatic Progression Generator** we choose chords based on the root pitch instead of Roman numerals—even though we'll continue to think of the chord progressions in terms of Roman numerals. The possible chord types include the three most common triads (diminished, minor, and major), the five standard seventh chords (major seventh, dominant seventh, minor seventh, half-diminished seventh, and diminished seventh), and a special chromatic chord—the dominant seventh flat-five (V^{7b5}). We can select a quality by choosing a point in the **Quality itable**, where this list of qualities is arranged from the bottom up. We can select a root by clicking on a point in the **Root itable**, where the pitches are arranged from

C to B from the bottom up. With these chord types built on any pitch, 108 different chords can be selected (9 x 12), and each of these chords can be transposed to five octave levels, inverted to first, second, and (for seventh chords) third inversion, and voiced in ten different ways. These parameters are chosen from the corresponding **itables**, similar to the **Diatonic Progression Generator**.

The following progression starts with a C dominant seventh chord which resolves to an F major chord a perfect fifth below (figure 8.12). That F major chord is followed by an F dominant seventh chord which resolves to a Bb major chord a perfect fifth below. The pattern continues in similar fashion, resulting in a chromatic circle-of-fifths progression. It is possible for the progression to continue chromatically from this final Ab and eventually return to C: Ab7 Db–Db7–Gb–Gb7–B–B7–E–E7–A–A7–D–D7–G–G7–C!

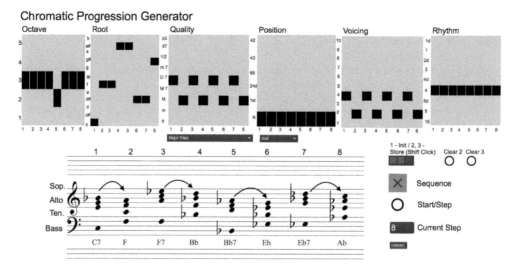

Figure 8.12: Chromatic circle-of-fifths progression in Max.

A similar chromatic descending-fifths pattern is heard in Antonio Carlos Jobim's song *If You Never Come to Me*, which includes these dominant seventh chords progressing by falling fifths: E7 → A7 → D7 → G7 → C7 → F7. In the published version of Jobim's song, the dominant seventh chords in this passage are extended with other tones (extended chords), which we're leaving out for the sake of simplicity.

8.9 Pivot Modulation

Music **modulates** from one key to another when a second key center is established as a new tonic. Modulations are longer than single tonicizations, and often involve multiple cadences in the new key. In fact, in order to modulate successfully, the music must convincingly sound as if a new key has been established. We can modulate from C to G major, as shown in figure 8.13. The D major first-inversion chord at 5 is outside the key of C major, but is it only a temporary excursion? Chord 5 is an applied dominant, a V^6/V resolving to V (D^6 → G), and then chords 7 → 8 are a D dominant seventh resolution to G major with a perfect authentic cadence. At this point, we have established new key.

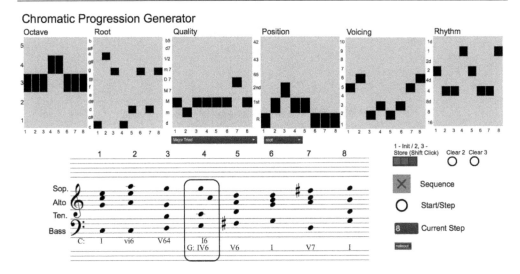

Figure 8.13: Modulation from C major to G major with a pivot chord (4) in Max.

In this modulation, we can also identify a **pivot chord**, which belongs to both keys, and which we will consider as the moment when we move from one key to the other, making it a **pivot modulation**. The encircled C major triad (chord 4) is I⁶ in C and IV⁶ in G, and with a chord in both keys, the modulation is made smooth.

We also notice that the Roman-numeral analysis has two lines, one for C major and one for G major. At the pivot chord there is a Roman-numeral analysis in both keys, but on either side, the analysis is either in C (chords 1–3), or G (chords 5–8).

The rhythm pattern also helps define the harmonic motion. Here the first four chords' rhythms are the same as the last four—giving extra emphasis to the pivot chord (C major first inversion) and the final G chord—the destination of the modulation.

8.10 Step-Up Modulation

Another type of modulation occurs when musical material is repeated and transposed up by a certain interval (often by a half or whole step): **step-up modulation**. Step-up modulation is common in popular music, but less typical in classical music, where a roughly equivalent type is called **sequential modulation**. Step-up or sequential modulation doesn't require applied chords, but instead requires transposing material chromatically. We hear the same music in two keys (the original key and the key to which we modulate). The modulation relies on this connection.

In the following example, we modulate from E minor to F minor (figure 8.14). Adding to the connection between the two halves of the music, the quality, position, voicing, and rhythm patterns for chords 1 → 4 are identical to those in 5 → 8. The **itables** for these chord parameters provide a visual cue of the pattern replication of the first four chords in the last four, with the second half being shifted up one semitone. Examples of a step-up modulation in popular music include Michael Jackson's *Man in the Mirror* and the outro of Stevie Wonder's *Knocks Me Off My Feet*.

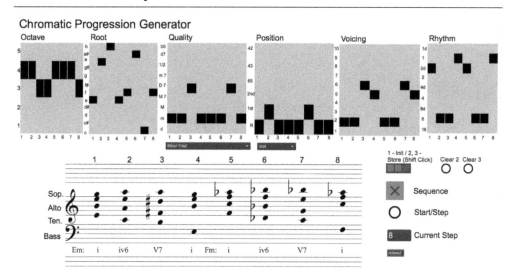

Figure 8.14: Step-up modulation from E minor to F minor in Max.

8.11 Descending-Fifths Progression with Chromatic Alterations

Using the descending-fifths progression discussed in Chapter 7 (pages 161–162) as a basis, we can create phrases that modulate to different keys, such as C major to A minor, and C to G major. The first is a modulation from the tonic to its relative minor or submediant (C to A minor), and second is from the tonic to the dominant (C to G). Both are common modulations. In the first example (figure 8.15), we mostly keep the original progression's descending fifths or ascending fourths root motion, except for chords 6–7 where the root motion moves a whole step up from D to E. Our chromatic alterations are that from chord 4 forward the G pitches are replaced with G#. The E dominant seventh chords resolve to A minor chords at 4 → 5 and 7 → 8. A modulation from C major to A minor (its relative minor) is smooth, as these are close keys—they share the same key signature.

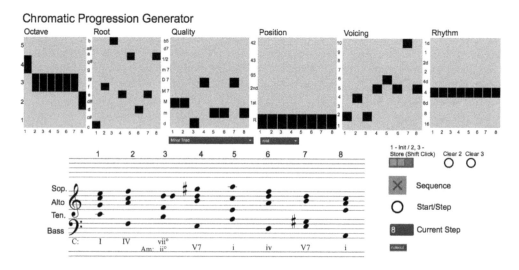

Figure 8.15: Descending-fifths modulation from C major to A minor in Max.

Using the descending-fifths progression again, we can modulate to G major with different chromatic alterations, as per figure 8.16. The chromatic alteration is F → F# in chord 7, and it creates a perfect authentic cadence to G in 7 → 8. Our voice-leading rules tell us that the tenor voice at 8 should double the G in the bass to avoid parallel perfect fifths between 7 and 8, but the **Chromatic Progression Generator** doesn't include voicings where the root is tripled, as this situation requires. Another detail to note is at chords 6 to 7. These two chords form a single harmonic unit, the **cadential** $^6_4$, a common chord elaboration. The second inversion G chord (chord 6) can be thought of as an embellishment to the D dominant seventh which follows it (chord 7). By convention, the two chords are notated as one Roman-numeral unit as V $^6_4$ $^7_5$$_3$.

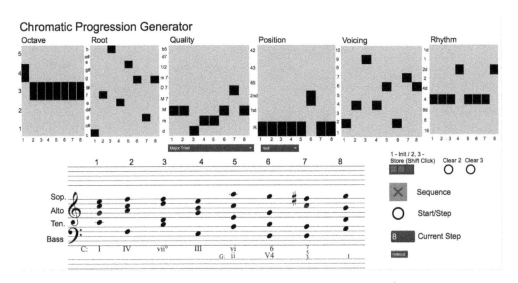

Figure 8.16: Descending-fifths modulation from C major to G major in Max.

8.12 Modal Mixture

Modal Mixture (sometimes called **Modal Interchange**) occurs when music in a major key incorporates elements from the parallel minor key, or when the minor key borrows from the parallel major key. The term **modal** can refer to music which uses modes, but in this context it refers to borrowing between major and minor *scales*. Our modern major and minor scales are in fact derived from two modes, the **Ionian** (major) and **Aeolian** (natural minor). A shift between major and minor is therefore also a shift in mode. Modal mixture can produce dramatic music, such as the opening to Richard Strauss's orchestral tone poem *Also Sprach Zarathustra*, familiar as the opening music heard in Stanley Kubrick's film *2001: A Space Odyssey* (figure 8.17).

The work opens with a low sustained C in the basses, organ, and contrabassoon. The trumpets then play C–G–C (ascending), and the entire orchestra plays a short, loud C major chord followed by a quieter sustained C minor chord. In the next phrase the chords are reversed: we hear a quick C minor chord followed by a sustained C major chord. The **Chromatic Progression Generator**'s following example (figure 8.17) sets chords 1 and 3 to the fastest rhythmic value, a sixteenth note, and chords 2 and 4 to the longest rhythmic values to mimic Strauss's music.

This awe-inspiring passage demonstrates how modal mixture can alternate major and minor chords with the same root. This simplified excerpt ends with the dominant chord at chord 8. After this famous opening, Strauss's tone poem continues with more than thirty minutes of music.

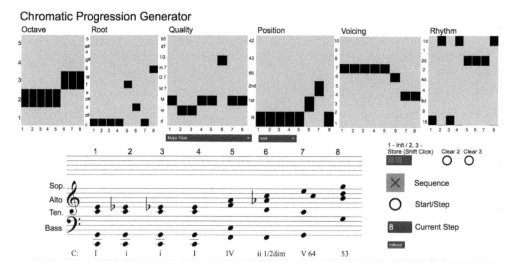

Figure 8.17: Strauss's *Also Sprach Zarathustra* (simplified): modal mixture in Max.

Modal mixture is the term used when major and minor modes are mixed together. An individual chord from the opposite (either major or minor) mode is a **borrowed** chord. The Strauss tone poem is in C major, but at chord 6 we have a D half-diminished seventh. This chord is borrowed from C minor, where it is the ii°⁷. Chords 2 and 3 are also borrowed chords from C minor.

Modal mixture includes borrowing tones and chords between the major and minor keys on the same pitch, as well as switching the mode of the tonic chord itself. With the possibility of chords borrowed from the parallel tonality (major to minor, or minor to major), we increase the number of available chords. Modal mixture and borrowed chords are common in all kinds of chromatic music. From classical music, Franz Schubert's *Winterreise (Winter Journey)* contains many striking examples. In popular music, we can hear modal mixture in Seal's *Kiss from a Rose* and in John Lennon and Paul McCartney's *Blackbird*.

8.13 Phrygian ♭II

The **Phrygian ♭II** chord is a major triad built on the *lowered* second scale degree. In C minor the chord is D♭–F–A♭. The F and A♭ are the fourth and sixth scale degrees of C natural minor respectively, and the D♭ is the lowered second scale degree. By including all the modes, the concept of *modal mixture* helps explain this chord. The C Phrygian mode has a D♭ as the second scale degree; we borrow this scale degree to create the chord. The Phrygian ♭II chord is available in all keys, but occurs more frequently in minor.

The Phrygian ♭II chord is often in first inversion, and is also known as a **Neapolitan sixth chord**. The root-position version is simply a Neapolitan chord. The flat sign in the name indicates that we are lowering the root pitch, but not necessarily with a flat. In E minor, for instance, the second scale degree is F#, but the ♭II chord is a major chord built on the lowered second scale degree, or F. Therefore, F major is ♭II in E minor.

Shown in figure 8.18 is a **Chromatic Progression Generator** with the chord progression in Hector Berlioz's song *Villanelle* from *Les nuits d'été* (*Summer Nights*) in F major. We hear a root position Phrygian ♭II (G♭ major) at chord 7.

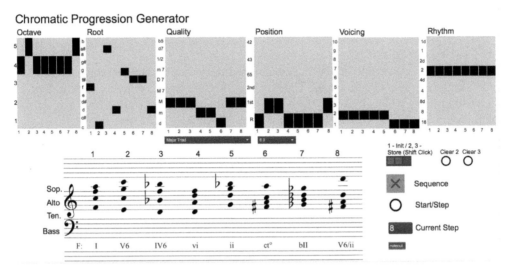

Figure 8.18: Berlioz's *Villanelle* (simplified)—the ♭II is at chord 7 in Max.

The F# diminished triad at chord 6 is a **common-tone diminished** chord, and labeled as ct°. A common-tone diminished chord with the same root as the preceding chord, the following chord, or both preceding and following chords, is considered an embellishment of the chord that has the same root. In this case, the common-tone diminished chord anticipates and embellishes the ♭II chord at chord 7. Berlioz uses this root position ♭II chord at this moment in the song to add emphasis to the singer's lyric "chills" or "*froids*" in the original French.

The Phrygian ♭II chord is also heard in Radiohead's *Pyramid Song* which alternates F# and G major chords throughout the song. Here, the G major chord is the ♭II chord. The song also includes modal mixture as F# major switches to F# minor at certain points.

8.14 $V^{7(\flat5)}$, Tritone Substitution, and Augmented Sixth Chords

We also can chromatically alter notes in the applied-dominant chord to create different kinds of harmony. One example is the $V^{7(\flat5)}$ chord, which can be voiced as the **French augmented sixth**. The French augmented sixth chord was used by many classical composers, whereas the $V^{7(\flat5)}$ is common in jazz composition and performance.

To understand where this chord comes from, we start with the applied dominant of V in C major, that is, V^7/V or a D dominant seventh chord resolving to the G major chord (figure 8.19). First, we alter this applied-dominant chord by lowering the fifth one semitone (mm. 3–4)—this is the $V^{7(\flat5)}$. Then we reposition the chord tones so that the lowered fifth goes into the bass, the third goes into the soprano, and the root and seventh become the alto and tenor voices (m. 5)—this is the French augmented sixth.

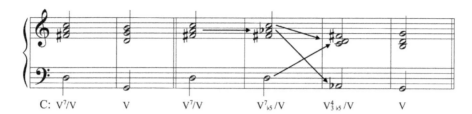

C: V⁷/V   V   V⁷/V   V⁷₍ᵦ₅₎/V   V⁴₃ ᵦ₅/V   V

Figure 8.19: Creating the French augmented sixth chord from V⁷/V basis.

The chord moves powerfully to the V (G major) chord because of the two semitones which approach the G from both directions. The French augmented sixth is similar to the **Italian augmented sixth,** which omits the D, and the **German augmented sixth,** which also omits the D and adds a note a perfect fifth above the bass (figure 8.20). Classical composers mostly used the augmented sixth chords in this position (the lowered fifth in the bass), whereas the V⁷ᵇ⁵ in popular music and jazz can be heard in any position.

C: Fr⁺⁶   It⁺⁶   Gr⁺⁶   V⁷₍ᵦ₅₎/V

Figure 8.20: The French, Italian, and German augmented sixth chords and the V⁷⁽ᵇ⁵⁾ chord.

The German augmented sixth in figure 8.20 adds an E♭ and omits the D; this E♭ is a lowered-ninth extension to the original V/V chord. Like the French and Italian, the German augmented sixth often moves to a cadential $^6_4$ (see page 187), a slight detour before the V chord to avoid parallel fifths. If we enharmonically respell the F# as a G♭, however, the chord becomes a more recognizable A♭ dominant seventh (figure 8.21).

When an A♭ dominant seventh chord resolves to a G major chord in jazz and popular music, it's called a **tritone substitution**. Instead of the usual D⁷ chord resolving to G, the A♭⁷ chord *substitutes* for the D⁷. This A♭⁷ is a tritone (a diminished fifth or augmented fourth) away from D. Tritone substitutions are common in jazz composition and performance and can be heard in many situations. Unlike the typical use of a German augmented sixth chord, the tritone substitution is not limited to a dominant-preparation function—a chord that precedes the dominant—nor is it limited in position. What the chords have in common is their dominant seventh sonority, and a downward stepwise resolution.

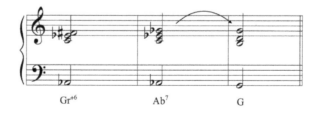

Gr⁺⁶   A♭⁷   G

Figure 8.21: The German augmented sixth and tritone substitution chords.

One can occasionally find the $V^{7(b5)}$ and tritone-substitution chords in the same musical work. In the following example (figure 8.22), we see the chords for mm. 3–10 of Cole Porter's *Easy to Love*. Chords 4 to 5 have the tritone substitution F^7 resolving to an E minor seventh chord (iii^7), and chords 6 to 7 have the $A^{7(b5)}$ resolving to a D minor seventh ($V^{7(b5)}/ii \rightarrow ii^7$). The flat five of the A7 chord is spelled (incorrectly) as a D#; it should be an E♭.

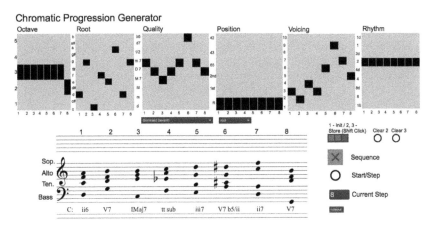

Figure 8.22: Porter's *Easy to Love* (simplified) mm. 3–10 in Max.

8.15 Max Patcher 12: *Chromatic Progression Generator*

The difference between **Diatonic Progression Generator** and **Chromatic Progression** is that with the diatonic version we select chords from diatonic collections, whereas in the chromatic version we can select any chord. The **Chromatic Progression Generator** can create diatonic progressions, and it can incorporate chromatic harmonies into a tonal progression. Both types of **Progression Generators** create a sequence of eight chords with different rhythms and allow for different octaves, positions, and voicings of chords. The basic layout in both patcher and presentation modes is the same (figure 8.23).

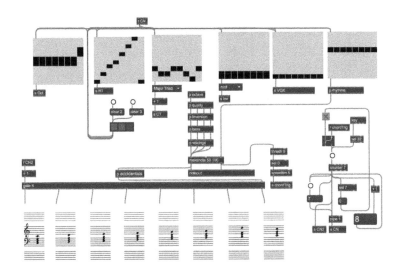

Figure 8.23: Chromatic Progression Generator **(patcher) in Max.**

In **Chromatic Progression Generator**, the root tone is selected by the second from left **itable** whose range corresponds to the twelve chromatic pitches. This **itable** outputs pitch-class numbers based on C=0. The root tone is then set to a **p octave** subpatcher whose function is identical to **Diatonic Progression Generator**'s **p octave** subpatcher (see pages 166–167). The pitch number at selected octave is then sent to the **p quality** subpatcher.

In the **p quality** subpatcher (figure 8.24) three semitone amounts are added to the root according to the chord type, to create four pitches. Table 8.2 shows the additions to the root that create each chord. The roots are always passed through unchanged, but the thirds, fifths, sevenths, and doubled chord tones are created by adding different numbers of semitones. The chord quality is set by the third from left **itable**. Its values are input to **p quality** by a **send/ receive** pair of objects (**s CT** /**r CT**).

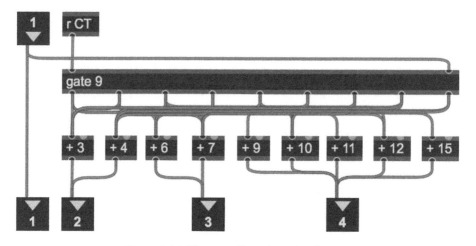

Figure 8.24: The p quality **subpatcher in Max.**

Table 8.2: Adding chord tones in p quality.

#/Chord type	Third	Fifth	Seventh or doubling
0 Diminished Triad	3	6	15
1 Minor Triad	3	7	12
2 Major Triad	4	7	12
3 Major Seventh	4	7	11
4 Dominant Seventh	4	7	10
5 Minor Seventh	3	7	10
6 Half-dim. Seventh	3	6	10
7 Dim. Seventh	3	6	9
8 Dom. Seventh b5	4	6	10

After the **p quality** subpatcher, the four-part chord is formed, and each note is sent to the **p inversion** subpatcher (figure 8.25). The **p inversion** subpatcher transposes certain notes down one octave to create inversions—a slightly different method than **Diatonic Progression Generator**'s, which transposed chord pitches up to create inversions. As an example, if the third and fifth are transposed down one octave, the triad will be in first inversion. The following table details this, with 0 indicating no transposition (tab. 8.3).

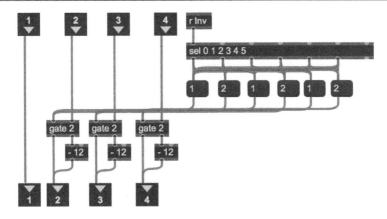

Figure 8.25: The p inversion **subpatcher in Max.**

Table 8.3: Transposition in p inversion.

Inversion	Third	Fifth	Seventh/Double
$^6_3$	−12	−12	0
$^6_4$	0	−12	0
$^6_5$	−12	−12	−12
$^4_3$	0	−12	−12
$^4_2$	0	0	−12

After the inversions are created, the **p bass** subpatcher isolates the bass (lowest) note of the chord. This **p bass** subpatcher is identical to that used in **Diatonic Progression Generator**. Its function is to isolate the bass note so that it will not be changed by the **p voicings** subpatcher, which creates different voicings.

Chromatic Progression Generator's **p voicings** subpatcher creates voicings by transposing chord tones up by various octave amounts (figure 8.26). Which chord tones are transposed is controlled by a **router 3 10**, which is in turn controlled by a **matrixctrl** and **coll 3by10**. The **coll 3by10** object has a list of sixty settings for the **matrixctrl** to route chord tones to various octave positions. Chord tones can be transposed up one, two, or three octaves. The **coll 3by10** object's sixty settings are needed to ensure that chord types are handled differently (for example, diminished chords will not double the root), and that the voicings avoid undesirable doublings.

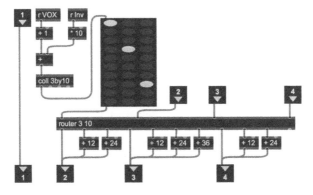

Figure 8.26: The p voicing **subpatcher in Max.**

After the voicing selection is made, the chords are sent to a **makenote/noteout** pair to be played, as well as to the **p accidentals** subpatcher (figure 8.27) to select sharps or flats for the **nsliders** and the musical notation display. The **Chromatic Progression Generator** selects which accidental to use based on the root tone and quality.

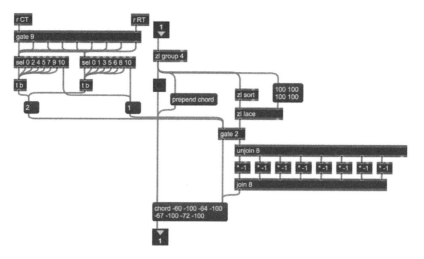

Figure 8.27: The p accidentals **subpatcher in Max.**

The function and layout of the transport controls is similar between the diatonic and chromatic versions, including **counter 7** and **sel 7** objects to progress through the sequence. Triggering chords in sequence is done by listening for the 0 velocity of chords (their endings), which bangs the counter and then the next chord until the eighth chord happens.

Chromatic Progression Generator also has a **preset** object for storing progressions and a **noteout** for transmitting progressions to other programs. The ability to transmit the progressions to Logic or Finale allows us to join multiple eight-chord progressions together and modify them in countless other ways.

8.16 Exercises

8.16.1 Exercise 1: Chromatic Harmony Progression Keyboard Exercises

Using Finale or Logic, create a keyboard exercise that uses a short progression with applied dominants, leading-tone chords, or both (resolving to chords in the major key), and transpose the progression to all the other major keys. The first example is a single-measure progression starting in C major which includes an applied dominant resolving to the supertonic (ii) chord (figure 8.28). The measure with the **I–vi⁷–V⁷/ii–ii** progression is copied into seven additional measures. M. 2 is transposed by an ascending *major second* (chromatic) (Finale's **Transposition** or Logic's **MIDI Transform Transposition**). To create a kind of perpetual step-up modulation, each measure after that is transposed by an amount one major second higher than the previous measure.

When we get to F# it makes sense in terms of the notation to transpose this measure up chromatically by a *diminished second*, which effectively transposes the key from F# major to Gb major, an enharmonic respelling. The Gb major is a little easier to read as it doesn't have double accidentals, and when we continue the modulations to Ab and Bb majors, the flat spellings of those keys is preferable. The complete sequence of keys will be: C, D, E, Gb, Ab, Bb, C. We can also do the same process with F, G, A, B, Db, Eb, F.

Figure 8.28: Step-up modulation exercise.

Another keyboard exercise is a chord progression in C major in triple meter that has an applied leading-tone diminished seventh chord resolving to a supertonic minor seventh, followed by an applied dominant seventh chord that resolves to V⁷, and ends back at I (figure 8.29).

We take these two measures and copy and paste them into mm. 3–4. Then, chromatically transpose the measures up a perfect fifth to G. Repeat the same process with mm. 5–6 into 7–8 and beyond, transposing each new segment up a perfect fifth or down a perfect fourth. Continue to all twelve major keys to create a chromatic harmony progression exercise.

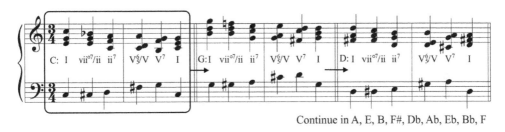

Continue in A, E, B, F#, Db, Ab, Eb, Bb, F

Figure 8.29: Chromatic harmony progression exercise.

8.16.2 Exercise 2: Chromatic Progression Generator Progressions

We can use the **Chromatic Progression Generator** to create eight-chord harmonic progressions heard in popular song accompaniments. We can find examples among thirty-two bar song-form pieces with eight-measure phrases (the form of these pieces is often AABA, where A and B are eight-measure phrases). Some examples even have just one harmony per measure, such as Jerome Kern's *All the Things You Are*. Once the chord root, chord quality, and inversion are input, we can vary the octave and voicing to create a smooth connection between the chords. The first line in table 8.4 has the chords of *All the Things You Are*, and lines 2–10 show other progressions to create:

Table 8.4: Chromatic Progression Generator chord progression exercises.

	1	2	3	4	5	6	7	8
1	Fm7	B♭m7	E♭7	A♭maj7	D♭maj7	G7	Cmaj7	Cmaj7
2	Cmaj7	Am7	Dm7	G7	Em7	Am7	Dm7	G7
3	Fm7	Fm7/E♭	D♭7	C7	B♭7	E♭7	C7	Fm7
4	F	Dm7	Gm7	C7	F	Dm	Am	F
5	E♭m	D	D♭	B♭m	E♭m	D	Em7	A7
6	C	C7/G	F	Fdim	C/E	D#dim	G7/D	C#dim
7	F7	B♭m	A♭7	D♭	E♭7	Cmin7/E♭	E♭7	A♭
8	A7/C#	D	B7/D#	E	E7	A/E	E7	A
9	Bmaj7	D7	Gmaj7	B♭7	E♭maj7	Am7	D7	Gmaj7
10	Gmaj7	Gm7	C7	Fmaj7	Fm7	B♭7	E♭7	D7

8.16.3 Exercise 3: Modify Chromatic Progression Generator for Random Generation

Using the same methods outlined in the Chapter 7 for the **Diatonic Progression Generator**, we can modify the **Chromatic Progression Generator** so that it has six buttons to generate values randomly for each **itable**. Randomly generated progressions are often harmonically incoherent, but we can use them as springboards to create more satisfying results by tweaking the parameters, and every so often chance will create a convincing progression.

Once again we can go further and think about how we could make these random generation processes more likely to succeed? What algorithmic programming would work? Or, to put it another way, what rules could we program into the patcher to create more convincing chromatic progressions? Developing a knowledge and understanding of progressions will be key to this task.

Chromatic Music

9.1 Atonal Music

For the most part, music theory instruction focuses on music with a key center (or tonic) that uses harmonic structures built in thirds or **tertian** harmony (triads, seventh chords, and extended chords). The chords used in traditional music, classical music up to the twentieth century, and most jazz, rock, and pop music are mostly tertian. Moreover, most music with tertian chords is **tonal** (having a tonal center or being in a major or minor key). The music might have many extended and chromatically altered chords, or lots of modulations and tonicizations, but if we hear a tonal center, it's tonal.

One composer who pushed the limits of tonal harmony by frequent modulations and far-ranging chromatic harmony was Max Reger. Listening to the first piece in Reger's *Monologe* (1902) for organ, for example, we might ask: is this music tonal? It can be hard to discern what key we are in, even at cadences. Modulations and chromatic harmonies fly by, and the music's tonal grounding seems to be always shifting. But Reger's music remains tertian, and the composer always indicates a key.

Reger's contemporaries in the early part of the twentieth century also pushed the limits of tonal harmony, and some began to question whether a tonal center was necessary, or whether one had to organize music with tertian harmony and major and minor scales. In the early twentieth century, composers such as Arnold Schoenberg and Edgard Varese started writing **atonal** music, music without tonality and without the clear use of traditional scales or tertian harmonies. The term atonal is somewhat controversial, but I'll use it to describe music that avoids key centers or tertian harmony. Other terms, such as non-tonal or pan-tonal, are favored by some music theorists.

Atonal music developed during a period when composers were using more and more chromatic elements (harmonies and melodies) in tonal music. Early atonal music and heavily chromatic music sometimes sound similar, as both rely on the chromatic scale. The techniques we'll discuss in this chapter using Logic, Finale, and Max could potentially be part of creating highly chromatic tonal music, but we'll focus on an atonal outcome to differentiate what we're doing here with those techniques covered in past chapters.

In atonal music theory we often identify musical structures (or groups of notes) by the number of pitches, or pitch classes, they contain. For instance, we name groups of three, four, or six pitches as **trichords**, **tetrachords**, or **hexachords**, respectively. The term *tetrachord* originally meant four scale tones spanning a perfect fourth, such as the first four pitches of a major scale, but the term can also describe any four pitches or pitch classes grouped together. We can discuss these groupings of pitches, also called **sets**, in different ways. Music theorists have developed a substantial conceptual basis for applying set theory to atonal music, and some well known atonal-music theory works are included in the bibliography.

To relate these pitch structures to traditional music theory concepts: triads are the tertian *subset* of the larger set of trichords, and seventh chords are the tertian *subset* of the larger set of tetrachords. Considering all the inversions and voicings as variants of the basic types of triads, there are four basic types (major, minor, diminished, and augmented), but there are twelve distinct trichords. That is, there are twelve ways to arrange three pitches within one octave that have a unique combination of interval classes. Similarly, we identify five traditional seventh chords (major, dominant, minor, half-diminished, and diminished) and we could add others, such as major minor seventh (a minor triad with a major seventh) or dominant seventh flat five. On the other hand, there are twenty-nine distinct chromatic tetrachords.

9.2 Trichords in Logic

We'll start discussing atonal music theory by randomly generating three-note chromatic (and non-tertian) trichords in Logic. To ensure that we only have non-tertian trichords with three different pitches, we will exclude triads and trichords with repeated notes. We'll think of them as motives and apply the same operations that we have applied to diatonic motives: transposition, inversion, retrograde, and combinations of these operations.

More broadly, however, the pitches in a set can be heard melodically or as a harmony. When a set's pitches sound together, it is a **simultaneity**. We can also consider the pitches of a trichord to be **ordered** (in a specific order, like a motive), or **unordered** (allowing for any ordering). Finally, we can think of the pitches of a set to be at specific octaves, or to be pitch classes (all the same pitch names at any octave), a concept we used in **Triad** and **Seventh Chord Generators**. All of these possibilities are analogous to the concepts we use for tonal music. A tonal melody can be made *from a chord*, and a melody uses scale pitches with a *specific ordering*. Chords can be at a specific *pitch level* (a C major closed-position triad on middle C), but we also recognize that all the multiple possibilities of arranging the three pitches C, E, and G are always a C major triad. In other words, in this chapter we will extend the concepts we have discussed in previous chapters to apply to atonal music.

Create trichords, and choose one to manipulate with motivic operations in Logic:

1. Set the time signature to $^3_4$.
2. Input three quarter-note middle Cs in m. 1.
3. Option-drag m. 1 into m. 2, and choose **Edit → Repeat Multiple**, selecting **18** for number of repeats so that we have a total of twenty measures with three middle C quarter notes in each measure.
4. Open **MIDI transform**, choose **Random Pitch** preset. Set the range parameter from **C4** to **C5** to limit all the pitches to one octave. Choose **Select and Operate** from **MIDI transform**.
5. View the notes in the **Score Editor** and listen to the playback.
6. To work with only atonal trichords with three different pitches, delete measures with triads, repeated pitches, or scale fragments.
7. In figure 9.1 we see the results of the process after ten measures were removed. M. 5 with a F–E–B trichord is selected.

Figure 9.1: Randomly generated trichords in Logic. M. 5 selected.

9.3 *Operations on Trichords*

We can transpose trichords with Logic's **MIDI Transform**. First, we'll remove all the other measures, and move the F–E–B trichord to m. 1. We'll copy and paste it into m. 2. After selecting m. 2, we open **MIDI Transform** and choose **Transposition** from **Presets**, and we **Add 1** (one semitone) and press **Operate Only**. We'll continue this copy, paste, and transpose process forward until we have twelve different trichords, and one final trichord with the same pitches as the first, but transposed up one octave (figure 9.2).

Figure 9.2: The F–E–B trichord transposed up successively by one semitone twelve times.

Transposing the trichord by three semitones gets us to the same trichord one octave up after four transpositions (figure 9.3), whereas transposing by four semitones gets us there after three transpositions. Finally, transposing by five semitones up (or seven semitones down) gets us back to the original after twelve transpositions. One interesting aspect of these transpositions is that while the trichords generated by a transposition of three semitones share pitch classes (mm. 1 and 3 both have B and F [or E#], and mm. 2 and 4 both have A♭ and D), transpositions of this trichord by four semitones generate trichords whose pitches are all unique. We can exploit these kinds of relationships to create contrasts or connections in composing atonal music.

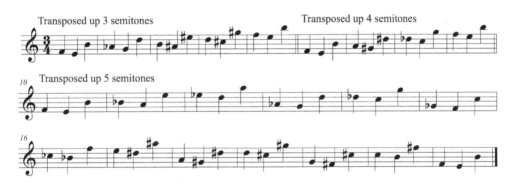

Figure 9.3: The F– E–B trichord transposed successively by semitone amounts.

We can also perform the operations of retrograde, inversion, and retrograde-inversion on the trichord with **MIDI Transform**. To retrograde the trichord, we first select it, then in **MIDI Transform** choose **Reverse Position** from the **Presets**. We then need to select the exact **Position** of the trichord by setting its start and end below the **Inside** setting. As the trichord takes up one measure, the start and end would typically look something like **4 1 1 1** to **5 1 1 1**. These numbers specify the measures, the beat, subdivision, and tick number. The beat, subdivision, and tick can all be set to one, and in this case we will be retrograding the notes between mm. 4 and 5.

To invert the trichord, we select **Reverse Pitch** from **MIDI Transform**'s **Preset** list. To invert the trichord around the starting pitch, we'll need to set the **Flip** to F4, the first note of the trichord. Choosing a different **Flip** (or axis of inversion) combines inversion with transposition. In figure 9.4 we see the original trichord (prime), its retrograded form, the inversion around the starting pitch, and the retrograde of the inversion.

Figure 9.4: Operations on a trichord.

Composing with these operations provides a means to generate melodic material based on a single source set, such as a trichord. In the following example, the F–E–B trichord appears four times in the melody, with various operations and rhythms. What **MIDI Transform** operations were required to transform the melody in m. 1 into the three next measures?

Figure 9.5: Tune and accompaniment based on the F–E–B trichord.

M. 2 is inverted and transposed up seven semitones. M. 3 is retrograded and transposed one semitone down, and m. 4 came about by retrograde inversion and a transposition by one semitone up. We also use the trichord to generate an accompaniment. The pitches of the trichord appear in the bass clef as simultaneities transposed down nine semitones in m. 1, down fourteen semitones in m. 2, down sixteen semitones in m.3, and down fourteen semitones again in m.4.

Early twentieth-century composers used non-tertian trichords, tetrachords, and other pitch structures as generative **cells** to create melodies and harmonies in **free atonal** music. A motivic cell is quite similar to a motive, but it can be used both melodically and harmonically (as a simultaneity). By using cells in multiple forms with transpositions, inversion, or combinations of these operations, composers create musical coherence in their music. Edgard Varese's *Octandre* (1923) is a good example of a free atonal piece which employs a four-note cell (a tetrachord) heard in various forms melodically and harmonically throughout. The motive (or cell) is played by the solo oboe at the beginning starting on G♭5, and at the end the motive transposed up three semitones to A5. The cell also appears throughout the piece as a simultaneity, and in other melodic forms. Whereas the major scale exerts a unifying force in tonal music, this kind of use of a generative **cell** is the unifying aspect of some atonal musical works.

9.4 Twelve-Tone Music

Another method in atonal music, the **twelve-tone technique**, became established through the teaching and writing of Arnold Schoenberg. Before developing the twelve-tone technique, Schoenberg wrote free atonal music, and his earliest music was (like Reger) highly chromatic but tonal.

Although it has never been a widely popular form of music, many composers in the twentieth century wrote twelve-tone music, and its basic principles are easily summarized. Twelve-tone technique starts with a **tone row** (or **series**) of all twelve chromatic pitches in a specific order. Each pitch appears in the row only once, which guarantees the row will have twelve distinct pitches. Any operation, or combination of operations, can be applied to the row: transposition, inversion, or retrograde. The row becomes the basic generative unit in a musical work. How composers create the row and how they use and manipulate the row varies considerably. Twelve-tone music can have many different qualities, including even tertian harmonies and harmonic consonance.

9.5 Creating Twelve-Tone Music with Finale

One relatively consonant-sounding twelve-tone work is Alban Berg's *Violin Concerto*. Berg was one of Schoenberg's more famous students, another being Anton Webern. The violin concerto row consists of many thirds, and many triads result—it's somewhat tertian and almost tonal sounding (figure 9.6).

In the following music, the row is presented in five forms; the first line represents the first or **prime** form. The triads heard in the prime-form row are G minor, F# diminished, and E major, which is followed by C#, D#, and F. The second line shows that the retrograde has the same triads in reversed order. An inverted form of the row is shown on the third line, and this form has C major, D diminished, and E♭ minor triads. The final three pitches of the inverted form are C#–B–A.

Figure 9.6: The tone row of Berg's *Violin Concerto* in five forms.

To create all the possible forms of the row, we can use the **Transposition** and **Canonic Utilities** tools in Finale. For instance, to create transposed rows, we copy and paste the row, select our new row, and from the **Transposition** tool select **Direction: Up or Down**, **Method: Chromatically**, the desired **Interval**, and press **OK** (figure 9.7).

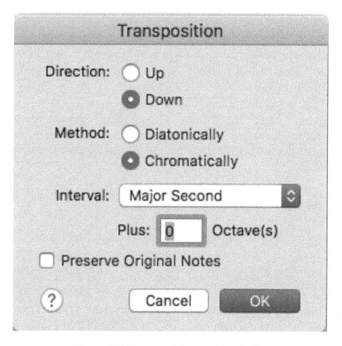

Figure 9.7: Transposition **tool in Finale.**

The fifth line of the music (figure 9.6) has the first-line version of the row transposed up a major third. When you transpose the prime form of the row in this way with Finale's **Transposition** tool the third measure's pitches will read as G#, B#, and D#. These pitches are a major third above the originals, but we can spell this more simply as an A♭ major triad. To change these pitches to the enharmonic spellings of A♭, C, E♭, we can again transpose this measure up chromatically (with the **Transposition** tool) by a *diminished second*. Transposition by a diminished second will produce the same pitches, but with enharmonic spellings a line or space above or below the original. Respelling chromatic transpositions can sometimes make them easier to read.

The original row in the first line of music is specifically designated as **P–7**, for prime 7 or the prime form starting on a G. The seven in this case is the starting note's pitch class (**pc**) number. We use C as pitch class 0, and count up from there for all the pitch-class numbers 0–11. In the third line, we have taken the original row in retrograde form. The **R–7** is the retrograde of the **P–7** form. Retrogrades are named by the non-retrograde form, in this case **P–7**. The **R–7** form ends with a G, or pitch class 7.

The **I–7** inversion in the fourth line is the original row inverted at a G. This inversion is also retrograded in line four. For all three operations we can use Finale's **Canonic Utilities**, performing transposition and inversion operations separately. In the following we see the settings for the **Canonic Utilities** for the inversion of the row after it has been transposed two octaves up to G5 (figure 9.8a). After transposing and inverting the row, we can retrograde it, by setting **Canonic Utilities** to **No Inversion**, **No Transposition** and checking the **Retrograde** box (figure 9.8b).

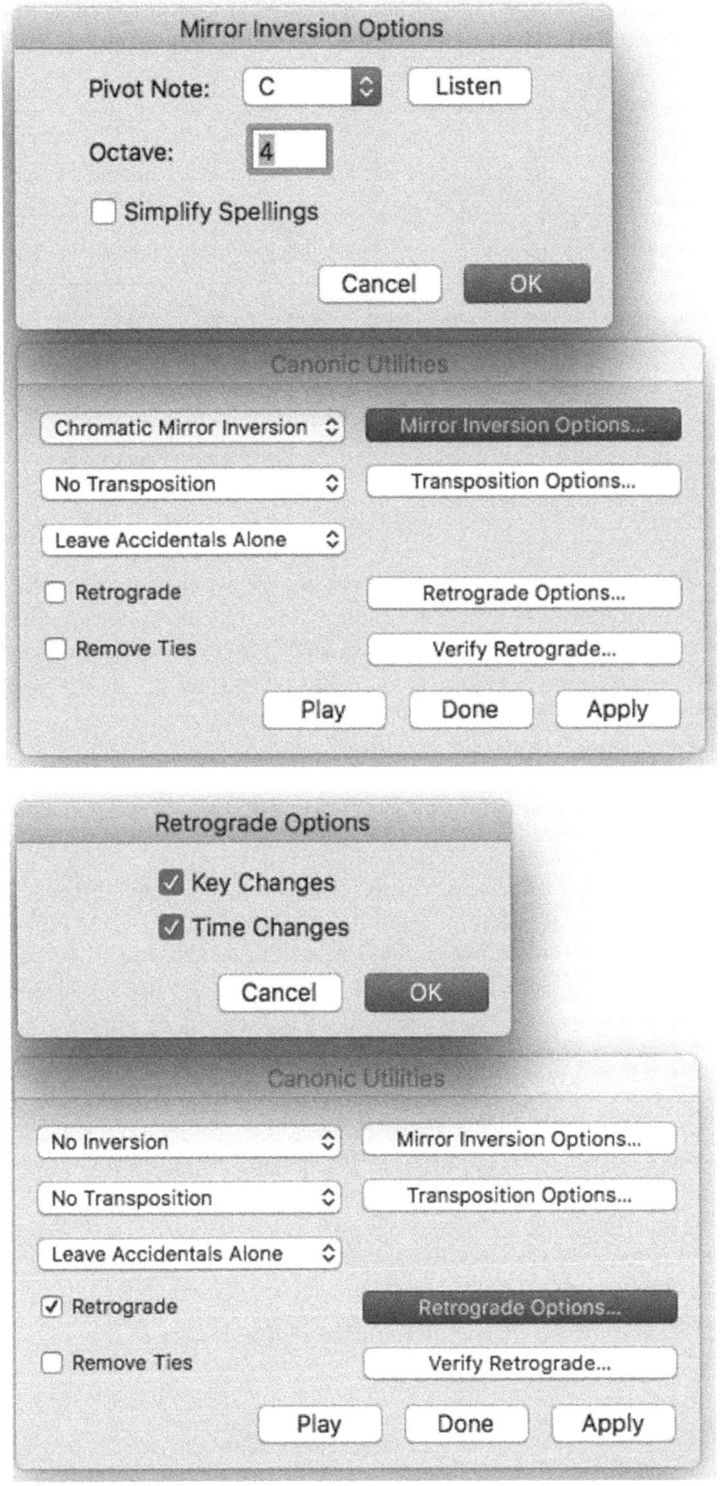

Figures 9.8a and 9.8b: Canonic Utilities Chromatic Mirror Inversion **and** Retrograde **in Finale.**

9.6 Twelve-Tone Matrix

TABLE 9.1: The 12 x 12 matrix based on the Berg tone row.

G	Bb	D	F#	A	C	E	G#	B	C#	D#	F
E	G	B	D#	F#	A	Db	F	Ab	Bb	C	D
C	Eb	G	B	D	F	A	C#	E	F#	G#	A#
G#	B	D#	G	Bb	Db	F	A	C	D	E	F#
F	Ab	C	E	G	Bb	D	F#	A	B	C#	Eb
D	F	A	C#	E	G	B	D#	F#	Ab	Bb	C
Bb	Db	F	A	C	Eb	G	B	D	E	F#	G#
F#	A	C#	F	G#	B	D#	G	Bbb	C	D	E
D#	F#	A#	D	F	Ab	C	E	G	A	B	C#
C#	E	G#	C	Eb	Gb	Bb	D	F	G	A	B
B	D	F#	A#	C#	E	G#	C	Eb	F	G	A
A	C	E	G#	B	D	F#	A#	C#	D#	F	G

The five lines of music shown in figure 9.6 represent only some of the possible row forms we can get from the original row. There are forty-eight forms in all, considering each of the four operations (prime, inversion, retrograde, and retrograde inversion) has twelve transpositions. These forty-eight forms are sometimes displayed in a twelve-tone **matrix** showing either pitch names (letters) or pitch classes (numbers) as per table 9.1. The prime forms are read from left to right, and the retrogrades are read from right to left. The inversions are read from top to bottom, and the retrogrades of the inversions are read from bottom to top. Finale's **Transposition** and **Canonic Utilities** tools make it easy to realize all the row forms.

One of the principles in twelve-tone composition is that the row also provides harmonic material. Because Berg's row has three qualities of triads (major, minor, and diminished), it follows that operating on the row with transpositions, inversions, and retrogrades (and combinations thereof) will result in all forms of these qualities of triads.

The row generates melodic and harmonic material for twelve-tone music, but the composer makes the musical *choices* about how to use the material. The following excerpt is the first complete statement of the tone row, and it demonstrates how tone rows can be both melody and harmony (figure 9.9). The tone row is numbered 0–11 in the violin part (top clef). Supporting this row statement in the accompaniment (grand staff) are row elements 8, 9, 10, and 11 as a chord in mm. 15–17 (to the first quarter), and row elements 0, 1, 2 as a broken chord in mm. 17–18. The G# in the orchestra and the E in the violin in m. 18 are both elements of the next statement of the row—a tone row **ellipsis**. Berg also includes chromatic passing tones in the treble clef of the accompaniment (F → F# → G; and G → G# → A → Bb).

Figure 9.9: Berg's *Violin Concerto*, mm. 15–18 (simplified).

9.7 Pitch Sets

Pitches can be grouped in different amounts to create the building blocks for atonal melody or harmony, and table 9.2 lists names for groups of pitches of different numbers—**pitch sets**. Each line in this table pairs two sets—**dyad** and **decachord**, trichord and **nonachord**, tetrachord with **octachord**, **pentachord** with **septachord**, and hexachord with hexachord. The set pairs (each line of the table) add up to twelve notes in each case, and if the pitches of each set are distinct from one another, the two sets together form a twelve-tone set. In this special case the sets are **complementary** (together forming a set made up of all twelve pitches).

Table 9.2: Pitch sets.

# of pitches	Pitch Class Sets		# of pitches
2	Dyad	Decachord	10
3	Trichord	Nonachord	9
4	Tetrachord	Octachord	8
5	Pentachord	Septachord	7
6	Hexachord		

Composers of the early twentieth century used pitch sets (tetrachords, pentachords, etc.) as a basis for harmony and melody in atonal music, and we can use tools in Logic and Finale to manipulate sets just as we have done for triads and seventh chords.

9.8 Manipulating Pitch Sets in Logic and Finale

The (D–G–A♭–C#) tetrachord seen in the first measure below (figure 9.10) was transposed up a major second three times in the next three measures using Finale's **Transposition** tool. In this context, the **Chromatically** setting ensures that the tetrachord's structure is replicated exactly.

Figure 9.10: Transposition Tool **used to transpose atonal tetrachords in Finale.**

Additionally, we can manipulate a tetrachord with the **Canonic Utilities** tool's settings **Chord Inversion Up** or **Chord Inversion Down**. Atonal tetrachords don't have roots per se, and therefore we don't identify its root position or inversions. But Finale's **Chord Inversion** rearranges the tetrachord in the same way that it inverts chords (figure 9.11).

Figure 9.11: Canonic Utilities Chord Inversion Up **for tetrachords in Finale.**

In the case of this tetrachord, we might notice that each of the major-second transpositions produces different pitches, and that the first three transpositions include all twelve pitches. Another interesting (and possibly useful) outcome of the operations is that the third transposition (m. 4 in figure 9.10) is identical to the second inversion (m. 3 in figure 9.11). We can also perform a melodic or mirror inversion on these tetrachords with **Canonic Utilities**. In the following example, we see the first tetrachord transposed up an octave, and then inverted around its lowest pitch, which is now D5. The tetrachord now extends downwards with the same intervals as we heard going up (figure 9.12), and this consistency of interval content creates an audible connection between the chords.

Figure 9.12: Canonic Utilities – Chromatic Mirror Inversion **of a tetrachord in Finale.**

Using Logic's **MIDI Transform Transposition** is another way to transpose tetrachords by semitones, as shown in figure 9.13. Here the number of semitones equals the chromatic interval size, and two semitones is equivalent to a major second.

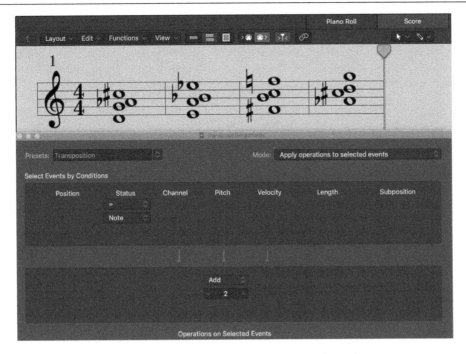

Figure 9.13: MIDI Transform: Transposition **in Logic.**

MIDI Transform: Reverse Pitch functions the same as **Chromatic Mirror Inversion**. In both cases we are inverting the entire structure around a single pitch. This pitch is the axis, **Pivot Note** (Finale), or **Flip** (Logic). In the following image, we see an atonal tetrachord inverted around its lowest pitch, a D5 (figure 9.14).

Figure 9.14: MIDI Transform: Reverse Pitch **in Logic.**

9.9 Chromatic Melody Generator

We can use the **Chromatic Melody Generator** to create melodies from pitch sets. Unlike the **Diatonic Melody Generator**, which creates melodies that are constrained to a major or minor scale, the **Chromatic Melody Generator** allows us to create melodies based on the chromatic scale.

Chromatic Melody Generator creates melodies based on three-, four-, five-, or six-note motives, and the motive is an ordered pitch set. The rhythm motive is created in the same way as in the **Diatonic Melody Generator**. Each generated melody consists of a given number of forms of the motive. If the motive is four notes, and we repeat it four times, the melody is sixteen notes. The motive can be transposed, inverted, retrograded, and retrograde inverted, or any combination of these. In the following, the **Chromatic Melody Generator**'s melody is created from the D–G–A♭–D♭ tetrachord in prime, retrograde, inversion, and retrograde-inversion forms, with the musical notation added below (figure 9.15).

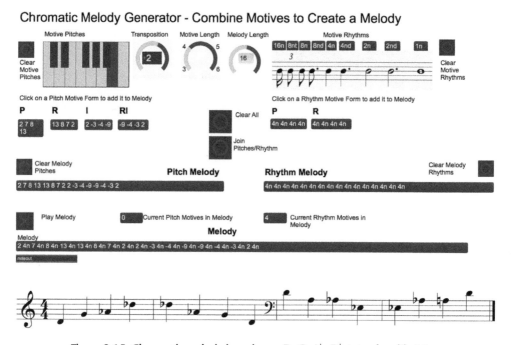

Figure 9.15: Chromatic melody based on a D–G–A♭–D♭ tetrachord in Max.

Chromatic Melody Generator's melodies appear in the **message** in the lower part of the screen with pairs of values for each note: a number representing pitch, and a note value for the rhythm, such as 4n (quarter note) or 8nd (dotted eighth note)—Max's standard set of note values. The pitch values are centered on middle C as value 0.

For pitches in the first octave above middle C, the values are the same as pitch classes. **Chromatic Melody Generator** represents the chromatic scale from C4 to B4 as 0 to 11. Higher pitches continue the numbering—C5 is 12, C#/D♭5 is 13, etc. Starting with B3, negative numbers are used, so that B3 is −1, B♭/A#3 is −2, A3 is −3, and these negative numbers continue as lower pitches for several octaves.

9.10 Two-Part Phrase Based on an All-Interval Tetrachord

Among the twenty-nine possible tetrachords are **all-interval tetrachords**, an example of which is C–C#–E–F#. By arranging these four pitches in different ways, all the intervals less than an octave can be created, as shown in the following table. As an example, C4 to C#4 is a minor second (m2), and C#4 to C5 is a major seventh (M7). These two intervals are inversions of one another (tab. 9.3).

Table 9.3: Intervals in all-interval tetrachord (C–C#–E–F#).

Pitches	Intervals
C–C#/C#–C	m2 or M7
C–E/E–C	M3 or m6
C–F#/F#–C	tritone
C#–E/E–C#	m3 or M6
C#–F#/F#–C#	p4 or p5
E–F#/F#–E	M2 or m7

We'll use this tetrachord to create a three-measure two-part phrase with **Chromatic Melody Generator**. The four forms of the tetrachord are shown in figure 9.16.

Figure 9.16: Four forms of C–C#–E–F# in Max.

To create a bass line for the three measures, we'll start with I (0), the inverse form, and follow it with a RI (−5), the retrograde inversion transposed down five semitones. The rhythms for these two tetrachords will be based on the rhythmic motive of a dotted half, quarter, dotted quarter, eighth, and we'll follow this by its retrograde. The **Chromatic Melody Generator** setting in figure 9.17 shows the bass line.

The melody uses the motive in three forms: (1) P +3 (the prime form transposed up three semitones); (2) P +5 (prime transposed up five semitones); (3) and I +12 (the inversion transposed up an octave). The rhythmic-motive forms used are: (1) dotted eighth, sixteenth, quarter, quarter; (2) the retrograde of the form; (3) the original rhythmic motive form. The bass line and melody are shown in musical notation below the patcher. The last melody note was extended so as to end with the bass line (figure 9.18).

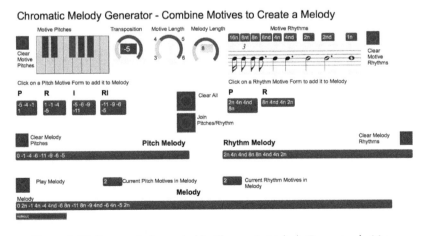

Figure 9.17: Bass melody created in Chromatic Melody Generator **in Max.**

Figure 9.18: Two-part phrase based on all-interval tetrachord.

The phrase is based solely on one all-interval tetrachord, and the sound of the all-interval tetrachords ensures an atonal and chromatic quality. In atonal music, the consistency of material, whether it's based on the use of pitch sets or tone rows, is often an important consideration. In that sense, atonal music shares a strong bond with tonal music, as tonal music achieves consistency by its use of tertian harmony.

9.11 Max Patcher 13: *Chromatic Melody Generator*

In the patcher presentation of the **Chromatic Melody Generator** (figure 9.19), we see that the upper left quadrant is for creating the pitch motive and the upper right quadrant is for creating the rhythm motive. The motives are joined together to make the pitch and rhythm melodies, and the two lists of pitches and rhythmic values are laced together to create the actual melody. Many of the subpatchers are essentially the same as those of the **Diatonic Melody Generator**. Significantly, there is no translation of pitches into scale degrees— something that makes the chromatic version less complicated than the diatonic version.

The **Chromatic Melody Generator** has the same subpatchers (**p SortAndTranspose**, **p Inversion**, and **p melodycount**), the same objects, and the same overall design as the diatonic version. To perform the melody, we simply add the value 60 to the numbers representing the melody pitches, so that our middle C (pitch 0) becomes MIDI note 60.

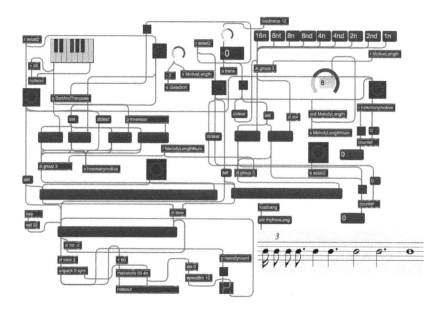

Figure 9.19: Chromatic Melody Generator **(patcher).**

9.12 Exercises

9.12.1 Exercise 1: Trichord and Tetrachord Music in Logic

Using the methods outlined in this chapter, create several phrases of music based on trichords and tetrachords. As you listen to the transposed, inverted, and retrograded forms of the trichords and tetrachords, think about creating different shapes with these various forms, such as a rising and falling shape, or a shape that alternates high notes with low notes. Copy and paste the forms of the sets into MIDI regions in tracks in Logic and create a soundscape by using all the tools at your disposal (Software instruments, MIDI FX, audio Plugins, looping, automation, panning, etc.)

9.12.2 Exercise 2: Use Finale to Create a Twelve-Tone Piano Prelude

The first step is to create a twelve-tone row or series. There are two things to remember for this process: (1) no pitch can appear twice; and (2) each of the twelve notes of the chromatic scale appears only once. Using Finale's **Canonic Utilities** and **Transposition**, create forty-eight versions of the tone row, including twelve versions of each category: transposition, retrograde, inversion, and retrograde inversion. Arrange these row forms into a matrix in a table with twelve columns and twelve rows.

Once you have all the possible row forms, select forms for melodies and accompaniment figures. You can also create chords from portions of a row, perhaps limiting yourself to dyads or trichords. But how you manipulate the row is a compositional choice. Consider yourself free to use forms however you'd like. Many twelve-tone composers avoided octaves and contiguous row-form repetitions, but there are many possible approaches.

9.12.3 Exercise 3: Bartok's String Quartet No. 5, Finale (Introduction)

The introduction of the last movement of Bela Bartok's String Quartet No. 5 sounds something like this (figure 9.20):

Figure 9.20: Bartok's String Quartet No. 5 (excerpt).

Recreate this passage with **Chromatic Melody Generator**, with six forms of the opening tetrachord. First, this opening tetrachord should be input an octave higher than notated in figure 9.20, then transposed down to this level. The remaining five measures can be derived from the opening motive by transposing and retrograding the motive. If you listen to the entire movement, you will hear the motive return at various points.

9.12.4 Exercise 4: Chopin's Etude, Opus 10, No. 2 in A Minor

Frederic Chopin, and other Romantic-era composers, sometimes used the chromatic scale in a tonal context. Using the **Chromatic Melody Generator** recreate this opening passage from

Chopin's Etude, Opus 10, No. 2 with eight forms of the first four notes (a tetrachord)—this is somewhat modified from the original, but sounds very similar (figure 9.21).

Figure 9.21: Chopin Etude, Opus 10, No. 2 (excerpt).

Notice how the chromatic scale is used throughout the piece. Nikolai Rimsky-Korsakov's *Flight of the Bumble Bee* employs the chromatic scale in a similar fashion.

9.12.5 Exercise 5: Modify Chromatic Melody Generator

Using the same techniques as outlined in Chapter 6 to modify the **Diatonic Melody Generator**, modify the **Chromatic Melody Generator** to randomly generate motives and melodies. Use your critical listening skills to select interesting and worthwhile motives and melodies to create music.

CHAPTER 10

Sound and Music Theory

10.1 *Music as Sound*

Our focus so far has been on using Logic, Max, and Finale to learn about music's rhythmic and pitch structures, and we have used MIDI, music notation, and Max programming in this pursuit. These programs also provide a window into sound itself by playing and recording sound and by displaying visualizations of the sound as **waveforms**. In this chapter, we'll discuss how these audio capabilities relate to music theory. In Logic, audio is played on **audio tracks**, and the program has many tools for editing and mixing audio. In Max, many objects (those with a tilde [~] after the object name) work with audio signals. As an example, **gate~** lets audio pass through when the gate is open and disconnects the pass-through when closed. Logic can also convert audio into MIDI data.

We know that the distance between two musical pitches is a musical interval measured by semitones, and that intervals are named with qualities and ordinal numbers (perfect fifth, minor third, etc.). But what elements of sound go into making a musical pitch? Why do a trumpet and a guitar sound so different when playing the *same* musical pitch? And what constitutes a musical interval, besides it being a certain number of semitones and having a recognizable sound?

10.2 *Sound and Frequency*

Sound is the perception of changing amounts of air pressure which come to our ears as **waves of compression** (air molecules being pushed closer together) and the opposite force, **rarefaction** (air molecules being spread apart). Air molecules are set into these opposite kinds of motion (compression and rarefaction) as musicians create the vibrations in the air with their voices or instruments. In the case of a violin, musical sounds are created when the bow causes the string to vibrate.

Logic can show the waveform of a violin playing a note—a completely different representation from the MIDI note in the **Piano Roll** or **Score** Editors (figure 10.1). In this image we see the continuous changes in air pressure caused by the violin's sound waves, shown at a vastly magnified time scale. The compression happens above the middle line, and the rarefaction happens below. The middle line is called the **0 line**—and a continuous signal on the 0 line would represent no change in air pressure and would result in no sound. Time moves from left to right; what's represented below is about 1/80th of a second.

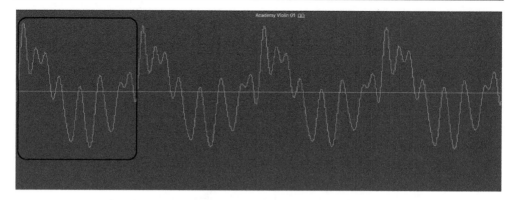

Figure 10.1: Violin tone showing waveform for the pitch E4 in Logic.

When these waves of compression and rarefaction are *cyclical* and repeat many times per second, we perceive *pitch*, as we do when listening to this violin note. One cycle of the waveform is marked off by the box, and we can see four repetitions of the cycle after this. If we count the number of the waveform's repetitions every second, the **cycles per second** or **cps**, we are measuring **frequency**. The pitch E4, as shown in figure 10.1, has 330 cps, or is at the frequency of 330 Hertz. We measure frequency by **Hertz** (Hz), the number of cycles per second.

Although pitch and frequency are related, pitch is *perceptual* and *relative*, whereas frequency is a *precise* measurement. The pitch A above middle C is understood to have a frequency of 440 Hz, but certain historical tunings might have placed the pitch at 415 Hz, and many European orchestras today tune this note to 443 Hz. Piano technicians will routinely tune pianos up or down a bit, depending on the circumstances. Piano technicians preparing a piano for a concert in a major concert hall might even consider the specific works being performed as they are tuning. The fact that *pitch* is a relative quantification may seem surprising, since electronic tuners are exact devices. But pitch's relative quality is not simply a matter of whether you tune your A4 to 440, 415, or 443 Hz, it's also a fundamental consideration in creating scales, intervals, and chords. Which frequencies are used in the notes of a major scale is not a simple issue. An understanding of frequency and pitch can help us learn about all these musical materials, as well as **timbre**, which is the sound quality of instruments and voices. First, however, we'll need to discuss some of the fundamental properties of sound.

10.3 Waveforms

Music technology allows us to see and hear music's waveforms, such as the violin tone, and it also allows us to create simple waveforms, such as a **sine wave**. We see the sine waveform in the upper part of the screen in figure 10.2. Its smooth shape is due to the fact that it is generated by the mathematical sine function! Like our violin tone, this waveform has a frequency of 330 Hz and is also the pitch E4. Compared to the violin, however, it sounds bland, unchanging, and hollow.

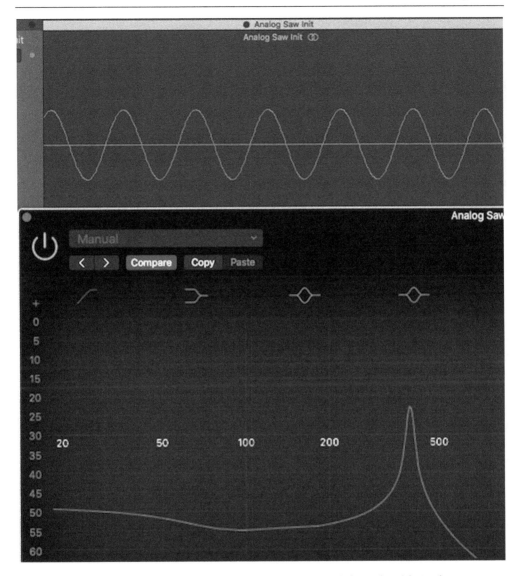

Figure 10.2: A sine wave and its frequency spectrum (Channel EQ) in Logic.

Below the waveform view, we see an analysis of the frequency content, a **frequency spectrum**. This view is from the **Analyzer** function of Logic's **Channel EQ** plugin. The peaks in a frequency spectrum show the loudness or energy of all the frequencies in the sound from 20 Hz to 20 kHz, which is also the range of human perception of frequencies. The sine wave frequency spectrum shows only a single peak of energy at 330 Hz. The frequency spectrum of the violin tone at the same pitch, on the other hand, has a peak at 330 Hz, and many other smaller and higher peaks as well (figure 10.3). Viewed in real time, this spectrum shows us that not only does the violin note contain more frequencies than the sine wave but also that the amplitude amounts of these frequency components are constantly changing. The sine wave frequency spectrum, on the other hand, remains unvarying.

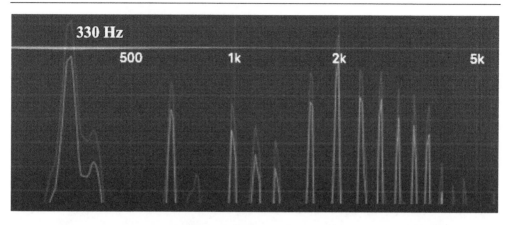

Figure 10.3: Channel EQ showing violin tone's frequency spectrum (fundamental frequency and overtones) in Logic.

10.4 Overtones and Timbre

When the violinist is playing the pitch E3, there is a first peak of frequency at 330 Hz (called the **fundamental** frequency), and additional peaks in the frequency spectrum at the frequencies of the **harmonic-overtone** series. The additional frequencies (overtones or partials) are whole-number multiples (2x, 3x, 4x, 5x, etc.) of the fundamental at 660, 990, 1320, 1650 Hz, etc. The overtone series is the key to understanding why the violin and the sine wave have such different timbres, even as they play the same pitch.

When we hear the violin tone, we don't hear the overtones as separate frequencies, but rather as one tone at the fundamental frequency (which has the greatest amplitude compared with the overtones). We can say that our brains perform a reverse **Fourier Transform** when we hear the sound—we subconsciously assimilate all the frequencies into one tone. The Fourier theorem tells us that any complex waveform frequency can be expressed as *the sum of multiple sine tones*, and the Fourier Transform is the process of taking a complex and cyclical waveform and separating it out into constituent frequencies. Our brain's reverse Fourier Transform sums together the overtones in the violin sound, and we perceive a richly timbred violin pitch at the fundamental, even as strengths of all the overtones are constantly changing.

How do timbre and the overtone series relate to music theory? To begin with, understanding musical timbre (and its basis in the overtone series) is helpful in the study of orchestration, instrumentation, and counterpoint—extensions and applications of music theory. A musical instrument's tone color is determined by which parts of the harmonic series it emphasizes. Practically speaking, a loud trumpet sound with its rich, bright, and forceful timbre contains many overtones. A clarinet, by contrast, emphasizes the odd-numbered overtones. How do these instruments combine effectively? Additionally, the overtone series can tell us about other aspects of music theory, specifically musical intervals and the quality of consonance and dissonance. Some music theorists have used digital analysis and visualization of music to explore music's organization (Cogan, 1984), and this area of study is now available to anyone with a computer and a DAW.

How can these separate frequencies be there when we don't hear them individually? With Max, we can demonstrate how our brains subconsciously perform this reverse Fourier Transform when we generate a **sawtooth** waveform, a synthesized waveform with multiple overtones (figure 10.4). We create the sawtooth by adding sine tones one by one as overtones (whole-number multiples), with each successive overtone having 1/Nth power, where N is equal to the overtone number. The image in the oscilloscope window will gradually morph from a sine tone to a sawtooth as we toggle on the overtones from left to right (the **toggles** are directly above the **gate~** objects). When we add them one by one, each new frequency will be perceived as we add it.

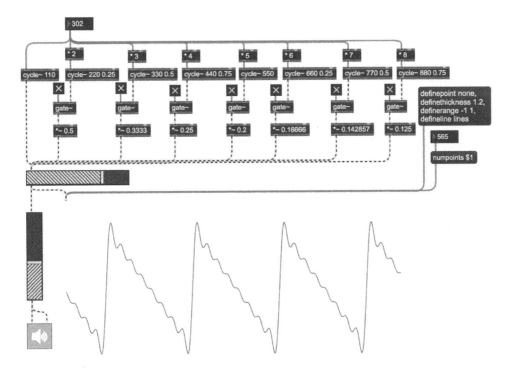

Figure 10.4: Summing sine waves to create a sawtooth wave **(patcher 14) in Max.**

When all the overtones are present, we can turn the volume to zero with the **gain~** object (a slider) on the left side of the patcher and then turn it back up to an audible level. As if by magic, we no longer hear the individual component frequencies! When we turn the volume back up, we hear only a single musical tone at the fundamental, because our brains gather the overtones together as one tone.

10.5 Musical Intervals and Just Intonation

Intervals are classified by ordinal number (seconds, thirds, fourths, etc.) and quality (major, minor, perfect, etc.) based on the number of semitones between the two pitches. Intervals are also classified as consonant or dissonant, and all of these attributes are part of music theory. From an acoustical point of view, however, musical intervals are formed as the ratio between two tones' fundamental's frequencies. The most universally recognized interval is the octave, with a ratio of 2:1. Octaves are universally recognized in all musical cultures and always have a 2:1 ratio.

Other musical-interval ratios can be determined in different ways, and these have changed over time and in different musical cultures. One historically significant basis for creating intervals is **Just intonation**, in which small whole-number ratios are used to determine intervals. These kinds of ratios are considered **pure**. We can demonstrate a major scale with just intonation by determining each scale-step frequency as a ratio of the tonic's fundamental frequency. In this case, we have chosen 220 Hz as the fundamental frequency for the A major scale; each scale-step's frequency is determined by the simple ratio shown in table 10.1.

Table 10.1: Just intonation frequency ratios for A major scale starting on A at 200 Hz.

A major scale based on just intonation								
Pitch	A	B	C#	D	E	F#	G#	A
Interval	Unis.	M2	M3	P4	P5	M6	M7	P8
Ratio	1:1	9:8	5:4	4:3	3:2	5:3	15:8	2:1
Multiply Fundamental	*1	*1.125	*1.25	*1.33r	*1.5	*1.66r	*1.875	*2
Freq. Hz.	220	245.5	275	293.33	330	366.66	412.5	440

The **Just intonation A major scale** patcher (figure 10.5) allows us to play the scale using the frequencies listed in table 10.1 (the Freq. Hz values). The first three notes play through the left channel, and the rest play through the right channel. We can play the entire scale by clicking on and off each note, or we can listen to intervals formed between one of the first three notes (A, B, C#) and one of the last five notes (C#, D, E, F#, G#, and A).

The notes and intervals formed by just intonation sound a bit foreign to our ears, as music today is tuned differently. The intervals formed between the starting tonic A and successive pitches are pure and are based on the simple ratios listed, and these sound in tune. Certain other intervals formed between other scale degrees are not pure, however, and they don't sound right. For instance, a pure B → D minor third has a ratio of 6:5 (the higher note should be 1.2 times the frequency of the lower note). The B → D minor third created here has a frequency ratio of 293.33 / 245.5 or 1.1948 . . ., noticeably different from 1.2 times the lower frequency. The C# → E minor third's frequency ratio, on the other hand, is 330 / 275 which is exactly 1.2. The B → D minor third has **acoustical beating** and sounds out of tune. Acoustical beating is an audible periodic variation in volume created when two frequencies that are close in pitch are played together—and it can also occur with these non-pure intervals. The somewhat out of tune B → E perfect fourth is 330 / 245.5, or 1.3441, higher than a pure 1.33r perfect fourth, while the C# → F# perfect fourth is 366.66 / 275, and is closer to 1.33r.

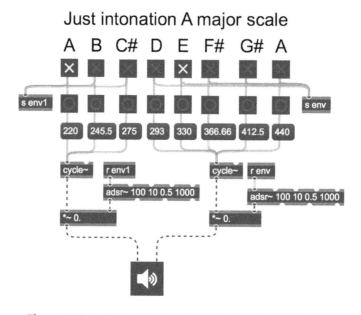

Figure 10.5: Just intonation A major scale **(patcher 15) in Max.**

Tuning anomalies such as these are the reason why just intonation is ultimately not a useful system for music with an expanded and chromatic palette of pitches and chords. But it's important to note that these pure intervals are found in the harmonic-overtone series. As they are based on whole-number multiples of a fundamental frequency, harmonic overtones have many of the same ratios as the just intonation intervals. In the following example, we build an overtone series by starting with A1 with a frequency of 55 Hz as the fundamental. The next two pitches in the series are A2 and E3. The perfect fifth's (A2–E3) frequency ratio is 3:2 (165:110), the same ratio we used in our just intonation A major scale, and the perfect fourth's ratio (E3–A4) is 4:3 (220:165) (figure 10.6).

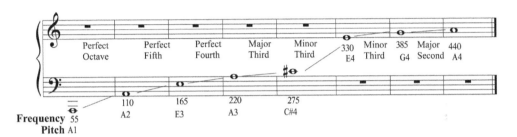

Figure 10.6: Harmonic overtone series.

One of the practical aspects of the Fourier theorem is that musical tones are comprised of frequency components in the harmonic series. If you have the A1 pitch in a chord, for example, you also have the E3 frequency as an additional component. This might explain why the fifth is the one chord tone in a triad which can be omitted without the triad losing its essential nature—the fifth's frequency is already present in the root. If you have an A, one of its overtone components is an E. The E will not be as loud as the fundamental A, but it's there. When an instrument is playing a musical pitch, the harmonic-series pitches decrease in energy (loudness) as you get higher in the series, but this second overtone (an octave and a fifth above the fundamental) is present enough to suggest that an A major triad can be represented by just an A and a C#.

10.6 Ratios and Intervals

Given that the harmonic series has intervals with these ratios that sound pure and clear, it would be logical to assume that musicians would produce musical scales from these intervals, as we did with the **Just Intonation A major scale**. Using the pure-interval ratios to create scales is possible but presents problems for chromatic music.

Pythagorean tuning, for instance, was based on the idea that if you used the 3:2 ratio of the perfect fifth, you could generate all the pitches in the chromatic scale. First, you can generate all the pitches by ascending fifths using the 3:2 ratio, and then by transposing them down by octaves (divide by two to transpose down one octave, divide by four to transpose down two octaves, etc.), you can put all pitches in the same octave. Eventually, one can derive a chromatic scale in one octave, based on generating ascending perfect fifths with the 3:2 ratio (table 10.2):

Table 10.2: The twelve chromatic pitches generated by ascending perfect fifths.

C1	G1	D2	A2	E3	B3	G♭,F#4	D♭,C#4	A♭,G#5	E♭,D#6	B♭,A#6	F7

The next pitch a perfect fifth up in the series after F7 is C8, seven octaves above where we started. The problem is that this C8, as generated based on this series of twelve 3:2 ratio perfect fifths, is a different frequency than that generated by a series of seven 2:1 octaves. This noticeable difference in frequency is called a **Pythagorean Comma**. The **Pythagorean Comma** patcher shown in figure 10.7 generates two signals, which will be heard on the left and right audio channels, respectively (figure 10.7). The fundamental frequency of A0 (27.5 Hz) in the left channel can be changed to produce a series of seven frequencies, each one of which doubles the previous frequency (ascending by octaves) until you reach A7 at 3520 Hz (27.5 x 2^7). The right channel produces a series of twelve frequencies, each one multiplies the previous frequency by 1.5 (ascending by pure perfect fifths) until you reach an A7 at the frequency of 3568.0242 Hz (27.5 x 1.5^{12}). But these two frequencies are noticeably different: 3520 Hz and 3568 Hz. Pythagorean tuning leads to other intonation problems as well and, like just intonation, has limited usefulness for any music beyond one-octave diatonic-scale melodies.

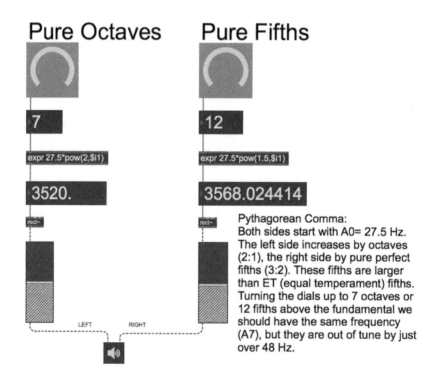

Pythagorean Comma:
Both sides start with A0= 27.5 Hz.
The left side increases by octaves
(2:1), the right side by pure perfect
fifths (3:2). These fifths are larger
than ET (equal temperament) fifths.
Turning the dials up to 7 octaves or
12 fifths above the fundamental we
should have the same frequency
(A7), but they are out of tune by just
over 48 Hz.

Figure 10.7: Pythagorean Comma **(patcher 16) in Max.**

10.7 Meantone and Equal Temperaments

Starting in the sixteenth century, musicians started modifying tuning systems to mitigate these limitations, leading to the development of **temperaments**. Among these were **meantone** temperaments, in which intervals are based on a slightly smaller-than-pure perfect fifth. Meantone temperaments strive to maintain purer thirds than those in just intonation, but are still limited when it comes to music that uses a wide range of pitches.

When playing a keyboard tuned in meantone temperament, you will hear that the primary chords sound sweet, but chords from distant keys can sound quite strange. Tuning a keyboard in meantone tuning requires that it be tuned in a specific key. Music played in that key sounds good, but music played in the key a half-step down won't sound as good. Certain distant chords will contain **wolf tones**, so named because they sound like a howling wolf (especially on an organ). Music theorists made changes to tuning systems throughout the seventeenth and eighteenth centuries, and eventually a system of **equal temperament** was widely adopted. In equal temperament each semitone is exactly the same ratio distance: the 12th root of 2 or 1.05946. The result is that equal-tempered keyboards can play in any key without having to be retuned, and they can modulate between all keys. The compromise of equal temperament is that many intervals are not at all pure, but this lack of pure intervals is spread throughout all the intervals and keys.

With our programs, we can explore temperament and tuning in various ways. The following Max patcher compares an A major triad with (1) equal temperament, (2) meantone temperament, and (3) just intonation (figure 10.8). Hearing them side by side, the equal-temperament triad is remarkably active sounding, with pronounced acoustical beating between the root and third. The just intonation chord, on the other hand, eliminates acoustical beating and sounds more static.

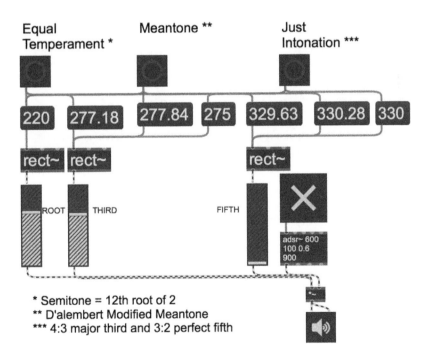

Figure 10.8: Triad with three temperaments (patcher 17) in Max.

One might even say that in comparison to the just intonation triad, the acoustical beating adds considerable roughness to the equal tempered triad. Modern listeners are, however, accustomed to equal temperament. In our patcher, we can use the faders to adjust the volume of the chord tones individually, allowing us to listen to the component intervals of the triads with these different tunings.

10.8 Logic Temperaments

For those who want to explore historical and alternative tuning systems, Logic provides temperament settings, available in a drop-down menu: **File → Project Settings → Tuning** (figure 10.9). The default setting is **Equal Tempered**, but from the **Fixed** category you can pick from a list of close to 100 different temperament systems which will alter the frequencies used to create all the musical tones. Playing music with chromatic harmony and modulations with many of these historical temperaments results in some strange sounds, but diatonic music that relies exclusively on primary triads often sounds sweeter and more consonant than when played in equal temperament (figure 10.10).

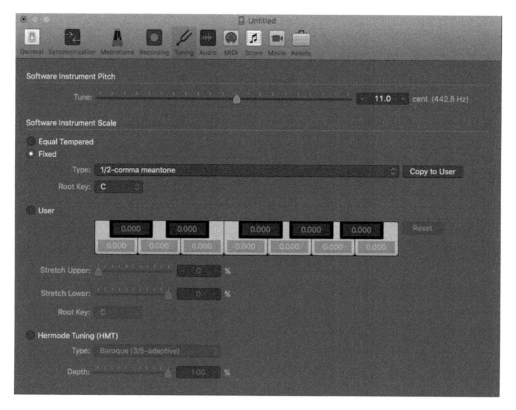

Figure 10.9: Tuning in Logic.

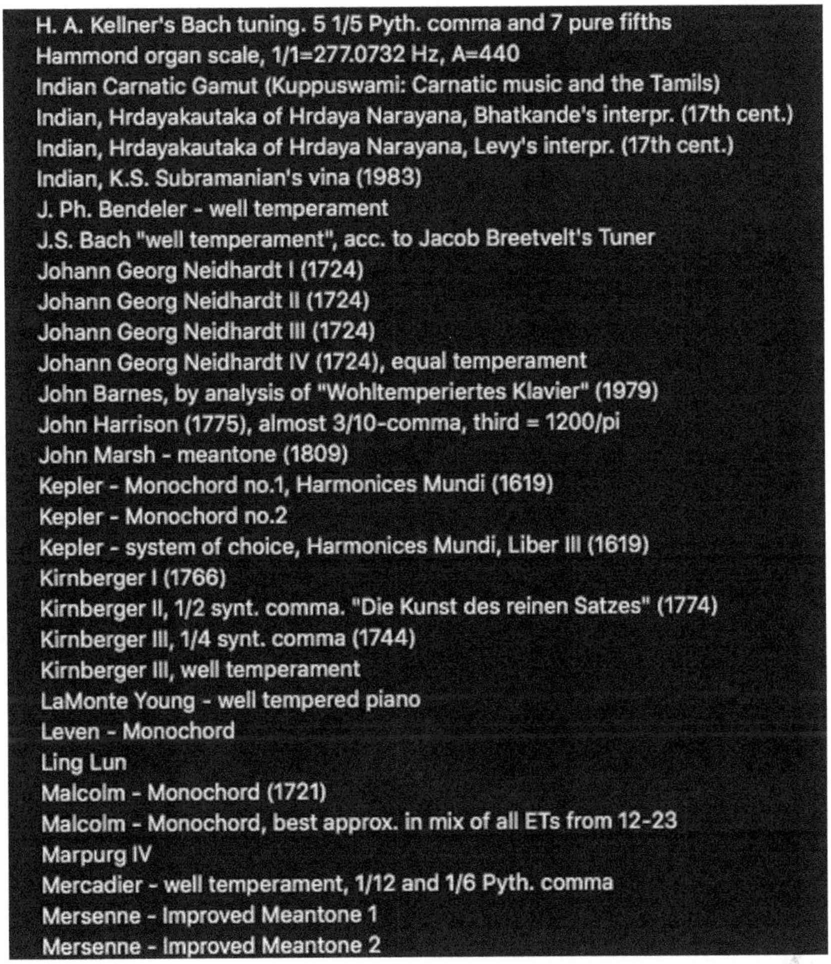

H. A. Kellner's Bach tuning. 5 1/5 Pyth. comma and 7 pure fifths
Hammond organ scale, 1/1=277.0732 Hz, A=440
Indian Carnatic Gamut (Kuppuswami: Carnatic music and the Tamils)
Indian, Hrdayakautaka of Hrdaya Narayana, Bhatkande's interpr. (17th cent.)
Indian, Hrdayakautaka of Hrdaya Narayana, Levy's interpr. (17th cent.)
Indian, K.S. Subramanian's vina (1983)
J. Ph. Bendeler - well temperament
J.S. Bach "well temperament", acc. to Jacob Breetvelt's Tuner
Johann Georg Neidhardt I (1724)
Johann Georg Neidhardt II (1724)
Johann Georg Neidhardt III (1724)
Johann Georg Neidhardt IV (1724), equal temperament
John Barnes, by analysis of "Wohltemperiertes Klavier" (1979)
John Harrison (1775), almost 3/10-comma, third = 1200/pi
John Marsh - meantone (1809)
Kepler - Monochord no.1, Harmonices Mundi (1619)
Kepler - Monochord no.2
Kepler - system of choice, Harmonices Mundi, Liber III (1619)
Kirnberger I (1766)
Kirnberger II, 1/2 synt. comma. "Die Kunst des reinen Satzes" (1774)
Kirnberger III, 1/4 synt. comma (1744)
Kirnberger III, well temperament
LaMonte Young - well tempered piano
Leven - Monochord
Ling Lun
Malcolm - Monochord (1721)
Malcolm - Monochord, best approx. in mix of all ETs from 12-23
Marpurg IV
Mercadier - well temperament, 1/12 and 1/6 Pyth. comma
Mersenne - Improved Meantone 1
Mersenne - Improved Meantone 2

Figure 10.10: Software Instrument Scales **in Logic.**

Once you have selected a temperament, you can **Copy to User**. The **User** keyboard then displays differences in **cents** between the temperament pitches and equal temperament in relation to the tonic note, which will always be 0 for every tuning. The cent is a measurement of pitch: one semitone is equal to 100 cents.

In order for a historical temperament to work in a given context, make sure the music's key is set in the **Key Signature** display of the **LCD**.

10.9 Max Patchers 14 – 17

Max patchers 14–17 all create musical sounds with basic waveform generators. These patchers are all shown in patcher mode, not presentation mode. Max's full name is comprised of three names: Max/MSP/Jitter. These three names reference the different capabilities and the different kinds of objects that we can use for those different capabilities. Max objects, named after Max Mathews (see Introduction), include all the MIDI and data objects that use the machine rate, that is, a slower computational rate than the audio or sampling rate. MSP objects work at the audio rate (or sampling rate) and can be used with audio signals. MSP are the initials of Max's first developer, Miller S. Puckette. Jitter objects can be used for the video capabilities. The word jitter refers to small delays in data transmissions, which are sometimes experienced as distortion.

10.9.1 Max Patcher 14: *Summing Sines to Make a Sawtooth Wave*

Summing Sines to Make a Sawtooth Wave adds multiple sine waves together. Summing waveforms is an example of **additive synthesis**, the broadest category of synthesis techniques in electronic and computer music. With the first four sine-wave generators, we see the principles that are used to create a sawtooth wave from multiple sine-wave generators (figure 10.11).

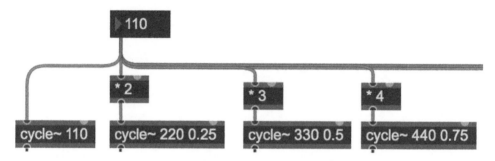

Figure 10.11: Four cycle~ **objects in Max.**

By default, the **cycle~** object generates a sine wave. The leftmost **cycle~** object's left inlet receives a value which sets the frequency for the waveform in Hz, and in this case receives a value for the frequency from a **number box**. This **fundamental frequency** is the basis for all the other frequencies. The second **cycle~** from the left is the fundamental multiplied by 2, the first harmonic. Each of the remaining **cycle~** objects in the patcher has a whole-number multiple of the fundamental frequency (3, 4, 5, 6, 7, 8), and the output of each **cycle~** object is sent to its own **gate~** object. These **gate~** objects allow the signal to pass when the **toggle** connected to the right inlet is on, and thus we are able to turn on and off individual overtones. Directly below each **gate~** object is a **multiply two signals (*~)** object with values between 0.5 to 0.125 as arguments. These **multiply two signals** objects multiply each signal by decreasing amounts, making the sine waves weaker as they go up in frequency.

The first argument written into the **cycle~** object is for the frequency (which is overridden when a value enters the left inlet). The second is for the phase off-set. The phase off-set determines when the waveform starts relative to its cycle. A phase off-set of 0 (or no phase off-set) has the wave starting at the beginning of the waveform, but a phase off-set of 0.5 starts it halfway through the cycle. Phase is usually represented as the 360° of a circle, so that halfway through the wave cycle is 180° or halfway around the circle. The signals are all phase off-set, and these phase off-sets are needed to avoid phase problems.

After passing through the **gate~** and **multiply two signals (*~)** objects the waveform signals are all sent to a **gain~** (a volume slider), and then the summed waveforms are sent to a **plot~** object, an object that appears as a large window on the screen and plots the waveform on a graph. To the left of the **plot~**, there is an **ezdac~** object. The **ezdac~** object transmits audio signals to a selected source or, by default, to the internal speakers. Clicking on the **ezdac~** object also turns the audio engine on and off.

Figure 10.12: The ezdac~ **object in Max.**

10.9.2 Max Patcher 15: *Just Intonation A Major Scale*

The **Just Intonation A Major Scale** patcher uses the **cycle~** object to create sine-wave signals with specific frequencies. The frequencies are based on just intonation instead of equal temperament. The signal in **Summing sines to create a sawtooth wave** was continuous, but could be turned off by turning the volume slider all the way down.

The more usual way to create musical tones with beginnings and endings in electronic music is to control the amplitude of a signal with an **amplitude envelope**. In **Just intonation A major scale**, an **adsr~** object (an amplitude envelope) controls **cycle~**'s signal amplitude by varying the value of **multiply two signals** (*~) over time (figure 10.13). The **adsr~** object is named after the standard four-stage amplitude: **attack**, **decay**, **sustain**, and **release**. The first, second, and fourth arguments for **adsr~** are given in milliseconds, while the third argument is given in an amplitude amount with a usable range of 0.0–1.0 (figure 10.13).

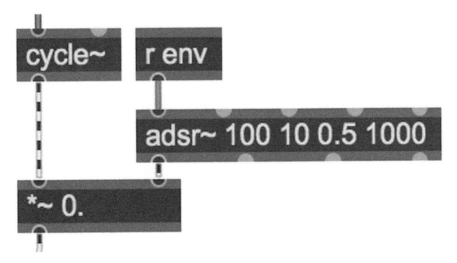

Figure 10.13: adsr~ **(amplitude envelope) in Max.**

The arguments function as follows: (1) when **adsr~** receives 1 in the left inlet, the volume increase from 0 to an initial maximum value over 100 milliseconds; (2) then decreases to a sustained lower amplitude level of 0.5 over 10 milliseconds; (3) when **adsr~** receives 0 in the left inlet, the amplitude reduces to 0 over 1000 milliseconds. These amplitude changes avoid the clicking noises that occur when an electronic signal is turned on or off abruptly. The 1 and 0 that turns **adsr~** on and off come from each scale tone's **toggle**. Each scale tone stays on while the **toggle** is on, so we can listen to the natural intervals of the scale.

10.9.3 Max Patcher 16: *Pythagorean Comma*

The Pythagorean Comma uses two **rect~** objects as the waveform generators for the left and right channels. The **rect~** object generates a **square wave** in its default setting. A square wave is a simple harmonic waveform that sounds a little bit like a clarinet. The benefit of using the square wave over the sine wave in this context is that, as its harmonic content is greater, it is more audible at lower amplitudes.

The frequencies of the **rect~** objects are provided by two **expression** objects (**expr**). Both channels start with A0 at 27.5 Hz. The octave frequencies are set by the expression $27.5*2^n$ (where n represents successive octaves), and the fifths by $27.5*1.5^n$ (where n represents successive fifths). Within the **expression** object's one argument (the expression), the variable n is represented by **$i1**. These three symbols can be read as "use the integer (i) entering this first inlet ($1)." In this way, we can change the n value to ascend by octaves or fifths. When these n numbers increase, the frequency is multiplied by an amount to produce a pitch either octaves or perfect fifths higher.

10.9.4 Max Patcher 17: *Triad with Three Temperaments*

The **Triad with Three Temperaments** patcher introduces no new programming concepts or objects. The three **rect~** objects are frequency-controlled by **messages** that don't change. There is a toggle to create an amplitude envelope for the triads, and the tuning system can be changed by the buttons at the top of the screen.

We might ask: instead of the **rect~** object, what would three **cycle~** objects sound like as waveform generators? Max also has a **saw~** object that produces a sawtooth wave, which has an even richer harmonic content. Substituting these waveforms will change the harmonic richness of the individual chord tones. The square waveform provides a good level of harmonic content to hear the differences between the triads tuned in three temperaments.

10.10 Exercises

10.10.1 Exercise 1: Diatonic and Chromatic Music Played with Different Temperaments

Select two pieces of music, one characteristically diatonic, the other characteristically chromatic. For example, you might choose a harpsichord piece by Henry Purcell for the diatonic, and a piano work by Franz Liszt for the chromatic. The diatonic work should have relatively few accidentals, and the chromatic work a fair amount. Find (or create your own) SMF of these pieces to play in Logic. An online search for "Henry Purcell, Free MIDI" and "Franz Liszt, free MIDI" returns several options.

Download the files and open them in separate Logic sessions. In Logic, go to **File** → **Project Settings** → **Tuning**. On the **Software Instrument Scale**, check **Fixed** and browse the historical tunings. Listen to the piece with different tunings, such as these four: (1) Equal Tempered; (2) Ramos de Pareja (1492); (3) Andreas Werckmeister III (1681); (4) ½ Comma meantone. For the historical tunings, make sure to set the **Root Key** to the key of the music. Play each piece with each of the tunings.

Compare the sound of the temperaments in terms of which notes, intervals, or chords stand out. Some parts might sound sweeter with the historical tunings than with the equal temperament, and some might sound quite strange.

10.10.2 Exercise 2: Create a Chromatic Scale by Ear in Max

By creating message boxes that control the frequency of a sine tone (**cycle~**), we can create an A major scale starting from A3/220 Hz and going up one octave to A4/440 Hz. Each pitch of the chromatic scale has its own **message**, and a **dial** with which you can control the frequency. Play the notes with the **kslider** keys and adjust each frequency by ear. The **kslider** keyboard outputs numbers 9 to 21. Other objects include **makenote 10 4n, sel 9 10 11 12 13 14 15 16 17 18 19 20 21**; **adsr~**; **divide two numbers (/ 127.)**; and **multiply two signals (*~)** (figure 10.14). The perfect fifth (at seven semitones above the low A) has a frequency of 332 in the following example—2 Hz higher than a pure perfect fifth of 330 Hz.

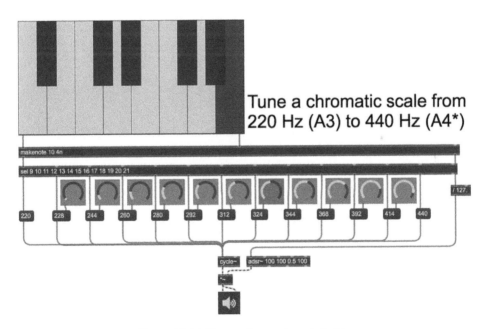

Figure 10.14: Tune a chromatic scale **in Max.**

Bibliography

Attali, Jacques. *Noise, the Political Economy of Music.* Minnesota, 1985.

Barbour, J. Murray. *Tuning and Temperament: A Historical Survey.* Da Capo, 1972.

Boulanger, Richard (editor). *The CSound Book.* MIT, 2000.

Burstein, L. Poundie and Joseph Straus. *Concise Introduction to Tonal Harmony.* W. W. Norton, 2016.

Chadabe, Joel. *Electric Sound: The Past and Promise of Electronic Music.* Prentice Hall, 1997.

Clendinning, Jane and Elizabeth Marvin. *Theory and Analysis.* 2nd ed. W.W. Norton, 2011.

Cogan, Robert. *New Images of Musical Sound.* Harvard University Press, 1984.

Cogan, Robert and Pozzi Escot. *Sonic Design: The Nature of Sound and Music.* Prentice Hall, 1976.

Cook, Gary. *Teaching Percussion.* 2nd ed., Schirmer, 1997.

Cooper, Grosvenor and Leonard Meyer. *The Rhythmic Structure of Music.* The University of Chicago Press, 1960.

Cope, David. *Experiments in Musical Intelligence.* A-R Editions, Inc., 1996.

Cope, David. *The Algorithmic Composer.* A-R Editions, 2000.

Cope, David. *Hidden Structure: Music Analysis Using Computers.* A-R Editions, 2008.

Edstrom, Brent. *Musicianship in the Digital Age.* Thomson, 2006.

Everett, Walter. *The Beatles as Musicians: Revolver through the Anthology.* Oxford University Press, 1999.

Everett, Walter. *The Foundations of Rock.* Oxford University Press, 2009.

Farnell, Andy. *Designing Sound.* MIT, 2010.

Forte, Allen. *The Structure of Atonal Music.* Yale University Press, 1973.

Freedman, Barbara. *Teaching Music Through Composition.* Oxford University Press, 2013.

Friedman, Michael. *Ear Training for Twentieth Century Music.* Yale University Press, 1990.

Gibson, Bill. *Sequencing, Samples, and Loops.* Hal Leonard, 2007.

Grout, Donald Jay. *A History of Western Music.* 3rd ed. WW Norton, 1980.

Guerin, Robert. *MIDI Power!* 2nd ed. Thomson Course Technology, 2006.

Hewitt, Michael. *Music Theory for Computer Musicians.* Course Technology, 2008.

Hewitt, Michael. *Harmony for Computer Musicians.* Course Technology, 2011.

Hindemith, Paul. *Elementary Training for Musicians.* Schott, 1949.

Hosken, Dan. *An Introduction to Music Technology,* 2nd ed., Routledge, 2015.

Huber, David. *Modern Recording Techniques,* 7th ed., Focal Press, 2010.

Johnson, Mark. *Finale 2014, A Trailblazer Guide.* Penelope Press, 2013.

Karpinski, Gary. *Aural Skills Acquisition.* Oxford University Press, 2000.

King, Andrew and Evangelos Himonides. *Music, Technology and Education.* Routledge, 2016.

Kosta, Stefan; et al. *Tonal Harmony.* 7th ed., McGraw Hill, 2013.

Manzo, V. J. *Max/MSP/Jitter for Music.* Oxford University Press, 2011.

Manzo, V. J. and William Kuhn. *Interactive Music.* Oxford University Press, 2016.

Mathews, M. The Digital Computer as a Musical Instrument, *Science,* Volume 142, Issue 3592, pp. 553–557, 1963.

Mulholland, Joe and Tom Hojnacki. *The Berklee Book of Jazz Harmony.* Berklee, 2013.

Nahmani, David. *Logic Pro X 10.1.* Pearson, 2015.

Ottman, Robert and Nancy Rogers. *Music for Sight Singing.* 8th ed., Pearson, 2011.

Patterson, Justin. *The Drum Programming Book.* Backbeat Books, 2015.

Perle, George. *The Listening Composer.* Univ. of California, 1990.

Perle, George. *Serial Composition and Atonality.* 6th ed., Univ. of California, 1991.

Piston, Walter and Mark DeVoto. *Harmony.* 5th ed., Norton, 1987.

Purse, Bill. *Finale Primer, 2014 Edition.* Alfred Music, 2014.

Rahn, John. *Basic Atonal Theory.* Schirmer, 1980.

Rothstein, Joseph. *MIDI, A Comprehensive Introduction.* 2nd ed., AR Editions, 1995.

Rowe, Robert. *Machine Musicianship.* MIT, 2001.

Schoenberg, Arnold. *Fundamentals of Musical Composition.* Faber and Faber, 1967.

Schoenberg, Arnold. *Theory of Harmony.* Univ. of California, 1978.

Slonimsky, Nicolas. *Thesaurus of Scales and Melodic Patterns*. Martino Fine Books, 2018.

Starer, Robert. *Rhythmic Training*. MCA Publishing, 1969.

Straus, Joseph. *Introduction to Post-Tonal Theory*. 4th ed., Norton, 2016.

Tymoczko, Dmitri. *A Geometry of Music.* Oxford University Press, 2011.

Watson, Scott. *Using Technology to Unlock Musical Creativity*. Oxford University Press, 2011.

Weisberg, Arthur. *Performing Twentieth Century Music*. Yale University Press, 1993.

Williams, David and Peter Webster. *Experiencing Music Technology*. 3rd ed., Thomson Schirmer, 1999.

Wilson, Scott, et al. (editors) *The Supercollider Book*. MIT, 2011.

Winkler, Todd. *Composing Interactive Music: Techniques and Ideas Using Max*. MIT, 2001.

Max Patchers and Objects

0) **Send and Receive** (pages xviii–xix)

+ (add two numbers)
counter
makenote
message
metro
notein/noteout
sel or select

1) **Drum Pattern** (pages 13–16)

comment
delay
toggle
transport, Global Transport

2) **Rhythm Generator** (pages 30–34)

attrui
button
midiinfo
pipe
random
send/receive (s/r)
stripnote
subpatcher
translate
trigger (t)
umenu
unjoin/join

3) **Mouse Click Melody** (pages 36–37)

Capture
key
loadbang
midiformat
midiflush
mousestate
onebang
pgmout
zl group/zl slice

4) **Pitch Generator** (pages 43–45)

* (multiply two numbers)
coll
decide
dial
ggate
kslider
nslider

5) **Scale Generator** (pages 55–58)

closebang
dial
gate
inspector
itable
kslider
number
patcher/presentation
preset

6) **Interval Identifier** (pages 60–61)

− (subtract two numbers)
> (compare numbers for greater than condition)
== (compare numbers for equal to condition)
abs
coll
inlet/outlet
nslider
subpatcher

7) **Triad Generator** (pages 86–92)

% (modulo—divide two numbers, output the remainder)
gate
loadmess
matrixctrl
midiin
midiparse
router
zl sort

8) **Triad Identifier** (pages 96–99)

match
quickthresh
switch
unpack
zl.sort
zl.stream

9) **Seventh Chord Generator** (pages 112–115)

pack

10) **Diatonic Melody Generator** (pages 140–144)

midiflush
seq
speedlim
unpack
zl.lace
zl.rev
zl.rot

11) **Diatonic Progression Generator** (page 164–173)

thresh

12) **Chromatic Progression Generator** (pages 191–194)

13) **Chromatic Melody Generator** (page 210)

14) **Summing Sines to make a Sawtooth Wave** (page 224)

*~ (multiply two signals)
cycle~
ezdac~
gate~
number box
slider~

15) **Just Intonation A Major Scale** (page 225)

adsr~

16) **Pythagorean Comma** (page 226)

rect~

17) **Triad with Three Temperaments** (page 226)

Credits

Index

accelerando 2, 16, 19
accidental: definition 41; and **Pitch Generator** 44; and scales 49–52; and **Scale Generator** 55; and chromatic intervals 58; and modes 61–63; and Logic **Score Editor** 74, 83, 183, 226; and **Triad Generator** 90; and Finale 103, 181; and **Seventh Chord Generator** 114; and **Diatonic Progression Generator** 162, 164–165, 172, 177, 183; and **Chromatic Progression Generator** 194
acoustical beating 218, 221–222
additive synthesis 224
adsr~ (Max) 225–227, 232
algorithmic xiii, xv, 20, 28, 30, 146–147, 164, 196, 228
Amazing Grace 178–179
APL (Audio Programming Language) xiii–xv
Apple Loop Beats (Logic) 20, 104, 123
applied dominant 177–184, 189, 194–195, 198
applied leading tone 182–183, 194–195
argument (Max) xiv, 13–16, 30, 44, 68, 90, 97–98, 102, 143, 147, 224–226
Arpeggiator (Logic) 115–118
arpeggio 115, 117
atonal 197–201, 205–207, 210
attrui (Max) 34
ASCII 102
AU DLS Synth 34, 36
Audio MIDI Setup xv, 72
audio track (Logic) 213
augmentation 135, 145
augmented sixth chord (French, Italian, German) 189–190
automation (Logic) 80, 83, 110, 211

Bach, J. S. 19, 136–137
bang (Max) xiv, 13–14, 30–33, 36–37, 57–58, 61, 68, 90–91
bar line 3, 7, 25, 55
Bartok, Bela 211
beat: definition 1–5, 7; and Logic **Grid** 9; and time signature 11; and **Drum Pattern** 14–17; and loops 20–23; and metric modulation 26–28; and **Rhythm Generator** 28–29, 38; and Logic **Arpeggiator** 117; and Finale **Click and Countoff** 124; and motivic analysis 137; and Logic **MIDI Transform Reverse Position** 199
Beats & Project (Logic) 93
Beethoven, Ludwig van 128, 145

Berg, Alban 197, 201, 204–205
Berlin, Irving 155
Berlioz, Hector 189
Bingo 104
block chord 115
borrowed chord 188
Boulez, Pierre 26
BPM (beats per minute) 1–2, 4–5, 10–11, 13, 17, 20, 27–30, 32, 37

cadence 152–154, 161–162, 173–174, 178–179, 184, 187, 197
cadential $^6_4$ 187, 190
Canonic Utilities (Finale) 48, 77–78, 84, 107–108, 119, 132, 136, 145, 174, 181, 202–204, 206, 211
capture (Max) 36–37
Carter, Elliott 26
Change Note Durations (Finale) 13, 135
Channel EQ Analyzer (Logic) 215–216
Chopin, Fréderic 115–117, 211–212
Chord Analysis (Finale) 94–96, 103
Chord Definition (Finale) 120, 179–180
chord substitution 120, 152, 189–191
chord tone 70, 87–91, 96–100, 107, 112–113, 118, 152, 167, 169, 171–172, 174, 219
Chord (Finale) 74–75, 84, 107, 119–120, 124, 179–181
Chord Trigger (Logic) xiv, 47, 71–74, 78–80, 82–85, 104–106, 109–110, 119–120, 123, 149, 151, 153–154, 156, 173–174, 178–179, 182–183
Chromatic Melody Generator (Max) 207–212
chromatic scale xvii, xix, 41, 49, 58, 70, 149–150, 178, 197, 207–208, 211–212, 219, 227
circle of fifths 50–51, 63, 110
clef 29, 40–41, 44, 48–49, 103–104, 138, 153–154
Click and Countoff (Finale) 124, 126
Cogan, Robert 216
Cohen, Leonard 182
coll (Max) 44, 60–61, 89, 113, 140, 143, 169, 171–172, 193
common time 3, 11, 14–15, 22, 30, 124, 135, 140
common tone 161
common-tone diminished chord 189
compare numbers for equal to condition (Max) 68
compression 213–214
Cope, David 164
counter (Max) xix, 57–58, 144, 166, 176, 194,
Count-in (Logic) 9

Covay, Don 149
Crazy (Aerosmith) 4
Cycle Area (Logic) 17
cycle~ (Max) 224–226

DAW (digital audio workstation) xiii–xv, 1, 216
decide (Max) 44
dial (Max) 35, 37, 44, 56, 58, 85–86. 92, 138, 142, 227
Diatonic Melody Generator (Max) xv, 138–141, 145–146, 207, 210, 212
Diatonic Progression Generator (Max) 156–157, 162, 164–173, 175, 177, 183–184, 191–193, 196
diminution 135, 145
Document Setup Wizard (Finale) 10, 64
dominant 40, 79, 81, 109, 140, 151–152, 154–155, 157, 183, 188
dominant function 152
dominant seventh 105, 108–109, 114, 117, 120, 122–124, 140, 159–161, 167–168, 177–178, 184, 186–187, 189, 195
downbeat 109
drone 149–150
Drum Groove (Finale) 20–22, 124–125
Drum Pattern (Max) 13–17, 28, 30
dump (Max) 36
Dylan, Bob 149–150

Echo (Logic) 5–6
enharmonic: definition 41–44; and scales 49–52; and intervals 58–59, 61; and Logic **Chord Trigger** 74; and Finale 76, 107, 181, 202; and **Triad Generator** 90, 103; and **Diatonic Progression Generator** 164; and **Chromatic Progression Generator** 194, 202
equal temperament 221–223, 225, 227
Exercise Wizard (Finale) 17
Expression (Finale) 2, 19
extended chord 119, 178, 184, 197
Extended Harmonies (Logic) 105–106, 120, 123
ezdac~ (Max) 224–225

Fields, Dorothy 127
figures (in Roman numeral analysis) 84, 105–110
fingering 66–67
Flex Pitch (Logic) 21
flip (Logic) 132, 145, 200, 207
Fourier transform 216–217, 219
fpic (Max) 31, 144
Franklin, Aretha 149–150
frequency 214–216
Frère Jacques 150–151
fundamental frequency 216–217

gate (Max) 87, 89–91, 113–114, 141, 143, 165, 167–169, 172
gate~ (Max) 213, 217, 224
General MIDI 28, 37
Global Transport (Max) 15, 28, 30, 34
Greensleeves 1–2

Grid (Logic) 7, 9
Grid mode (Logic **Arpeggiator**) 115, 117–118
Guitar Hero 34

half step 41, 45, 54
Hamilton, Nancy 124–125
Handel, G. F. 127
harmonic analysis 79, 84–85
harmonic motive/sequence 162
harmonic overtones 219
Hart, Lorenz 109–110, 182–183
Hertz (Hz) 214
hexachord 205
hook 128

IAC (Interapplication Communication) xv, 72–73, 79, 173
Implode Music (Finale) 65
interval class 98, 198
Interval Identifier (Max) 59–61, 67
interval 45–47, 213; inversion of 48; and minor scales 52–53; chromatic 58–59; identification of 59–61, 67–69; reading (natural intervals) 64–65; and triads 70, 74, 96–98; and seventh chords 105, 107, 112, 122; and extended chords 119–120; and melody 127–128, 131, 136; and root motion interval 151, 162, 185; and atonal music 202, 206; and frequency 217–221
itable (Max) 56–58, 67, 158, 165–167, 168, 171, 176, 183, 192, 196

Jackson, Michael 185
Jobim, A. C. 184
just intonation 217–225

Kern, Jerome 127, 195–196
key (Max) 37, 102
key 49–52, 55, 78, 104, 110, 131, 137, 144, 150–151, 161; relative and parallel keys 51–52; and **Triad Generator** 85–86; and **Diatonic Melody Generator** 138–140, 143, 145; and **Diatonic Progression Generator** 156–157, 162, 164–167, 172, 175; and Finale **Spelling Tables** 76–77; close and distant keys 183; modulation of keys 183–187, 194–195
key signature 10, 177
Key Signature (Finale) 54, 62, 64–65
Kodaly 17
kslider (Max) 45, 56, 87, 100, 102, 122, 138, 140, 227

LCD (Liquid Crystal Display) (Logic) 1, 3–4, 49, 51, 63, 80, 92–93, 223
leading tone 40, 79, 81, 152, 157, 159–161, 172
ledger lines 41
Lennon, John 161, 182, 188
Lewis, Morgan 124
Liszt, Franz 226
loadbang (Max) 37, 58
loadmess (Max) 92
loop 20–23, 37–38

makenote (Max) xix, 13–14, 31, 33, 44, 56, 92, 102, 143–144, 165–166, 194, 227

Marley, Bob 161

match (Max) 98–99

Mathews, Max xiv, 223

matrix 204

matrixctrl (matrix switch control) (Max) 89, 169, 171, 193

McCartney, Paul 161, 182, 188

Meade, Norman 155

measure 2–4, 11, 13–17

meantone temperament 220–221, 227

mediant 40, 79, 81, 152, 157, 161, 167, 177

melodic inversion 48, 131–134

message (Max) xix, 13–15, 34, 37, 44–45, 56, 61, 67, 91, 96, 98, 100, 102, 138–139, 142–144, 208, 226–227

meter 3–4, 16, 20, 29, 127, 195; and Finale 10–11, and Max 13–15

metric modulation 26–28

metro (Max) xix, 14–16, 30, 56–58, 176

Metronome (Logic) 2, 9, 17

middle C xix, 38, 40–41, 49, 58, 68, 70, 90, 102, 129, 138, 143, 167, 198, 208, 210, 214

MIDI setup (Finale) xvi

MIDI Transform (Logic) 48–49, 63–64, 78, 84, 108–110, 129–130, 132, 135–136, 145, 173–174, 194, 198–200, 206–217

MIDI Yoke xv

Mitchell, Joni 155

modal mixture (modal interchange) 187–189

modes 52, 61–63, 66–67

modulation (harmonic) 177, 183–187, 194–195, 197, 222

modulo (Max) 90, 98

motive 127–148, 162–164, 200

motivic analysis 136–137

Mouret, J. J. 38

Mouse Click Melody (Max) 34–39

mousestate (Max) 37

Mozart, W. A. 109

multiply two numbers (Max) 91

multiply two signals (Max) 224–225, 227

Neapolitan sixth *see* phrygian ♭II

non-chord tones 149–151

note number: for percussion sounds 33; and pitch names 44; and C major scale 57–59; and triads 87; and accidentals in Max 90

note durations (note or rhythmic values): 4–7, 10, 12–13, 16–17, 32, 135; and Max 14–15, 30–31, 86, 88, 142, 157, 210

notein (Max) xix, 36, 56, 60, 87

noteout (Max) xvi, 13–15, 34–37, 44, 55–57, 102, 111, 145, 157, 165, 172, 194

nslider (Max) 44, 61, 85, 90–91, 100–102, 111, 114, 121–122, 165, 172

Oats, Peas, Beans and Barley Grow 151–152

object (max) xviii–xix

octave 41, 45–46, 48

ordinal number 46

Page, Jimmy 161

Parker, Charlie 39

patcher xv–xvii

patcher mode (Max) 30–31, 34, 36, 43, 55, 60, 86, 96, 140–141, 146–147, 165, 223

Pencil (Logic) 1, 19

pgmount (Max) 37

phrase (musical) 17, 35, 37, 62, 129, 131, 133, 178, 187, 208–210; definition 152

phrygian ♭II 188–189

Piano Roll Editor (Logic) 5, 9, 23, 40–42, 46, 52, 94, 129–130, 133

pickup (anacrusis) 6–7, 10–11

pipe (Max) 31, 33, 56

pitch class 90, 202, 205

Pitch Generator (Max) 42–45

pitch set 205–207, 210

pivot (Finale) 132, 136, 145, 174

pivot modulation 184–185

Plant, Robert 161

plot~ (Max) 224

polyphonic mode (Max, for **nsliders**) 165

Porter, Cole 191

position (root and inversions): and triads 70–71; and Finale and Logic 77–78, 93, 96, 103; and **Triad Generator** 84–89; and **Triad Identifier** 96–99; and **Triad Quiz** 100–102; and seventh chords 107–110; and **Seventh Chord Generator** 113

power chord 160

PPQN (part per quarter note) *see* tick

preset (Max) 56–57, 67, 194

proportional tempi *see* metric modulation

Puckette, Miller S. 224

Purcell, Henry 19, 226

Pythagorean tuning 219–220

quantization (rhythmic) 7–9

quickthresh (Max) 97

Radiohead 189

random (Max) 30, 44, 68, 102, 122, 146–147, 175–176

Random Pitch (Logic) 63–64, 129, 198

receive (Max) 31–33, 91, 102, 147–148, 166–167, 172, 175, 192

rect~ (Max) 226

Reger, Max 197, 201

Reich, Steve 20

rest (rhythmic duration) 5, 12, 32

retrograde 119, 131–133, 136, 138–142, 144–145, 198–204, 208–211

Rhythm Generator (Max) xv, 28–34, 37–38, 55, 146

Rhythmic Subdivisions (Finale) 118

Rhythmic values *see* note durations

Rimsky-Korsakov, Nikolai 26, 212

ritardando 2, 16, 19, 153

Rodgers, Richard 109–110, 182–183

Roman numeral 79, 81, 85, 105, 108, 156, 165, 167, 175
router (Max) 89, 113, 169, 171, 193,

Santy Anno 7
scale degree 40–41, 45, 52, 56, 77, 79, 81, 108–110, 117, 138–140, 143, 167, 188, 210, 218
Scale Generator (Max) xv, 54–58, 67
Scale Quantize (Logic) 52–53, 61–63, 66, 130–132, 144–145
Schoenberg, Arnold 197, 201
Schubert, Franz Peter 149
Score Editor (Logic) xiii, 5, 7, 9–10, 19, 22, 29, 38, 40, 45, 49, 54–55, 74, 79–80, 106, 110, 117, 131, 198
Score Settings (Finale) 10–11
Seal 188
secondary dominant *see* applied dominant
sel, select (Max) xix, 30, 34, 37, 56, 58, 90, 102, 113–114, 144, 166, 168–169, 172, 176, 194, 227
semitone (half step): definition 41; and intervals 46–51; and **Scale Generator** 56–57; and **Interval Identifier** 59–61; and **Interval Quiz** 67–68; and **Spelling Table** 77; and circle of fifths 80, 83; and **Triad Generator** 87–88; and **Triad Identifier** 98–99; and **Seventh Chord Generator** 112–113; and melody 130, 132; and **Diatonic Melody Generator** 142–143; and **Diatonic Progression Generator** 167; and **Chord Definition** 180; and **Chromatic Progression Generator** 185, 189–190, 192; and pitch set 199–200, 206; and **Chromatic Melody Generator** 209; and frequency and temperament 213, 217, 221, 223, 227
send (Max) *see* **receive** (Max)
sequence 131–132, 145; and harmony 162–164
set (Max) 37, 44, 144
Seventh Chord Generator (Max) 111–115, 121–123
Shenandoah 104
Signature Global Tracks (Logic) 50–51
Simple Entry (Finale) 11–13, 16, 64, 103, 118
sine wave 214–217, 224
SmartMusic 17
SMF (Standard MIDI File) 19, 26, 75–77, 124, 179, 181, 226
SMPTE (Society of Motion Picture and Television Engineers) 2
Speedy Entry (Finale) 11–12, 13, 25, 118
Spelling Table (Finale) 76
staff, staves, grand 40–42
Step-input keyboard (Logic) 9–10, 23
Stockhausen, Karlheinz 20
Strauss, Johann 127
Strauss, Richard 26, 187–188
Stravinsky, Igor 26
stripnote (Max) 34, 36, 56, 60, 87
stuck note 35, 37
subdominant 40, 79, 81, 123, 161, 178, 181
subdominant function 152, 177
submediant 40, 79, 81, 152, 161, 177, 186
subpatcher (Max) 31, 32, 68–69, 86–88, 90–92, 97–99, 102–103, 112–114, 122–123, 140–143, 147–148, 165–172, 175–176, 192–194

subtonic 81
supertonic 40, 79, 81, 168, 177, 194–195
switch (Max) 89, 97, 99

Takadimi 17
Tempo Global Track (Logic) 1–2, 19
Tempo Marks (Finale) 2
Tempo Tap (Finale) 19
tempo xiv, 1–2, 10–11, 15–16, 19, 20, 26–28, 32, 34–35, 127, 153
tendency tones 149–150, 159–160
tertian 197–198, 200–201, 210
tetrachord: 197, 200, 205–212; all-interval tetrachord 208–210
The Oak and the Ash 137
The Water is Wide 35
tick 2, 29, 199
tie 7
Time (Logic) 2–3
Time Handle (Logic) 25, 133
time signature 3–4, 10–11, 16, 26–27, 40, 124, 140, 154, 174, 198
Time Signature (Finale) 11
Todd Winkler xiv
tone row 201–202, 204, 211
tonic: and scale 40; and keys 51; and **Scale Generator** 56–57; and Finale 64; and diatonic collection of triads 79, 81; and blues 123; and **Diatonic Melody Generator** 138, 140; and harmonic progressions 150–155, 159–164; and **Diatonic Progression Generator** 166–168; and Logic **Chord Trigger** 173; and chromatic harmony 177–178; and Finale **Chord** tool 180–181; and **Chromatic Progression Generator** 183–184, 188; and atonal music 197; and tuning and temperament 217–218; and Logic **Tuning** 223
tonic function 150, 152
tonicization 177
translate (Max) 32–33
Transposer (Logic) xiv, 65–66, 123, 140
Transposition (Finale) 47, 65, 77, 118–119, 131, 136–137, 145, 154–155, 174, 181, 202, 206, 211
Triad Generator (Max) xv, 84–92, 100, 111–113, 122
Triad Identifier (Max) 96–99
trichord 198–200, 205, 211
triplet 7, 10–12, 15–16, 22–24, 26, 28
tritone 59, 190, 209
tritone substitution 189–191
Tuning (Logic) 222–223
Tuplet Definition (Finale) 25
tuplet: 22–26; nested tuplet 26
twelve-tone technique 201–205, 211

unjoin (Max) 31, 33, 141
upbeat 3

Varese, Edgard 197, 200
voice leading 157–160

voicing: open vs. closed 70; and **Triad Generator** 85–86, 88–89, 92; and Logic's **LCD Chord** 93; and **Triad Identifier** 98; and **Triad Quiz** 102; and **Seventh Chord Generator** 111, 113, 115; and Logic's **Chord Trigger** 123; and **Diatonic Progression Generator** 156–158, 165, 169–171; and **Chromatic Progression Generator** 191, 193

waveform 213–216, 223–224, 226
whole step 41, 185, 186

wolf tone 221
Wonder, Stevie 145, 185

zl.clear (Max) 144
zl.group (Max) 36, 60, 91, 97, 141–142, 144, 147, 172
zl.lace (Max) 91, 142–143, 172
zl.rev (Max) 142
zl.rot (Max) 143, 147
zl.slice (Max) 37, 60, 143, 147
zl.sort (Max) 91, 97, 172
zl.stream (Max) 97